COMPUTER SCIENCE, TECHNOLOGY AND APPLICATIONS

DIGITAL TECHNOLOGY

ADVANCES IN RESEARCH AND APPLICATIONS

W0010644

COMPUTER SCIENCE, TECHNOLOGY AND APPLICATIONS

Additional books and e-books in this series can be found
on Nova's website under the Series tab.

COMPUTER SCIENCE, TECHNOLOGY AND APPLICATIONS

DIGITAL TECHNOLOGY

ADVANCES IN RESEARCH AND APPLICATIONS

MICHELLE F. WRIGHT
EDITOR

nova
science publishers
New York

Copyright © 2019 by Nova Science Publishers, Inc.

NOTICE TO THE READER

Library of Congress Cataloging-in-Publication Data

Names: Wright, Michelle F., editor.
Title: Digital technology : advances in research and applications /
  Michelle F. Wright, editor.
Description: New York : Nova Science Publishers, 2019. | Series: Computer
  science, technology and applications | Includes bibliographical
  references and index. |
Identifiers: LCCN 2019043003 (print) | LCCN 2019043004 (ebook) | ISBN
  9781536164381 (hardcover) | ISBN 9781536164398 (adobe pdf)
Subjects: LCSH: Human-computer interaction. | Electronic digital computers.
Classification: LCC QA76.9.H85 D496 2018 (print) | LCC QA76.9.H85 (ebook)
  | DDC 004.01/9--dc23
LC record available at https://lccn.loc.gov/2019043003
LC ebook record available at https://lccn.loc.gov/2019043004

Published by Nova Science Publishers, Inc. † *New York*

CONTENTS

PREFACE

To date considerable attention or, in some cases alarm, has been given to the risks and consequences of digital technologies use for adolescents and emerging adults (known as "youth" throughout the rest of this section). Digital technologies are embedded in the lives of many youth. Considering that youth spend substantial time with their peers, it is not surprising that many online risks involve their peers, friends, and romantic partners as significant contexts of the online experience. Many youth report that they were sent violent, vulgar, or sexual content from someone they had a pre-existing relationship with. In addition, some youth perpetrate, experience, and/or witness hateful, vulgar, or nasty online messages. Bullying and offensive content are widespread on the Internet, and youth are particularly concerned with such experiences. There is considerable concern with the impact of digital technologies use, specifically addiction that can occur. Another concern is youth exposure to unsafe content, such as videos that promote dangerous lifestyles, like anorexia. Though receiving less attention than other online risks, fake news is another concern for youth when using digital technologies. Ultimately, digital technologies have afforded youth with many avenues to explore their morality and ethics, sexuality, and identity. Therefore, the primary aim of this book was to describe the role of digital technologies in youths' lives, and how they navigate developmental tasks and issues utilizing these technologies. To do this, the book will synthesize the research on digital technology use and how these technologies can hinder or help youths' development, formation, and exploration of morality and ethics, sexuality, and identity.

ORGANIZATION OF THE BOOK

The book is organized based on the type of risk or opportunity experienced by youth through digital technologies. There is some overlap of information between some chapters, particularly in the chapters on cyberbullying. Different terminologies might be used to refer to the subjects of the chapters, such as some authors might refer to teens, adolescents, young people, youth, pupils or students, and emerging adults. Although different terminologies might be used throughout the chapters, authors make it clear which developmental age group or groups their chapter addresses. There are 12 chapters included in this book. A brief summary of these chapters follows:

The author of Chapter 1 begins by describing the debate that continues to persist regarding the conceptualization of cyberbullying. She addresses concerns about whether there are theoretical justifications for classifying traditional bullying and cyberbullying similarly or differently. In the chapter, she describes results of a study in which the severity of different forms of traditional bullying and cyberbullying are investigated. Based on the findings, it was concluded that comparing the severity of the different types of bullying is difficult, which increases the difficulty with discussing cyberbullying without reference to specific forms of this behavior.

In Chapter 2, the authors discuss the multi-faceted effects digital culture has on bystanders in cyberspace. The additional aim of the chapter is to discuss bystander effects in traditional and digital environments and the roles of digital bystanders and digital upstanders.

Utilizing Bronfenbrenner's ecological framework, the aim of Chapter 3 was to explore Polish teachers' perceptions of cyberbullying, their beliefs about the effects of either being exposed to or engaging in cyberbullying on students' psychological well-being, and their perceptions of safety and support for preventing cyberbullying in schools. The authors concluded that teachers had awareness about cyberbullying, as well as the support both within and outside of the school environment. However, teachers acknowledged the need for further guidance in the management of cyberbullying incidents.

Chapter 4 focuses on characterizing cyberbullying and the associated psychological factors impacting junior-high school students, with the primary aim to share efficacy information about Project IMPACT. Project IMPACT involves a 10 hour program of multi-faceted cyberbullying prevention focused on self-control, empathy (online and offline), awareness of factors that influence aggression escalation, and awareness of mediated communication. The findings revealed that the activities helped students develop knowledge about the social functioning of cyberspace and reduced cyberbullying perpetration.

The concept of sexting and its definitions are described at the beginning of Chapter 5. The authors then discuss the frequency of sexting, with specific focus on sending, receiving, and forwarding messages. They also explain the importance of the peer context and gender differences in sexting. The chapter concludes with recommendations for encouraging healthy practices in intimate communication between adolescents.

The purpose of Chapter 6 is to review literature on the general trends on social media engagement, online communities, and how they may be used as tools for connection and coping. The authors discuss memes, self-deprecating humor, anonymous thread discussions, and echo chambers. Overall, the authors approach the chapter by describing both the positive and negative aspects of social media as a source of connection and coping. They also consider the developmental potential of social media for young people.

Chapter 7 describes the negative issues associated with smartphone use, specifically cyberbullying, cyber shaming, and phone snubbing or phubbing. The chapter further describes the use of smartphones for social media and how such a practice can promote social comparison, potentially increasing distress.

Chapter 8 explains problematic internet use (PIU) by discussing the benefits and risks of digital technology use, behavioral addictions, and the classification and measurement of PIU. The author continues by discussing the prevalence of PIU among adolescents, and the associated demographic, biological and genetic, behavioral, psychological, and social predictors and negative outcomes of PIU. Concluding the chapter are recommendations for research and practice.

The concern addressed in Chapter 9 is increasing suicide rates among adolescents in the United States. The author argues that this concern is spurred by the heavy digital technology use of young people. In the rest of the chapter, the author evaluates the evidence as to whether digital technology use is responsible for the changes in adolescent health and well-being over the past several decades.

The author of Chapter 10 argues that problematic use of digital technologies increases the rise of online aggression, including hate speech, shitstorms, and cyberbullying, as well as promotes digital lies. The underlying theme of the chapter is that the way people process information online influences the formation of opinion, which are highly influenced by the use of digital technologies. Strategies are proposed within the chapter to prevent or stop the issues promoted by digital technology use.

Chapter 11 discusses results of a study on the comments of people in response to proanorexia videos on YouTube. The authors found that proanas tended to defend their in-group identity and distinguish themselves from hateful (non-proana) outsiders. Proanas adhered to extreme categorizations that reinforced deviant attributes and stigma associated with their identity. Such extreme adherence to deviate attributes may strengthen the attractiveness of the risky in-group.

The author of Chapter 12 explores the idea that technology is similar to skin for adolescents and emerging adults. Their use of digital technologies allows for protection, regulation, and communication. Similar to skin, the author argues that adolescents and emerging adults do not fully recognize or understand the impact of digital technologies on their identity development, thinking processes, and daily functioning.

In: Digital Technology
Editor: Michelle F. Wright

ISBN: 978-1-53616-438-1
© 2019 Nova Science Publishers, Inc.

Chapter 1

TRADITIONAL BULLYING AND CYBERBULLYING: A THEORETICAL AND EMPIRICAL COMPARISON BASED ON CORRELATIONS AND SEVERITY

*Julia Fluck**, *PhD*

Chair of School Pedagogy and Educational Research,
RWTH Aachen University,
Institute of Educational Science, Germany

ABSTRACT

Early cyberbullying research has addressed the question, whether the phenomenon is simply "old wine in new bottles" (Li, 2007). To date, researchers still do not agree on a common conceptualization of cyberbullying. Is it a form of bullying like physical, verbal, and relational bullying? Or are traditional bullying and cyberbullying two different

* Corresponding Author's E-mail: julia.fluck@rwth-aachen.de.

constructs, that merely share some common features? This chapter addresses the issue of bullying in a digital age – what is the relationship between traditional bullying and cyberbullying? The chapter reviews the theoretical discussions as well as the existing evidence on cyberbullying. In addition, empirical data is used in order to analyze the relationship between cyberbullying and traditional bullying. The empirical study shows, on the one hand, that the persons involved in the two types of bullying are often, but not always the same. However, the role someone plays remains rather stable across contexts. This study also investigates the severity for different forms of traditional bullying and cyberbullying. It becomes apparent that both traditional and cyberbullying are heterogeneous constructs, which is why severity cannot be considered higher or lower per se for any of the two types. This illustrates that it is pretty much impossible to research and discuss cyberbullying without regarding specific forms. Based on the insights drawn from the literature and the data, resulting conclusions for research and practice are discussed.

DEFINITIONS AND FORMS OF TRADITIONAL BULLYING AND CYBERBULLYING

New media play an important role in the everyday life of children and adolescents (Schmidt, Paus-Hasenbrink, & Hasenbrink, 2011). Teenagers communicate online, play online games together, post pictures and videos on social networking sites, and consider the number of facebook friends or followers an indicator for popularity (Golub; 2014; Savage, 2012). New technologies always bear the risk for being abused for cruel or criminal activities (Drucker, & Gumpert, 2000). Therefore, youths are also subject to technical risks such as spam or hacker attacks and social risks such as being contacted by strangers, viewing violent or sexually explicit content online, or experiencing cyber aggression or even cyber bullying (Teimouri et al., 2015; Vandebosch, & van Cleemput, 2008).

According to Smith, Mahdavi, Carvalho, Fisher, Russell, and Tippett (2008), cyberbullying is "an aggressive, intentional act carried out by a group or individual, *using electronic forms of contact*, repeatedly and over time against a victim who cannot easily defend him or herself" (p. 376). Thus, based on this definition, the sole distinction between traditional and cyberbullying is the fact, that it is carried out using new information and communication technology. Both types of bullying by definition require repetition, intent to hurt, and an imbalance of power between perpetrator and victim (Olweus, 1993).

Some authors argue, however, that singular acts of internet aggression, such as uploading a derogatory video on YouTube constitutes bullying, in which the aspect of repetition is immanent to the technology (Dooley, Pyżalski, & Cross, 2009). The person in the video is victimized over and over again, each time another internet user watches the video. Other forms of cyberbullying, such as sending offensive messages by email or chat, require repeated acts from the perpetrator (Langos, 2012). A solution would be to understand repetition not as repeated acts of the bully but as an ongoing *or* repeated experience of victimization from the victims' point of view (Fawzi, 2009).

The criterion "imbalance of power" is also critically discussed in the literature. Since physical strength does not play a role in internet communications, some authors argue, that imbalance of power should not be a definition criterion of cyberbullying (Roberto, & Eden, 2010; Wolak, Mitchell, & Finkelhor, 2006; Wingate, Minney & Guadagno, 2013). Even with traditional bullying, however, physical strength is not the only way in which a perpetrator can be more powerful than the victim (Smith, Del Barrio, & Tokunaga, 2013). The number of friends and supporters of a bully can also make him or her superior to the victim. This aspect plays as big a role online as it does offline (Savage, 2012). Also, victims of cyberbullying still feel helpless towards the attacks, which justifies speaking of a power differential, even if this power differential is immanent to the technology (Dooley, et al., 2009). It does not make a lot of sense, though, to assume that the perpetrators' strength lies in a higher amount of knowledge and skills when it comes to new media, since "both those who are cyber-bullied and those who cyberbully may have similar media knowledge as they both use these technologies for communication purposes" (Grigg, 2010 p. 145).

Focus group studies with children and adolescents confirm the assumption that the definition criteria of cyberbullying should be the same as for traditional bullying; Menesini et al., (2012) found out that imbalance of power is considered the most important criterion for cyberbullying by youths. Vandebosch and van Cleemput (2008) identified the following three conditions which need to be given for youths to consider a behavior "cyberbullying": First, the bully must have a clear intention to hurt the victim and a feeling of hurt must be experienced by the victim. Second, the attacks must be part of an ongoing pattern of several aggressive acts. Third, in any dyad of bully and victim, the victim must feel helpless due to being less powerful than the bully.

While definition criteria for traditional bullying and cyberbullying should be the same, there are some differences when it comes to particular forms of aggressive acts. Traditional forms of bullying include physical (e.g., kicking, punching, beating), verbal (e.g., calling names, threatening, mocking, offending) and relational forms (e.g., spreading rumors) of aggression (Klett, 2005; Smith, & Brain, 2000). Cyberbullying is generally considered to be verbal and/or relational (Vandebosch, & van Cleemput, 2008; Wright, & Li, 2013), and can appear in the following types of actions (Willard, 2007):

- *Harassment*: repetitiously sending insulting or threatening messages to another person by e-mail, SMS, instant messaging or in chatrooms.
- *Denigration*: spreading rumors via electronic communication devices.
- *Outing & trickery*: a message revealing personal information, which the victim sent to someone in confidence, is forwarded to other people in order to compromise the victim.
- *Exclusion* is equivalent to exclusion in real life and means withholding the opportunity of taking part in social activities. In an online context this could be excluding someone from multiplayer games, chats, or other platforms.

Some forms of cyberbullying are similar to comparable kinds of traditional bullying, e.g., spreading rumors online versus offline. Other forms are specific to cyberbullying, such as programming a website with derogatory material on the victim, are distinct from traditional bullying (Calvete, Orue, Estevez, Villardon, & Padilla, 2010).

TRADITIONAL BULLYING AND CYBERBULLYING IN RELATION TO EACH OTHER

Early studies on cyberbullying mainly addressed the following two research questions: What is the extent of the problem (prevalence) and how is it different from traditional bullying (Riebel, Jaeger, & Fischer, 2009)? This latter question is difficult to answer. First publications on cyberbullying mostly addressed differences between the two bullying types (Willard, 2007). Only much later, those differences became subject of empirical studies. Some of those differences mentioned in literature are:

- Cyberbullying can reach a greater audience than traditional bullying since the internet is a medium for mass communication. Theoretically, information in the web can be shared with millions of other internet users within minutes (Heirman & Walrave, 2008).
- On the internet, bullies can act anonymously. Thus, the victim might not know where an attack comes from (Smith, 2012; Walker, Craven, & Tokunaga, 2013).
- Willard (2007) claims that when a bully is unable to see the emotional reaction of a victim he or she does not know when to stop. Channel reduction theory (Winterhoff-Spurk, & Vitouch, 1989) supports this assumption but Doering (2003) discusses this argument critically by pointing out that there are social rules online as well as offline and that bullies in both contexts willingly and knowingly choose to ignore those rules.
- The role of bystanders is different on the internet. While in real life they can step in and stop the bully from further hurting the victim, this is much harder to do online. However, by liking and sharing

offensive content, third parties play a crucial role when it comes to determine the extent of the victimization (Markey, 2000).

- As already discussed above, power differentials between bullies and victims are different in the virtual world, where physical strength does not play a role (Perren et al., 2012).
- Cyberbullying is even more difficult for grown-ups to detect than traditional forms of bullying (Walker et al., 2013). Thus, bullies hardly have to fear any consequences, which according to the theory of planned behavior (Ajzen, 1985) increases an already existing motivation to act aggressively (Festl, 2015).

Although cyberbullying has the potential to be anonymous and public, studies also show that most virtual attacks are private, not public (Festl, 2015) and that most victims know – or can at least guess – who the bully is (Ybarra, 2004). Still, those two aspects are usually mentioned in order to support the argument that cyberbullying is more severe than traditional bullying. Indeed, it seems that public and anonymous attacks cause more stress (Kowalski & Limber, 2007; Pieschl, Kuhlmann, & Porsch, 2014) and that - in comparison with traditional bullying - cyberbullying leads to an increased level of anxiety, psychosomatic stress, and depression (Campbell, Spears, Butler, & Kift, 2012). However, a study by Sticca and Perren (2013) sheds some more light on the effect of publicity and anonymity. Participants were given different scenarios and had to rate them according to how severe they considered the bullying. Scenarios varied by publicity and anonymity, but those two aspects were combined with cases of traditional as well as cyber bullying. Results show that cyberbullying scenarios were not generally rated more severe than traditional bullying scenarios. The differences in severity ratings can be explained by effects of anonymity and publicity: Cases where bullying (regardless if it is traditional or cyber) happens in public are rated significantly more severe than when the bullying only happens between perpetrator and victim. Also, bullying is rated as significantly more severe when the bully remains unknown to the victim. Considering that many instances of cyberbullying are neither public nor anonymous, it would be wrong to assume that cyberbullying is generally more severe than traditional bullying.

When it comes to the question how traditional and cyberbullying relate to each other, according to Craven, Marsh, & Parada (2013), there exist two different perspectives (see Figure 1).

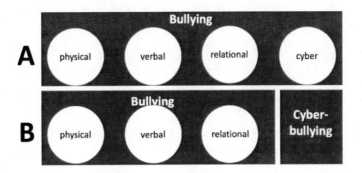

Figure 1. Perspectives on types of bullying.

Perspective A: Bullying as a Generic Term of Traditional and Cyber Bullying

Some researchers argue that cyberbullying is just one more tool in the bullies' toolbox of aggressive behaviors. From this perspective, it is one of several types of bullying (Cook, Williams, Guerra, & Sadek, 2010). Although it has some distinct features, it shares its most important aspects with bullying in general, for example when it comes to definition criteria. Olweus (2012) draws rather radical conclusions from this perspectives and questions the necessity of separate research and intervention for cyberbullying. Instead, he argues that since cyberbullying is just another kind of bullying, research and prevention should simply keep focusing on traditional bullying. Olweus tries to prove the adequacy of his approach with the argument that only a very small percentage of cyber victims are not victims of traditional bullying as well. Thus, Olweus (2012) uses the investigation of *correlations* to support his arguments. This, however, is only one approach to address the problem.

Perspective B: Cyberbullying and Bullying as Distinct Forms of Aggressive Behavior

Another perspective on cyberbullying focuses more on the differences than on the common aspects of both types of bullying. From this perspective, bullying (with its sub-types physical, verbal and relational bullying) and cyberbullying are rather similar, but nonetheless distinct types of aggressive behavior. When researchers have this perspective on cyberbullying, they argue in favor of cyberbullying having its own definition criteria (Menesini et al., 2012), which can be somewhat different to those of traditional bullying. Arguments for this approach focus on the special features of cyberbullying. Smith (2012) for instance points out the effects of anonymity and channel reduction as well as the effects of cyberbullying on the victims' physical and mental health to support the hypothesis, that cyberbullying is a distinct – and more severe – form of bullying.

Whether perspective A or perspective B is more valid seems to be a paradigm. Both perspectives arguments can be supported with arguments and empirical data. Researchers do not agree on this point, but perhaps they do not have to. What we can draw from this discussion, however, is that there are two approaches to investigate the relationship between traditional bullying and cyberbullying: Correlation and severity.

Most studies on cyberbullying use correlation-based methods, such as Pearson correlations, regression, internal consistency or factor analysis, in order to investigate cyber-bullying scales, to compute correlations with traditional bullying or to regress it on predicting constructs. But correlation-based methods might be susceptible to methodological artifacts. One of the problems with aggression data is low incidence, leading to zero-inflated data, i.e., the majority of people have had no victimization experiences at all, which results in skewed distributions. Another problem is a high poly-victimization across several forms of aggression (Finkelhor, 2008). Poly-victimization means that people who are victims of one type of aggressive behavior (e.g., violence in schools) also experience other types, such as family violence. A high correlation between two types of aggressive behavior, therefore, cannot prove whether they are both part of the same construct. High correlations between traditional bullying and cyberbullying factors could be due to the fact that many participants hardly experience any victimization at all and those who do, experience different forms of victimization at the same time. A high correlation per se does not necessarily mean that two constructs are "the same"; it can merely *falsify* the hypothesis that they are *not* the same.

To further investigate the relationship between traditional and cyberbullying, it is therefore helpful to use the aspect of severity as another approach to understanding the problem (Fluck, 2018). Severity is sometimes measured by comparing the consequences of victimization online and offline. As Olweus (2012) points out, however, this is problematic since only a very small percentage of victims experience only cyberbullying and no traditional bullying. Therefore, study results on the health effects of cyberbullying are confounded with traditional bullying. However, severity can also be assessed by considering children and adolescents as experts of their own living environment and asking them directly to rate different forms of bullying in terms of severity.

The following two sub-sections will discuss the relationship between traditional and cyber bullying in terms of these two approaches (see Figure 2). In each sub-section, theoretical arguments and empirical data from existing studies will be reviewed first. Second, results of the author's own empirical study will be presented and discussed in order to shed some more light on the issue at hand.

These data were collected in a 2015 study with 488 adolescents in the German state of Rhineland-Palatinate. Approximately 60.9% were male and 38.9% female (one person chose not to answer the item on gender). The age ranged from 12 to 17 years ($M = 14.86$ years, $SD = 1.12$). Participants were asked about their involvement in each bullying and cyberbullying (*yes vs. no*) and about the role they played there [*If you already have experiences with (cyber)bullying, would you say that ...(1) I am always a victim; (2) I am mostly a victim, but sometimes I also bully; (3) I am equally often a bully and a victim; (4) I am sometimes a victim, but mostly a bully; (5) I am always a bully*]. The participants were presented with 11 forms of traditional bullying (see below) and 7 forms of cyberbullying and were asked to rate each form for severity [*How bad is it when someone ... (1) not bad at all ... (4) very bad*].

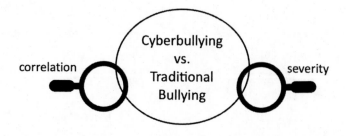

Figure 2. Approaches to investigating the relationship between types of bullying.

CORRELATIONS OF BULLYING BEHAVIOR ON- AND OFFLINE

Early studies have focused on the correlation between perpetrator behavior online and offline, and between victimization experiences online and offline as well as whether cyberbullies have been victimized in real life at an earlier time. This last correlation of online perpetration and offline victimization has also been called "The revenge of the nerds" hypothesis.

Correlations can only answer the question whether the people who take up a certain role in one context (online) also take up this role in another context (offline). This does not necessarily mean, that bullying online and offline *are* the same. However, if the persons involved take up the same role across different contexts, we can conclude that the phenomena of traditional and cyberbullying are very similar and can possibly even be explained by the same psychological and social mechanisms.

At least a third of the persons involved in cyberbullying are also involved in traditional forms of bullying (Ybarra, Diener-West, & Leaf, 2007). But the amount of overlap is probably a lot higher, as other studies suggest. Riebel et al. (2009) report that 84% of cyberbullies also acted as bullies in real life and 78% of cyberbullying victims were also victims offline. Data from their study also support the "revenge of the nerds" hypothesis, with 59% of the online bullies also reporting that they were victims in real life.

Wachs and Wolf (2011) found a correlation of $\varphi = .512$ between bully-status online and offline. According to a meta-analysis, the mean correlation coefficient for bullies across several studies is $r = .47$ (Modecki, Minchin, Harbaugh, Guerra, & Runions, 2014). Williams and Guerra (2007) point out that the correlation is dependent on the forms of cyberbullying. Verbal bullying is associated higher ($r = .87$) with cyberbullying than physical bullying ($r = .66$).

The effects for victims are somewhat smaller but still significant. The mean correlation across several studies for victim status online and offline is $r = .40$ (Modecki et al., 2014). Differential effects of the form also play a role (Randa, Nobles, & Reyns, 2015). As Olweus (2012) points out, there are only very few victims of cyberbullying who are not also bullied in real life. Kowalski, Giumetti, Schroeder, and Lattaner (2014) speak of between 10% to 15% of cybervictims who are only victimized online. It seems that not all cases of traditional bullying go on in cyberspace, but most bullying constellations online seem to be founded offline (Cross, Lester, & Barnes, 2015; Sourander et al., 2010). Few longitudinal studies support the assumption, that traditional bullying was a problem first, which was then transported into cyberspace (Del Rey, Elipe, & Ortega-Ruiz, 2012; Gradinger, Strohmeier, Schiller, Stefanek, & Spiel, 2012a; Pornari & Wood, 2010).

In this study, a new approach was used to investigate the roles of adolescents in bullying and cyberbullying. A large amount of those who are involved in bullying are not either victims or bullies, but so-called bully/victims. Those persons are the victim in some interpersonal constellations, but at the same time, in other interpersonal constellations, they are the bullies. This group is at least as big as the group of victims (Kowalski et al., 2014). Also, Finkelhor (2008) argues that bullies and victims often share the same psychological predictors, so it is difficult to separate them in two different groups, especially if they play different roles in different constellations. To avoid the "dyadic bias" (Espelage & Swearer, 2003) of dividing the persons into bullies and victims only, participation status was in a first step assessed with a dichotomous variable. Those who claimed that they have participated in bullying were then asked in a second step, which role they played. The results are displayed in Tables 1 and 2.

The cross-tabulation of participation in traditional bullying and cyberbullying shows that the majority of those who carry out and/or experience bullying online also carry out/experience it offline and vice versa ($chi^2_{(df=1)}$ = 79.069, p < .001). However, with a correlation of φ = .408 (p < .001), this concordance is far from perfect. There still exist many persons who are involved in one form, but not in the other.

Table 1. Cross-tabulation of participation in different types of bullying

		participation in cyberbullying		sum
		no	Yes	
participation in traditional bullying	no	253	20	273
	yes	119	84	203
	sum	372	104	476

Table 2. Cross tabulation of roles in different types of bullying

		role in cyberbullying					sum
		V	B/V	B/V	B/V	B	sum
role in traditional bullying	V	12	4	0	0	0	16
	B/V	6	7	1	2	0	16
	B/V	1	0	15	2	1	19
	B/V	0	0	3	5	2	10
	B	0	0	0	3	16	19
	sum	19	11	19	12	19	80

Annotation: V = victim only; B/V = sometimes bully, but mostly victim; B/V = sometimes bully, sometimes victim; **B**/V = mostly bully, but sometimes victim; B = bully only.

A view on the specific roles, that participants play in such bullying contexts, shows a closer relationship between the characteristics of online versus offline bullying. Adolescents in this study tend to play the same role online as they do offline. A Spearman correlation of r = .892 (p < .001) illustrates how large the effect is.

The meaning of these findings is discussed in the conclusions section. The following sub-section completes the investigation of the research question by taking a closer look on severity.

SEVERITY

Previous studies on severity either address the question, whether traditional bullying is more severe than cyberbullying or they compare different forms of cyberbullying according to their severity. According to Campbell et al., (2012), participants rated traditional bullying as more severe than cyberbullying – in spite of the heavier impact on psychological wellbeing, which cyberbullying had in this particular study. Slonje and Smith (2008) showed that cyberbullying that happens by text-based communication is rated less severe than traditional bullying, but when cyberbullying includes pictures or video material, it is considered more severe than traditional bullying.

Studies on the severity of cyberbullying forms also show differences between the forms. Outing/Trickery is considered more severe than harassment or denigration. The latter two are in turn considered to be more severe than exclusion (Pieschl et al., 2014). Focus-groups by Schultze-Krumbholz, Höher, Fiebig, and Scheithauer (2014) revealed a very low severity of cyber exclusion in comparison to other forms. The authors question if this form should be considered cyberbullying at all, since – as the participants said – the perpetrator "doesn't really do anything" (p. 372).

Since some forms of cyberbullying are closely related to traditional forms, while some others do not have any traditional equivalents (see above), it is important to take different forms into consideration, when comparing traditional bullying and cyberbullying. This study tries to fill this gap in literature and compares the severity of different forms of traditional as well as different forms of cyberbullying. Table 3 shows the results. The most severe forms are blackmail (traditional) outing/trickery by picture and denigration by picture (both cyber), physical attacks, and threats (both traditional). The least severe forms are mean talk and calling names (both traditional), harassment by text (cyber), mockery (traditional), and cyber exclusion.

Table 3. Severity of different bullying forms

Item	N	Minimum	Maximum	Mean	SD
Blackmail *	478	1	4	3.74	.598
Outing/Trick picture #	476	1	4	3.72	.602
Denigration picture #	476	1	4	3.59	.727
Physical attacks *	478	1	4	3.49	.757
Threats *	474	1	4	3.44	.705
Outing/Trickery text #	479	1	4	3.44	.737
Denigration Text #	478	1	4	3.37	.772
Destroying friendships *	476	1	4	3.36	.816
Spreading rumours *	476	1	4	3.26	.782
Damaging property *	478	1	4	3.25	.795
Harassment picture #	478	1	4	3.20	.753
Traditional exclusion *	478	1	4	2.77	.873
Mean talk *	476	1	4	2.75	.853
Calling names *	478	1	4	2.72	.845
Harassment text #	477	1	4	2.67	.809
Mocking someone *	477	1	4	2.55	.919
Cyber exlcusion #	476	1	4	2.19	.892

Annotation: Forms of traditional bullying are marked with an asterisk, forms of cyberbullying are marked with a hasthtag. Standard deviations give information about how unanimously the persons rated the severity of a form.

The data do not allow any general conclusions on the severity of traditional and cyberbullying. Some forms of cyberbullying are more severe, some less severe than traditional forms. It is interesting, though, that exclusion is rated more severe when it happens in real life whereas denigration (both text and picture based) is rated more severe when it happens online than when rumors are spread offline. Thus, there is not a consistent pattern to be found that equivalent forms are generally more severe in one context.

In order to illustrate the relationship between the items, multidimensional scaling was carried out, a graphical method for investigating the similarity and dissimilarity of different items (Borg, 2010), based on a correlation matrix. The method scales the items on a usually two-dimensional space. Similar items are graphed closely together, while dissimilar items are graphed further apart.

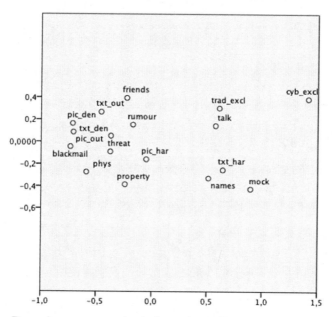

Annotation: Damaging property, physical attacks, calling names, mocking someone, talking about someone in a mean way, spreading rumors, blackmail, destroying friendships, threats and (traditional) exclusion, cyber exclusion as well as text and picture based forms of harassment, denigration and outing/trickery.

Figure 3. Multidimensional scaling based on similarity of severity ratings for forms of traditional bullying.

The fit of a multidimensional scaling model can be assessed with the STRESS test. The analysis at hand yielded a STRESS I value of .12954 and a STRESS II value of .25803. According to Kruskal & Wish (1978), STRESS values > .2 suggest misfit of the model. Thus, it can be assumed that more than two dimensions are needed to explain differences in the data. However, the results yield some interesting insights into the nature of the relationship between traditional bullying and cyberbullying.

Figure 3 does not show any distinguishable clusters for forms of traditional and cyberbullying. Some forms are considered similar to each other, although they are carried out in different contexts. Name calling (traditional), mockery (traditional), and harassment (cyber) by text, for instance, are very similar in perceived severity. Text as well as picture-based forms of denigration (cyber) and outing/trickery (cyber) are much closer to traditional forms, such as physical attacks and property damage, than they are to cyber-exclusion.

Multidimension scaling therefore supports the results of the comparison of means. The question on severity of traditional bullying versus severity of cyber bullying cannot be answered without considering the properties of the separate forms of each type.

CONCLUSION

This chapter investigates the relationship between traditional bullying and cyberbullying. Is cyberbullying a different phenomenon or is it the same as traditional bullying and merely happens in another context?

The results of this and previous studies on *correlations* show that the conclusion by Ybarra and Mitchell (2004) is still valid: Traditional bullying and cyberbullying are very similar phenomena, which at the same time are still in some aspects different from one another. Therefore, the persons involved in the two types of bullying are not always the same. It is a new finding from this study that the role someone plays remains rather stable across contexts. Thus, the conclusion from this part of the study is that cyberbullying and traditional bullying have more aspects in common than they have aspects that separate them.

The approach of *severity* makes clear that both traditional and cyberbullying are heterogeneous constructs, which is why severity cannot be considered higher or lower *per se* for any of the two types. This illustrates that it is pretty much impossible to research and discuss cyberbullying without regarding its forms. Some forms of cyberbullying are more similar to forms of traditional bullying than to others forms of cyberbullying.

Based on the insights in this chapter, we can conclude that the two perspectives of A and B (as described above and depicted in Figure 1, see also Craven et al., 2013) are both not sufficient as adequate models of bullying and cyberbullying. A more appropriate view is depicted in Figure 4.

Since the roles participants play are stable across contexts, cyberbullying and traditional bullying are both heterogeneous concerning its forms and the forms within one type are sometimes more distinct to one another than across types, it makes sense to assume a common construct (bullying) for both types on a superior level. The close relationship between both types of bullying is concordant with perspective A. But perspective A (see above) does not account for the fact that there are no separate clusters for the forms cyberbullying and the forms of traditional bullying. A new perspective C could explain the data better. This third perspective, however, still needs to be confirmed based on empirical data.

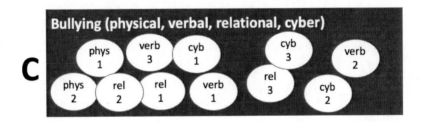

Figure 4. A third perspective on types of bullying.

Both correlation and severity approaches to investigate the relationship between traditional bullying and cyberbullying show us that there are some differences between both types of bullying. Such differences justify separate research and intervention for cyberbullying (Smith, 2012). All in all, though, traditional bullying and cyberbullying have more features in common than distinguishing elements. This suggests that cyberbullying is much more a social problem than a problem of media abuse. Just as the definite means of language can be used for an indefinite number of creations by the speaker (Schmidt, 2006), including hurtful speech, other forms of communication can and will be (Drucker & Gumpert, 2000) abused in order to hurt others. While media knowledge (e.g., concerning privacy online, risky online behavior etc.) should continue to be part of cyberbullying prevention courses, the focus should still be on the social aspects of the problem, including how (potential) bullies can vent feelings of anger and frustration without harassing others and how (potential) victims can deal with aggressive attacks online as well as offline and how they can cope with negative effects of bullying, such as anxiety and depression.

REFERENCES

Ajzen, I. (1985). From intentions to actions: A theory of planned behavior. In J. Kuhl & J. Beckmann (Eds.), *Action control: From cognition to behavior* (pp. 11-39). Berlin: Springer.

Borg, I. (2010). Multidimensionale Skalierung. In C. Wolf & H. Best (Eds.), *Handbuch der sozialwissenschaftlichen Datenanalyse* [*Handbook of social science data analysis*] (pp. 291-419). Wiesbaden: Springer VS.

Calvete, E., Orue, I., Estévez, A., Villardón, L., & Padilla, P. (2010). Cyberbullying in adolescents: Modalities and aggressors' profile. *Computers in Human Behavior, 26*, 1128–1135.

Campbell, M., Spears, B., Slee, P., Butler, D., & Kift, S. (2012). Victims' perceptions of traditional and cyberbullying, and the psychosocial correlates of their victimisation. *Emotional and Behavioural Difficulties, 17*, 389–401.

Cook, C. R., Williams, K. R., Guerra, N. G., Kim, T. E., & Sadek, S. (2010). Predictors of bullying and victimization in childhood and adolescence: A meta-analytic investigation. *School Psychology Quarterly, 25*, 65–83.

Craven, R. G., Marsh, H. W., & Parada, R. H. (2013). Potent ways forward: New multidimensional theoretical structural models of cyberbullying, cyber targetization and bystander behaviors and their potential relations to traditional bullying constructs. In S. Bauman, D. Cross & J. L. Walker (Eds.), *Principles of cyberbullying research* (pp. 68–86). New York, NY: Routledge.

Cross, D., Lester, L., & Barnes, A. (2015). A longitudinal study of the social and emotional predictors and consequences of cyber and traditional bullying victimisation. *International Journal of Public Health, 60,* 207–217.

Del Rey, R., Elipe, P., & Ortega-Ruiz, R. (2012). Bullying and cyberbullying: Overlapping and predictive value of the co-occurrence. *Psicothema, 24,* 608-613.

Dooley, J. J., Pyżalski, J., & Cross, D. (2009). Cyberbullying versus face-to-face bullying. *Zeitschrift für Psychologie, 217,* 182–188.

Drucker, S., & Gumpert, G. (2000). Cybercrime and punishment. *Critical Studies in Media Communication, 17,* 133-158.

Espelage, D. L., & Swearer, S. M. (2003). Research on school bullying and victimization: What have we learned and where do we go from here? *School Psychology Review, 32*(3), 365–383.

Fawzi, N. (2009). *Cyber-Mobbing. Ursachen und Auswirkungen von Mobbing im Internet.* Baden-Baden: Nomos.

Festl, R. (2015). *Täter im Internet: Eine Analyse individueller und struktureller Erklärungsfaktoren von Cybermobbing im Schulkontext* [*Offenders on the Internet: An analysis of individual and structural explanatory factors of cyberbullying in the school context*]. Wiesbaden: VS Verlag für Sozialwissenschaften.

Finkelhor, D. (2008). *Childhood victimization: Violence, crime and abuse in the lives of young people.* New York: Oxford University Press.

Fluck, J. (2018). Investigating the Comparability of Two Multi-Item-Scales for Cyber Bullying Measurement. *International Journal of Environmental Research and Public Health,* 15(11), http://dx.doi.org/10.3390/ijerph15112356.

Golub, K. (2013) *Subject access to information.* Santa-Barbara, CA: ABC-Clio.

Gradinger, P., Strohmeier, D., Schiller, E. M., Stefanek, E., & Spiel, C. (2012a). Cyber-victimization and popularity in early adolescence: Stability and predictive associations. *European Journal of Developmental Psychology, 9,* 228-243.

Grigg, D. W. (2010). Cyber-aggression: Definition and concept of cyberbullying. *Australian Journal of Guidance and Counselling, 20,* 143-156.

Heirman, W., & Walrave, M. (2008). Assessing concerns and issues about the mediation of technology in cyberbullying. *Cyberpsychology: Journal of Psychosocial Research on Cyberspace, 2*, 1.

Klett, K. (2005). *Gewalt an Schulen - Eine deutschlandweite Online-Schülerbefragung zur Gewaltsituation an Schulen* [*Violence in schools - A Germany-wide online pupil survey on the violence situation in schools*]. Köln: Philosophische Fakultät.

Kowalski, R. M., Giumetti, G. W., Schroeder, A. N., & Lattanner, M. R. (2014). Bullying in the digital age: A critical review and meta-analysis of cyberbullying research among youth. *Psychological Bulletin, 140*, 1073–1137.

Kowalski, R. M., & Limber, S. P. (2007). Electronic bullying among middle school students. *Journal of Adolescent Health, 41*, S22–S30.

Kruskal, J. B., & Wish, M. (1978). *Multidimensional Scaling*. Beverly Hills: Sage.

Langos, C. (2012). Cyberbullying: The challenge to define. *CyberPsychology, Behavior & Social Networking, 15*, 285-289.

Li, Q. (2007). New bottle but old wine: A research of cyberbullying in schools. *Computers in human behavior, 23*(4), 1777-1791.

Markey, P. M. (2000). Bystander intervention in computer-mediated communication. *Computers in Human Behavior, 16*, 183–188.

Menesini, E., Nocentini, A., Palladino, B. E., Frisén, A., Berne, S., Ortega-Ruiz, R., et al., (2012). Cyberbullying definition among adolescents: A comparison across six European countries. *Cyberpsychology, Behavior, and Social Networking, 15*, 455–463.

Modecki, K. L., Minchin, J., Harbaugh, A. G., Guerra, N. G., & Runions, K. C. (2014). Bullying prevalence across contexts: A meta-analysis measuring cyber and traditional bullying. *Journal of Adolescent Health, 55*, 602-611.

Olweus, D. (1993). *Bullying at school: What we know and what we can do*. Oxford: Cambridge.

Olweus, D. (2012). Cyberbullying: An overrated phenomenon? *European Journal of Developmental Psychology, 9*, 520–538.

Perren, S., Corcoran, L., Cowie, H., Dehue, F., Garcia, D., McGuckin, C., et al., (2012). Tackling cyberbullying: Review of empirical evidence regardingf successful responses by students, parents, and schools. *International Journal of Conflict and Violence, 6*, 283-293.

Pieschl, S., Kuhlmann, C., & Porsch, T. (2014). Beware of publicity! Perceived distress of negative cyber incidents and implications for defining cyberbullying. *Journal of School Violence, 14*(1), 111–132.

Pornari, C. D., & Wood, J. (2010). Peer and cyber aggression in secondary school students: The role of moral disengagement, hostile attribution bias, and outcome expectancies. *Aggressive Behavior, 36*, 81-94.

Randa, R., Nobles, M., & Reyns, B. (2015). Is cyberbullying a stand alone construct? Using quantitative analysis to evaluate a 21st century social question. *Societies, 5*(1), 171–186.

Riebel, J., Jäger, R. S., & Fischer, U. (2009). Cyberbullying in Germany – an exploration of prevalence, overlapping with real life bullying and coping strategies. *Psychology Science Quarterly, 51*, 298-314.

Roberto, A. J., & Eden, J. (2010). Cyberbullying: Aggressive communication in the digital age. In T. A. Avtgis & A. S. Rancer (Eds.), *Arguments, aggression, and conflict: New directions in theory and research* (pp. 198-216). New York: Routledge.

Savage, M. (2012). *Developing a Measure of Cyberbullying Perpetration and Victimization.* Tempe: Arizona State University.

Schmidt, M. (2006). *Bewegungsverben und ihre semantischen Weiterentwicklungen im Russischen [Verbs of movement and their derivatives].* Tübingen University: Master thesis.

Schmidt, J., Paus-Hasenbrink, I., & Hasenbrink, U. (2011). *Heranwachsen mit dem Social Web. Zur Rolle von Web 2.0-Angeboten im Alltag von Jugendlichen und jungen Erwachsenen (Schriftenreihe Medienforschung der LfM, Band 62) [Growing up with the social web. On the Role of Web 2.0 Services in Everyday Life of Adolescents and Young Adults (LfM Media Research Series, Volume 62)].* Berlin: Vistas.

Schultze-Krumbholz, A., Höher, J., Fiebig, J., & Scheithauer, H. (2014). Wie definieren Jugendliche in Deutschland Cybermobbing? Eine Fokusgruppenstudie unter Jugendlichen einer deutschen Großstadt

[How do young people in Germany define cyberbullying? A focus group study among young people in a German city]. *Praxis der Kinderpsychologie und Kinderpsychiatrie, 63*, 361-378.

Slonje, R., & Smith, P. K. (2008). Cyberbullying: Another main type of bullying? *Scandinavian Journal of Psychology, 49*, 147–154.

Smith, P. K. (2012). Cyberbullying: Challenges and opportunities for a research program—A response to Olweus (2012). *European Journal of Developmental Psychology, 9*, 553–558.

Smith, P. K., & Brain, P. (2000). Bullying in schools: Lessons from tow decades of research. *Aggressive Behavior, 26*, 1–9.

Smith, P. K., Del Barrio, C., & Tokunaga, R. S. (2013). Definitions of bullying and cyberbullying: How useful are the terms? In S. Bauman, D. Cross & J. L. Walker (Eds.), *Principles of cyberbullying research* (pp. 26–40). New York: Routledge.

Smith, P. K., Mahdavi, J., Carvalho, M., Fisher, S., Russell, S., & Tippett, N. (2008). Cyberbullying: Its nature and impact in secondary school pupils. *Journal of Child Psychology and Psychiatry, 49*, 376–385.

Sticca, F., & Perren, S. (2013). Is cyberbullying worse than traditional bullying? Examining the differential roles of medium, publicity, and anonymity for the perceived severity of bullying. *Journal of Youth and Adolescence, 42*, 739–750.

Teimouri, M., Hassan, M. S., Griffiths, M., Benrazavi, S. R., Bolong, J., Daud, A., et al., (2015). Assessing the validity of western measurement of online risks to children in an Asian context. *Child Indicators Research, 9*(2), 407-428.

Vandebosch, H., & van Cleemput, K. (2008). Defining cyberbullying: A qualitative research into the perceptions of youngsters. *CyberPsychology & Behavior, 11*(4), 499–503.

Wachs, S., & Wolf, K. D. (2011). Zusammenhänge zwischen Cyberbullying und Bullying – erste Ergebnisse aus einer Selbstberichtsstudie [Links between cyberbullying and bullying - first results from a self-report study]. *Praxis der Kinderpsychologie und Kinderpsychiatrie, 60*, 735-744.

Walker, J. L., Craven, R. G., & Tokunaga, R. S. (2013). Introduction. In S. Bauman, D. Cross & J. L. Walker (Eds.), *Principles of cyberbullying research* (pp. 3–20). New York: Routledge.

Willard, N. E. (2007). *Cyberbullying and cyberthreats: Responding to the challenge of online social aggression, threats, and distress.* Champaign: Research Press.

Williams, K. R., & Guerra, N. G. (2007). Prevalence and predictors of internet bullying. *The Journal of adolescent health: official publication of the Society for Adolescent Medicine, 41*(6 Suppl 1), S14-21.

Wingate, V. S., Minney, J. A., & Guadagno, R. E. (2013). Sticks and stones may break your bones, but words will always hurt you: A review of cyberbullying. *Social influence, 8,* 87-106.

Winterhoff-Spurk, P., & Vitouch, P. (1989). Mediale Individual kommunikation [Individual medial communication]. In J. Groebel & P. Winterhoff-Spurk (Hrsg.), *Empirische Medienpsychologie* (pp. 247-257). Weinheim: PVU.

Wolak, J., Mitchell, K., & Finkelhor, D. (2006). *Online victimization of youth: five years later.* Alexandria: National Center for Missing and Exploited Children.

Wright, M. F., & Li, Y. (2013). Normative beliefs about aggression and cyber aggression among young adults: A longitudinal investigation. *Aggressive Behavior, 39*(3), 161–170.

Ybarra, M. L. (2004). Linkages between depressive symptomatology and internet harassment among young regular internet users. *Cyber Psychology & Behavior, 7*(2), 247–257.

Ybarra, M. L., & Mitchell, K. J. (2004). Online aggressor/targets, aggressors and targets: a comparison of associated youth characteristics. *The journal of child psychology and psychiatry, 35,* 1308–1316.

In: Digital Technology   ISBN: 978-1-53616-438-1
Editor: Michelle F. Wright   © 2019 Nova Science Publishers, Inc.

Chapter 2

DIGITAL BYSTANDERS: MULTI-TIERED CONSIDERATIONS IN EXAMINING THE BYSTANDER'S ROLES TO CYBERBULLYING

Mickie Wong-Lo[1,*], Randy Gonzalez[2]
and Lyndal M. Bullock[3]
[1]Biola University, School of Education, La Mirada, CA, US
[2]Biola University, Rosemead School of Psychology,
La Mirada, CA, US
[3]University of North Texas, College of Education, Denton, TX, US

ABSTRACT

The innovation of technology has re-conceptualized the traditional notion of human interaction and social connection. Communicating with friends through the use of stationary has been overshadowed by the usage of abbreviated lingos and emoticons in social mediated chat rooms and

* Corresponding Author's E-mail: mickie.wong-lo@biola.edu.

instant messaging. Self-expressions are being validated by the number of *follows* or *likes* from peers in one's social platforms, while the demonstration of opinions on any particular issue can go 'viral' with a simple click of a *share* arrow. Such technological possibilities have created virtual realities where global accessibility is seamless with unlimited possibilities to stay connected. Simultaneously, these virtual environments can also be transformed into places of disconnect, loneliness, and hopelessness for victims of digitally aggressive behaviors. Thus, similar digital influences could present unique manifestations in the characteristics of roles (e.g., instigators, victims, bystanders) involved in cyberbullying incidents. To examine the multi-faceted effects digital culture has on the conventional roles of bystanders, three primary area topics will be discussed: (a) bystanders effect in traditional and digital environments, (b) roles of digital bystanders, and (c) digital upstanders.

INTRODUCTION

Social media continues to revolutionize peer connections and prompts people to examine their own digital relevance. From the glamorized promotion of being the next "influencers" to the urgency of "building a following," the digital era has altered the worth of human relationship to an arithmetical value which represents "subscribers" and "followers." YouTube's Creator Blog (2018, para. 2) noted that "In the last year, the number of channels with over 1 million subscribers has increased by 75%." Within the social networking conglomerate, such value and online presence generate monetary revenue from notable brand advertisers and sponsorships. The incentive-driven ideal encapsulates the social media culture and attracts those who seek the perceived lucrative lifestyle with an ever-increasing fan base to fuel their virtual popularity and financial support. However, the reality of fame in social media comes at a cost where privacy is easily compromised as one's life is magnified among the millions of digital bystanders.

The trendiness of digital presence has garnered a readily available space for victims of cyberbullying to share their personal stories and emotional struggles. Many utilize cyberspace to connect with those facing similar challenges, in hopes of providing and receiving support from their online communities. However, the same cyberspace can also showcase a side of victimization that sends shock-waves across social media networks. Since the early 2000s, documented cases of cybersuicide via live stream or recorded (e.g., Abraham Biggs, Amanda Todd, Naika Venant, Oceane) have highlighted the responsibilities of digital bystanders and prompted researchers to reexamine the bystander effect in digital platforms (Darley & Latane, 1968; Polder-Verkiel, 2012; Wong-Lo & Bullock, 2014). Consequent to the global awareness of cyberbullying, public policy and legislative changes have provided positive impact with the development of prevention and intervention programs. Nevertheless, such awareness also revealed vast areas of negative effects cyberbullying has on its victims, in particular the prominence of responses from digital bystanders. To examine the multi-faceted effects digital culture has on the conventional roles of bystanders, three primary area topics will be discussed: (a) bystanders effect in traditional and digital environments, (b) roles of digital bystanders, and (c) digital upstanders.

BYSTANDER EFFECT IN TRADITIONAL AND DIGITAL ENVIRONMENTS

Latane and Darley's (1970) groundbreaking work documented empirical findings that explored the determinants of bystander responses in unexpected circumstances (i.e., case of Kitty Genovese), which continues to influence researchers examining the impact of victimization and how it can be transformed by the responses of witnesses or bystanders. Specifically, Latane and Darley captured the multi-faceted responses of bystanders under their bystander intervention model, which illustrated five sequential decision-making stages of bystanders that determine their intervention pathway in situational circumstances (Anker & Feeley, 2011; Latane & Darley, 1970; Wong-Lo & Bullock, 2014). Lante and Darley's bystander intervention model consists of the following stages - stage one: *Notice the event*, which verifies that the bystander is aware of the situation; stage two:

Interpret the event as an emergency, in which the bystander must determine if the situation at hand classifies as an emergency or requires one's further assistance; stage three: *Accept responsibility for the situation*, which requires the bystander to decide whether or not to accept personal responsibility for intervening with the situation; and stage four: *Knowledge and implementation of intervention*, which requires that the bystander self-assess his/her own abilities to intervene in the situation (Anker & Feeley, 2011; Fleishman, 1980; Hudson & Bruckman, 2004; Latane & Darley, 1970; Wiesenthal, Austrom, & Silverman, 1983; Wong-Lo & Bullock, 2014). Furthermore, Latane and Darley (1970) documented four contributing mechanisms of the bystander effect - First, *Self-awareness*, where one's action is dependent on the audience presence at the time of the event; Second, *Social cues*, where one's action is dependent on the actions or non-actions of others in the environment; Third, *Blocking*, where one's action is prevented by the action of another bystander, and Fourth, *Diffuse responsibility*, where one's action is dependent on the bystanders population, in which the larger the audience, the greater the likelihood for one to feel obligated to take action. Consequently, Latane and Darley's research has inspired subsequent scholars to apply and validate their *bystander effect* theory and/or related bystanders factors on non-emergency circumstances (e.g., Anker & Feeley, 2011; Hudson & Bruckman, 2004) as well as under digital platforms (e.g., Rivers et al., 2009; Machackova et al., 2018; Wright & Wachs, 2018; Wong-Lo & Bullock, 2014).

ROLES OF DIGITAL BYSTANDERS

Research on cyberbullying continues to highlight the complexities of its socially intricate phenomenon and its manifestation across social media platforms (Festl & Quandt, 2013; Hinduja & Patchin, 2007; Kowalski, Limber, & Agatson, 2008; Raskauskas & Stoltz, 2007; Tokunaga, 2010; Wong-Lo & Bullock, 2011; Wong-Lo, Bullock, & Gable, 2011; Ybarra & Mitchell, 2004). Further, research continues to verify the multi-dimensional consideration to understand the factors associated with each incident of cyberbullying (i.e., Englander, 2013; Horowitz & Bollinger, 2014; Schoffstall & Cohen, 2011; Tokunaga, 2010). While there are common traits (i.e., roles involved and intention), each cyberbullying case presents qualities that are as unique as each person involved (i.e., aggressor, victim, bystander).

With the global accessibility of digital environments (e.g., social media platforms; forums; blogs), a simple command of 'send', 'share', 'upload', or 'live' grants content creators an immediate online presence of a target audience to access their personal videos or livestream an event in real time. Similar to cases of cyberbullying via text messages where an intimate dialogue between two individuals can instantly be exposed to strangers without the victim's awareness or consent, with livestream, moments are shared in real time and the opportunity for exposure to digital aggression becomes more instantaneous. The repercussions of such exposure categorizes individuals involved in distinctive roles and responsibilities. Unique to the role of bystanders in cyberbullying incidents, bystanders engage in a decision-making process (e.g., bystander intervention model) that can instantaneously determine their roles under each circumstance (Wong-Lo & Bullock, 2014). Depending on the environmental variables (e.g., via text messages, video recordings, livestream) of the cyberbullying case, the reactions of the digital bystanders can guide the course and duration of the victimization cycle (Machackova & Pfetsch, 2016; Salmivalli, 2014).

Furthermore, studies have recognized contributing factors associated with bystander responses within online environments (Barliska, Szuster, & Winiewski, 2013; Kowalski, 2008; Kraft, 2011; Machackova & Pfetsch, 2016; Machackova et al., 2018). For example, in 2017, 14-year-old girl Naika Venant livestreamed herself hanging from a glass door frame in the bathroom of her home. When her friend saw the video stream, police was called immediately, unfortunately, the police arrived too late to the scene and Naika had committed suicide. In 2008, 19-year-old boy Abraham Biggs Jr. committed suicide in front of a webcam with viewers 'egged him on'. While both cases (and others) have resulted in death by suicide, the distinction in the responses of the digital bystanders between both cases affirm the significance in their roles and responses.

Ambiguity is one of the many aspects in online platforms that provides digital bystanders a sense of virtual protection from retaliation or unwanted attention. It is also an environment where their action or inaction to witnessing a harmful situation can alter the outcome of an event. Researchers have examined the level of involvement by digital bystanders and have identified factors such as diffusion of responsibility, fear of being ridiculed or tormented by bullies, and lack of support from adults, and the fear of losing technology privileges and unfamiliarity of the characteristics of cyberbullying (Hinduja & Patchin, 2008; Kraft, 2011; Latane & Darley, 1970; Olweus, 1993; Wong-Lo, 2009; Wong-Lo & Bullock, 2014). Others, such as Machackova and Pfetsch (2016) noted that unlike traditional bystanders, digital bystanders do not have to be direct witnesses during the display of online aggressive behaviors, which allows for distance from fully understanding the impact of the victimization and to evaluate the severity of the situation. Additionally, Machachova and colleagues (2018) extended their research to examine the differences of responses to digital aggression among 'supportive' versus 'passive' adolescents, in which they found the significant role that 'immediate empathic response' has on the digital bystanders in providing support to victims. Olenik-Shemesh and colleagues (2017) identified age and gender as contributing factors in the level of involvement by digital bystanders. They found that 'active' bystanders were characterized as older and with a healthy social support, while the 'passive' bystanders were characterized as younger and had less social support (Olenik-Shemesh, Heiman, & Eden, 2017). In regards to gender differences, it was reported that "more girls than boys expressed a fear of intervening" (p. 41). Furthermore, Barlinska and colleagues (2018) examined the roles of 'affective' versus 'cognitive empathy' have on the level of engagement by digital bystanders. In their findings, it was noted that "only cognitive empathy increases the likelihood of intervening bystander behavior... neither affective empathy induction, previous experience of cyberperpetration, cybervictimization, nor gender affected the engagement in prosocial bystander behavior" (p. 1). On the other hand, Obermaiser and colleagues (2016) found the decision to intervene by digital bystanders are correlated to the perceived severity of the cyberbullying incident and the number of bystander witnesses to the event. Additionally, their findings shed light on the 'feeling of responsibility' as delineated in Latane and Darley's (1970) bystander effect model, in which, the bystanders' intention to intervene is influenced by variables such as *Diffuse responsibility*, where one's action is dependent on the bystanders population and *Accept responsibility for the situation*, in which the bystander decides whether or not to accept personal responsibility for intervening with the situation.

DIGITAL UPSTANDERS

To generate a sense of empowerment for witnesses of online mistreatment, it is sensible to consider the digital bystander's ability to report online bullying without potential repercussion from the perpetrator or indirectly worsening the online aggressive behaviors. Since the inception of cyberbullying research, intervention and prevention programs continue to expand to innovative strategies such as online privacy protection, anonymous reporting, and technological safeguards to create additional assurances in promoting upstander behaviors for bystanders that may feel unsafe to report or fear of retaliation. As depicted by Latane and Darley (1970), the stage of *Knowledge and implementation of intervention* requires the bystander to self-evaluate his/her own abilities to effectively intervene in the bullying situation and is recognized as the significant precursor in the transition of a bystander to uphold the role of an upstander (Anker & Feeley, 2011; Christopherson, 2007; Hudson & Bruckman, 2004; Polder-Verkiel, 2012). The acquisition of knowledge and practical skills strengthens an individual's perception of his/her ability to intervene and predicts the likelihood to actively respond to malicious or unjust situations (Polder-Verkiel, 2012; Schoffstall & Cohen, 2011) as well as predicts if a bystander will be prepared when an opportunity to assume the role of an upstander arises (Merrell, 2004; Mishna, Cook, Sanini, Wu, & MacFadden, 2010; Wong-Lo, Bullock, & Gable, 2011).

With the complexities of each cyberbullying case, strategies recommended for digital bystanders should be comprehensively structured and uniquely considered. Multi-disciplinary approaches (e.g., social-ecological, behavioral, psychological) are critical practices to promote upstander characteristics (e.g., Cunningham & Sandhu, 2007; Hinduja & Patchin, 2012; Perkins, Craig, & Perkins, 2011). Community-based frameworks and the cultivation of digital citizenship have been adopted as strategies to capture the significance of external influences to advocacy (e.g., Olweus, 1994; Merrell, 2004; Prinstein, Boergers, & Vernberg, 2001; Seals & Young, 2003; Barlinska, Szuster, & Winiewski, 2013; Bearden, 2016). Specifically, Bearden (2016) emphasized the value of stakeholders (e.g., parents, students, school personnel, community professionals) being involved in establishing a 'comprehensive digital citizenship program' to promote and practice upstanders behaviors as the digital culture continues to evolve.

CONCLUSION

It is well-established that the influence of social media will continue to transform our digital culture and shape the mindsets of technologically savvy generations. Therefore, a multi-tiered approach must be considered to fully comprehend the complexities in the roles of digital bystanders. In situations where millions of digital bystanders can be present at a cyberbullying incident via recording or livestream, it is imperative to first recognize the human aspects of each online witness and to avoid preconceived assumptions that each action/inaction is due to the cohesive practice or belief of the entire digital community. Along with the spectrum of empirical findings on the bystander effect, one undeniable factor is the power of peer influence when an individual is confronted with unfamiliar circumstances. Such influence becomes the catalyst of ones' 'next' step in the decision making process to intervene or abdicate involvement. This 'next' step is expressed by an array of associated factors that researchers continue to unearth in an effort to further awareness about an intricate phenomenon of digital behavior.

REFERENCES

Anker, A., & Feeley, T. H. (2011). Are nonparticipants in prosocial behavior merely innocent bystanders? *Health Communication*, 26, 13-24.

Barlinska, J., Szuster, A., & Winiewski, M. (2013). Cyberbullying among adolescent bystanders: Role of the communication medium, form of violence, and empathy. *Journal of Community & Applied Social Psychology*, 23(1), 37-51.

Barlinska, J., Szuster, A., & Winiewski, M. (2018). Cyberbullying among adolescent bystanders: Role of affective versus cognitive empathy in increasing prosocial cyberbystander behavior. *Frontiers in Psychology*, 9, 1-19.

Bearden, S. (2016). *Digital citizenship*. Thousand Oaks, CA: Corwin/Sage.

Bever, L. (2017). Naika Venant. Retrieved from *The Chicago Tribune*.

Christopherson, K. M. (2007). The positive and negative implications of anonymity in internet social interactions. *Computers in Human Behavior*, 23(6), 3038-3056.

Cunningham, N. J., & Sandhu, D. S. (2007). A comprehensive approach to school-community violence prevention. *Professional School Counseling*, 4, 126-133.

Darley, J. M., & Latane, B. (1970). Bystander intervention in emergencies: Diffusion of responsibility. *Journal of Personality and Social Psychology*, 8(4), 377-383.

Dasgupta, R. (2017). Oceane. Retrieved from *The Guardian*.

Englander, E. K. (2013). *Bullying and cyberbullying: What every educator needs to know*. Cambridge, MA: Harvard Education Press.

Festl, R., & Quandt, T. (2013). Social relations and cyberbullying: The influence of individual and structural attributes on victimization and perpetration via the Internet. *Human Communication Research*, 39(1), 101-126.

Fleishman, J. A. (1980). Collective action as helping behavior: Effects of responsibility diffusion on contributions to public good. *Journal of Personality and Social Psychology*, 38, 629-637.

Friedman, E. (2008, November 21). Florida teen live-streams his suicide. Retrieved from *Reuters*.

Hinduja, S., & Patchin, J. (2007). Offline consequences of online victimization: School violence and delinquency. *Journal of School Violence*, 6(3), 89-112.

Hinduja, S., & Patchin, J. W. (2008). Cyberbullying: An exploratory analysis of factors related to offending and victimization. *Deviant Behavior*, 29(2), 129-156.

Horowitz, M., & Bollinger, D. (2014). *Cyberbullying in social media within educational institutions*. Lanham, MD: Rowman & Littlefield.

Hudson, J., & Bruckman, A. (2004). The bystander effect: A lens for understanding patterns of participation. *The Journal of the Learning Sciences*, 13(2), 165-195.

Kowalski, R. M., Limber, S. P., & Agatston, P. W. (2008). *Cyberbullying: Bullying in the digital age*. Malden, MA: Blackwell.

Kowalski, R. M. (2008). Cyber bullying: Recognizing and treating victim and aggressor. *Psychiatric Times*, 25, 1-2.

Kraft, E. (2011). *Online bystanders: Are they the key to preventing cyberbullying*. Retrieved from http://www.elementalethics.com/files/Ellen_Kraft_PhD.pdf.

Latane, B., & Darley, J. M. (1970). *The unresponsive bystander: Why doesn't he help? New* York, NY: Appleton-Century-Crofts.

Machackova, H., & Pfetsch, J. (2016). Bystanders' responses to offline bullying and cyberbullying: The role of empathy and normative belief about aggression. *Scandinavian Journal of Psychology*, 57, 169-176.

Merrell, R. (2004). The impact of drama intervention program on response of the bystander to bullying situation. *Aggressive Behavior*, 29, 1-14.

Mishna, F., Cook, C., Saini, M., Wu, M. J., & MacFadden, R. (2010). Interventions to prevent and reduce cyber abuse of youth. *Research on Social Work Practice*, 1(1), 1-10.

Obermaiser, M., Fawzi, N., & Koch, T. (2016). Bystanding or standing by? How the number of bystanders effects the intention to intervene in cyberbullying. *New Media & Society*, 18(8), 1491-1507.

Olenik-Shemesh, D., Heiman, T., & Eden, S. (2017). Bystanders' behavior in cyberbullying episodes: Active and passive patterns in the context of personal-social-emotional factors. *Journal of Interpersonal Violence*, 32(1) 23-48.

Olweus, D. (1993). *Bullying at school: What we know and what we can do.* Oxford, UK: Blackwell.

Olweus, D. (1994). Bullying at school: Basic facts and effects of a school based intervention program. *Journal of Child Psychology and Psychiatry*, 35, 1171-1190.

Perkins, H. W., Craig, D. W., & Perkins, J. M. (2011). Using social norms to reduce bullying: A research intervention among adolescents in five middle schools. *Group Process & Intergroup Relations*, 14(5), 705-706.

Polder-Verkiel, S. E. (2012). Online responsibility: Bad samaritanism and the influence of internet mediation. *Science and Engineering Ethics*, 18(1), 117-141.

Prinstein, M. J., Boergers, J., & Vernberg, E. M. (2001). Overt and relational aggression in adolescents: Social-psychological adjustment of aggressors and victims. *Journal of Clinical Psychology*, 30, 479-491.

Raskausaka, J., & Stoltz, A. (2007). Involvement in traditional and electronic bullying among adolescents. *Developmental Psychology*, 43(3), 564-575.

Rivers, I., Poteat, V. P., Noret, N., & Ashurst, N. (2009). Observing bullying at school: The mental health implications of witness status. *School Psychology Quarterly*, 24, 211-223.

Salmivalli, C. (2014). Participants roles in bullying: How can peer bystanders be utilized in interventions? *Theory into Practice*, 53, 286-292.

Schoffstall, C., & Cohen, R. (2011). Cyber Aggression: The relation between online offenders and offline social competence. *Social Development*, 20(3), 587-604.

Seals, D., & Young, J. (2003). Bullying and victimization: Prevalence and relationship to gender, grade level, ethnicity, self-esteem and depression. *Adolescence*, 38, 735-747.

Tokunaga, R. S. (2010). Following you home from school: A critical review and synthesis of research on cyberbullying victimization. *Computers in Human Behavior*, 26, 277-287.

Wiesenthal, D. L., Austrom, D., & Silverman, I. (1983). Diffusion of responsibility in charitable donations. *Basic and Applied Social Psychology*, 4, 17-27.

Wong-Lo, M. (2009). *Cyberbullying: Responses of Adolescents and Parents toward Digital Aggression*. Denton, Texas. Retrieved from UNT Digital Library. http://digital.library.unt.edu/ark:/67531/metadc 12215/.

Wong-Lo, M., & Bullock, L. M. (2011). Digital aggression: Cyberworld meets school bullies. *Preventing School Failure*, 55(2), 64-70.

Wong-Lo, M., Bullock, L. M., & Gable, R. A. (2011). Cyberbullying: Practices to face digital aggression. *Emotional and Behavioural Difficulties*, 16(3), 317-325.

Wong-Lo, M., & Bullock, L. (2014). Digital metamorphosis: Examination of the bystander culture in cyberbullying. *Aggression and Violent Behavior*, 19(4), 418-422.

Wright, M., & Wachs, S. (2018). Does parental mediation moderate the longitudinal association among bystanders and perpetrators and victims of cyberbullying? *Journal of Social Science*, 7, 231.

Ybarra, M., & Mitchell, K. (2004). Online aggressors, victims, and aggressor/victims: A comparison of associated youth characteristics. *Journal of Child Psychology and Psychiatry*, 45(7), 1308-1316.

YouTube's Creator Blog (2018). *Million Subscriber Statistic*. Retrieved from https://youtube creators.googleblog.com/2018/10/a-final-update-on-our-priorities-for.html.

In: Digital Technology ISBN: 978-1-53616-438-1
Editor: Michelle F. Wright © 2019 Nova Science Publishers, Inc.

Chapter 3

POLISH TEACHERS AND CYBERBULLYING: A QUALITATIVE EXPLORATION OF THE STAKEHOLDERS' PERCEPTIONS AND EXPERIENCE OF THE PHENOMENON

Magda Marczak[1],*, PhD and Iain Coyne[2], PhD
[1]Coventry University, Coventry, UK
[2]Loughborough University, Loughborough, UK

ABSTRACT

Cyberbullying refers to bullying and harassment of others using new electronic technologies, the most popular being the internet and mobile phone. For young people the internet is an everyday means of communication and information gathering. Very often their social life after school consists of participating in chat rooms and social network websites. Using Bronfenbrenner's ecological framework (1979, 1989), this study aims to investigate Polish teachers' perceptions of cyberbullying, the effect of either being exposed to or engaging in cyberbullying on students'

---

* Corresponding Author's E-mail: Magdalena.Marczak@coventry.ac.uk.

psychological well-being and the importance of safety and support available in schools. Cyberbullying in secondary education is explored from the stakeholders' perspective using a qualitative method of enquiry. A total of 23 teachers participated in the semi-structured interviews. Participants whilst sharing their beliefs about cyberbullying identified its dangers, characteristics, and reasons behind perpetrating cyberbullying. Furthermore, whilst teachers' responses highlighted their awareness of available support both within and outside the school environment, they implored the need for further guidance in management of cyberbullying incidents. The current chapter highlights the value of Bronfenbrenner's ecological framework (1979, 1989) whilst trying to understand a relatively new phenomenon of cyberbullying among young people from the teachers' perspective. It is argued that this can be helpful when evaluating current and designing future interventions aiming at cyberbullying prevention and management.

Keywords: teachers, students, cyberbullying, consequences, support

INTRODUCTION

This chapter is intended to provide an understanding of cyberbullying phenomenon in schools among young people from the teachers' perspective. This chapter discusses the vital role teachers play in prevention and management of cyberbullying. Teachers' work involves managing the learning environment around a social dynamic of fluid relationships. In order to achieve required academic goals, teachers have to support their students not only in navigating the demands placed upon them by learning, but also by their social, emotional, and peer relationships. The latter can include dealing with the different forms of adolescent aggression including cyberbullying. Throughout the chapter the importance of understanding teachers' perceptions of cyberbullying is emphasised as the necessary first step to help them develop a good recognition of this phenomenon and develop skills to deal with it. Consideration is first given to cyberbullying in the global research context (the conceptualization and the prevalence and the impact on young people) to help the reader appreciate the importance of this work on a wider scale and not only in Poland, where the research project is based.

Following this, research undertaken by the authors is presented. Based on in-depth interviews with 23 teachers (74% females) from four different schools from the region of Lodz in Poland, the research was able to capture teachers' perceptions of cyberbullying, their understanding of its impact on young people's health and lives, their readiness to act when incidents of cyberbullying take place and finally the support the teachers voiced they need to help them prevent and manage cyberbullying within educational settings (Marczak, 2014). In conclusion the chapter highlights the value of Bronfenbrenner's ecological framework (1979) when evaluating current and designing future interventions aiming at cyberbullying prevention and management.

DEFINING CYBERBULLYING

It has been widely acknowledged that the nature of bullying has changed as technology has become a more integral and established means of communication (NSPCC, 2013). Young people in particular are drawn to different forms of technology and use it regularly. While the Pew Research Center 2018 study show that 45% of teenagers are online almost constantly, 72% reported checking for messages or notifications as soon as they wake up at least sometimes (with 44% doing it often; Jlang, 2018). These numbers are even higher for Polish young people, as results from Nastolatki 3.0 survey show 80% are either constantly online or go online on numerous occasions throughout the day (Tanaś, Kamieniecki, Bochenek, Wrońska, Lange, Fila, & Loba 2017). The Internet provides many benefits including connecting with others and access to vast information, however there are risks related to privacy, security, and harassment. Development of social media sites and online forums has encouraged new avenues through which bullying can occur, for example creating 'fake' online profiles and revenge porn (Ministry of Justice, 2015; Hinduja & Patchin, 2014). In addition, readily available access to the Internet has opened the door to a new phenomenon commonly known as cyberbullying (other names include cyber victimization, online victimization, and online aggression). Bullying through online technology increases anonymity, resulting in the perpetrator feeling unrestricted in what they say (Hinduja & Patchin, 2014). As there is a lack of direct social interaction, this may also give rise to a lack of awareness about the impact of bullying on the victim (Hinduja & Patchin, 2014). Furthermore, technology has enabled bullying to become a 24 hour experience that invades both public and private spaces (Betts & Spenser, 2017).

This new form of bullying has been termed technology assisted violence or cyberbullying and has been defined by Smith et al. (2008, p. 376) as:

> "an aggressive, intentional act carried out by a group or individual, using electronic forms of contact, repeatedly and over time against a victim who cannot easily defend him or herself."

There is no legal definition of cyberbullying (The Children's Society and Young Minds, 2018), which may lead to inconsistencies in how the term is understood. Within the literature, there is an ongoing debate regarding the key characteristics and defining features of cyberbullying (Olweus & Limber, 2018; Marczak & Coyne, 2016), including how power imbalance, intention, and repetition are understood (Marczak & Coyne, 2016). Smith et al. (2008) discussed frequency as a defining feature of cyberbullying; however it has been argued that a single act, such as posting online or creating a false profile, may in fact be classed as cyberbullying; in this case, it is possible for a wide audience to repeatedly access the online material which may cause continual harm to the individual targeted (Marczak & Coyne, 2016). As with more traditional forms of bullying, the definition of cyberbullying is subjective; it is dependent on the victim's perception and interpretation of their experience.

YOUNG PEOPLE AND THE PREVALENCE
OF CYBERBULLYING

The World Health Organisation (2014) recognizes the differing definitions and terms used to define young people, which include youth and adolescents. They define young people as aged between 10 and 24, a definition which encompasses both terms 'child' and 'adolescent.'

Cyberbullying appears to occur among people of all ages. However, most research has examined this phenomenon in young people, children and adolescents (Tokunaga, 2010). The reported prevalence rates for cyberbullying, across such studies, have ranged from about 10 to 72% (for example, Dehue, Bolman, & Völlink, 2008; Hinduja & Patchin, 2008; Juvonen & Gross, 2008; Kowalski & Limber, 2007; Li, 2007; Mishna, Cook, Gadalla, Daciuk, & Solomon, 2010; Patchin & Hinduja, 2006; Raskauskas & Stoltz, 2007; Schneider, O'Donnell, Stueve, & Coulter, 2012; Williams & Guerra, 2007). A recent meta-analysis of data from 80 such studies has suggested that prevalence rates for cyberbullying among young people are 15% for victimization and 16% for perpetration (Modecki, Minchin, Harbaugh, Guerra, & Runions, 2014).

The wide variation in reported rates across studies tends to reflect a difference in focus of a particular research study and the demographics of participants involved, in the measures and methods used, and in differences over time, between countries, cultures, and schools. Such differences make comparisons across studies and summarizing data difficult. When a restrictive time frame was used when asking young people when a cyberbullying incident took place (such as within the last year; DeHue, Bolman, & Völlink, 2008; Williams & Guerra, 2007; Wolak, Mitchell, & Finkelhor, 2007; Ybarra, 2004; Ybarra & Mitchell, 2008) the reported prevalence rates were lower than in the studies with no time frame imposed (Juvonen & Gross, 2008; Mishna et al. 2010; Raskauskas & Stoltz, 2007). Kowalski, Giumetti, Schroeder, and Lattanner (2014) also argued that the reported prevalence rates of cyberbullying depend largely on the means and method of communication being the most popular among the participants sample at the time of the research being conducted.

A significant part of childhood now includes life online, with an estimated 61% of UK young people creating social media accounts before the age of 13 (The Children's Society and Young Minds, 2018). EU Kids Online survey findings (Pyżalski, Zdrodowska, Tomczyk, & Abramczuk, 2019) show that 42.2% of girls and 53.5% of boys aged 9-10 also have a social media account; these numbers increase to 79.9% for girls and 78.6% for boys aged 11 to 19. At a young age, children are exposed to the double-edged sword that is technology, which gives both opportunities for connectedness and growth, but also the potential for harm. According to the 2018 EU Kids Online survey, conducted on 356 young people aged 9-17 years old, prevalence rates for Poland show that 12.4% of young people experienced cyberbullying at least once a month, 8.7% at least once a week, 16% everyday, and 35.4% a few times in last year (Pyżalski et al., 2019); a rise from 6% in 2011 for 960 young people aged 9 to 16 (Kirwil, 2011). These statistics reflect current growth rates and highlight the increasing need to understand and support young people who have experienced cyberbullying.

RISK FACTORS

A considerable amount of studies has tried to identify risk factors associated with cyberbullying perpetration and cyberbullies' motivation. These included beliefs about aggression (Ang, Huan, & Florell, 2014; Ang, Tan, & Talib Mansor, 2011; Kowalski et al. 2014), moral disengagement and lower emphatic responsiveness (Steffgen, König, Pfetsch, & Melzer, 2011), and exposure to violent online games (Lam, Cheng, & Liu, 2013) as well as poor parenting style (Floros, Siomos, Fisoun, Dafouli, & Geroukalis, 2013), parental unemployment (Arslan, Savaser, Hallett, & Balci, 2012), and poor parental control (Shapka, & Law, 2013). Sparse research has investigated the predictors of cyberbullying and their similarities and differences to those associated with traditional bullying (Marczak & Coyne, 2015).

Research also showed that cyber victimization is associated with intensive use of the Internet (Wolak et al., 2007), and poor body image for girls and nonheteronormative identification of young people (Guan, Kanagasundram, Ann, Hui, & Mun, 2016). Other predictive factors of cyber victimization include location of the computer at home and a lack of awareness of the risks involved in going online (Hinduja & Patchin, 2009; Sengupta & Chaudhuri, 2011).

IMPACT OF CYBERBULLYING ON YOUNG PEOPLE

There have been many quantitative studies which have shown that cyberbullying victimization in young people is associated with increased symptoms of depression (Bonanno & Hymel, 2013; Erdur Bakera & Tanrikulu, 2010; Landstedt & Persson, 2014; Chang, Lee, Chiu, His, Huang, & Pan 2013; Schneider, O'Donnell, Stueve, & Coulter, 2012). Schneider et al. (2012) found that 33.9% of young people who were victims of cyberbullying experienced symptoms of depression. Research has also shown that young people who had experienced cyberbullying victimization were more likely to have suicidal thoughts and they were 1.9 times more likely to have attempted suicide compared to people who have not experienced cyberbullying (Hinduja & Patchin, 2010). Therefore, such findings suggest that the psychological impact of being a victim of cyberbullying could be associated with life threatening consequences (Bonanno & Hymel, 2013). There is also evidence to suggest that cyberbullying victimization is associated with how the 'self' is perceived, particularly in relation to self-esteem (Brewer & Kerslake, 2015; Patchin & Hinduja, 2010; Brighi et. al., 2012), with cyber-victims having significantly lower self-esteem compared to those who have not experienced cyberbullying (Patchin & Hinduja, 2010).

Given the impact of cyberbullying victimization on mental health, it is unsurprising that research also highlights the impact of cyberbullying on social connectedness. Brighi et al. (2012) suggest that the lack of connection with parents and peers increases with the severity of cyberbullying victimization. Similarly, Spears, Taddeo, Daly, Stretton, and Karklins (2015) reported that victims of cyberbullying were significantly less likely to feel socially connected compared to those who did not experience cyberbullying. Brewer and Kerslake (2015) also found a significant positive correlation between cyberbullying and loneliness.

BACKGROUND OR CURRENT STUDY

The advancement of technology provided teachers with the opportunity to engage young people in lessons through the use of online material and thus provide them with positive experiences associated with the Internet use (Byron, 2008; Ertmer & Ottenbreit-Leftwich, 2010). However, research show that intensive use of the Internet emerged as a risk factor for child cyber victimization (Wolak et al., 2007). Additionally, teachers have a responsibility to supervise children when they use the internet, while promoting awareness of e-safety issues (Patchin & Hinduja, 2006; Popović-Ćitić, Djurić, & Cvetković, 2011). Teachers play a key role when providing education in terms of not only assisting in academic goal achievement but also providing emotional and social support to young people (Macaulay et al., 2018). Teachers are often the first adults dealing with student bullying/ cyberbullying—related incidents (Schmitz, Hoffman & Bickford, 2012; Oldenburg et al., 2015). Thus, understanding teachers' perceptions of the cyberbullying phenomenon can help develop new strategies to encourage young people to seek help and in turn to help teachers prevent, identify and manage cyberbullying incidents.

ECOLOGICAL MODEL

The World Health Organization used Bronfenbrenner's (1979) ecological system model to aggressive behavior to understand the multiple causes of aggressive behavior (1999, 2002). Within the model risk factors contributing to aggressive behavior have been identified as operating at four different levels (individual, relationship, family, and societal; Bronfenbrenner, 1979). A parallel method was proposed by Sutton and Smith (1999) to understand school bullying. Marczak's (2014) constructed an approach that allowed to further an understanding of cyberbullying using the four levels of the ecological model, together with the risk factors identified by research on school bullying and youth offending. Adapted model for school bullying is shown in Figure 1.

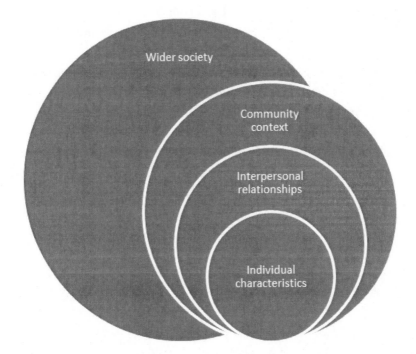

Figure 1. Ecological model for understanding school bullying (adapted from World Health Organization, 2002).

The first level of the ecological model focuses on the personal characteristics of the individual that play a role in the development of victimization or bullying behavior (e.g., the child's temperament). The second level of the model focuses on an individual's interpersonal relationships (i.e., with their family or friends) and how these may heighten the risk of being victimized or engaging in bullying behaviors. This could include factors such as parental style (Baldry & Farrington, 2000) and friendship relationships (Cairns, Leung, Buchanan & Caims, 1995). The third level of the model examines the community and more precisely the schools and neighborhoods as an ambience in which interpersonal relationships happen and attempts to establish which of them relate to an increased risk of either victimization or an occurrence of bullying behaviors. The identified risk factors on this level may encompass social circumstances (such as the care-givers being of no fixed abode, frequent relocations of the family and living within a heterogonous population), and economic factors (such as high levels of unemployment, likelihood of witnessing crime in terms of getting involved in gangs, guns and drug-dealing activities). Thus, the last mentioned characteristics of an immediate community can penetrate into school communities and act as encouragement for violent attitudes and behaviors. The fourth and the last level of the ecological model considers the wider societal factors that may affect the rates of violence. These include the established social and cultural norms supporting violence as an acceptable way of conflict resolution or a solution to a political conflict, undermining child welfare and giving priority to parental rights within a family home and possibly putting the child in danger and supporting male dominance over women and children. Other societal factors, such as the educational, economic, and social policies responsible for the economic or social inequality between groups in society, can also be included at this level (Askew, 1989; Carter, 2002; O'Moore, Kirkham & Smith, 1997).

Marczak's (2014) approach highlights that cyberbullying behaviors emerge from a complex intersection of young person's individual characteristics (such as personality and disposition) which continue to be modified as they move around the different context during childhood and early adolescence. Individual and social contextual factors are intertwined with one another, and they influence each other in a reciprocal manner. The proposed ecological model consists of four interrelated systems encompassing a number of factors or events with regards to cyberbullying, cyber victimization, and cyberbullying prevention and management (Marczak, 2014). The four systems include:

- the microsystem - individual characteristics of cyberbully/cyber-victim such as age, gender and individual differences that an individual brings to their behavior and which may increase the likelihood of being a cyberbully or a cybervictim;
- the mesosystem - interpersonal relationships such as parent-child relationships and home difficulties, and peer relationships and associated social support;
- the exosystem - school community context such as school environment, school climate, and teacher–student relationship;
- the macrosystem - wider society such as cultural norms and beliefs, media portrayal of violence, media industry – usage of IT for educational and personal purposes, access to medium, community environmental factors and intervention programmes.

Research investigating cyberbullying tends to examine the phenomenon from only one perspective (victim). Research investigating teachers' perceptions or understanding of the cyberbullying phenomena continues to be limited. This chapter presents cyberbullying as perceived by the self-selected group of Polish teachers.

METHOD AND FINDINGS

This study was conducted in the region of in the region of Łódź (województwo łódzkie) in Poland. Twenty-three teachers [17] females (74%) and 6 males (16%)] participated in semi-structured interviews. The interviews were analyzed using thematic analysis, a flexible and useful tool which can potentially provide a rich, detailed, and yet complex, account of data. From their accounts, seven codebooks were identified. The codebooks included Internet, Perspicacity, Seen through the eyes of bystander, Threat to self and well-being, Readiness to act, and Avoidance and Support (Table 1).

Table 1. Codebooks with identified main themes and subthemes

Cyberbullying phenomenon		
Codebook	**Main themes**	**Subthemes**
Codebook 1: 'Internet'	Use	-Educational -Personal
	Access to medium	-Improvement -Hindrance
Codebook 2: 'Perspicacity'	Understanding of the phenomenon	-Personal experience -Means -Medium -Technique
	Beliefs about cyberbullying	-Reasons -Dangers -Characteristics
Codebook 3: 'Threat to self and well-being'	Consequences for cyber-victim	-Threat to own health -Threat to social life
	Consequences for cyberbully	- At school -In personal life
Codebook 4: 'Readiness to act'	Action taken by cyber-victim	
	Action taken by teacher/school	-School staff involvement -Organisational characteristics
Codebook 5: 'Seen through the eyes of bystander'	Cyberbully	-Social immaturity -Emotional disturbance -Lack of perspective taking
	Cyber-victim	
Codebook 6:'Avoidance'	Avoidance in accessing support	
	Factors preventing problem solving	
Codebook 7:'Support'	Future solutions	
	Ability to identify	

The *Internet* codebook which emerged through the data analysis focused on participants' views in terms of the Internet and the risks and opportunities associated with its use by young people, was linked to three out of four layers of the ecological model. Results presented in the *Internet* codebook confirmed the increased popularity of Internet-related technologies among young people, with participants commenting on two main reasons for using the net; these being educational and personal purposes.

"They are trying to find information as are not used to looking in books anymore so the most often they are using Internet to do so", teacher 4, line 4 – 6

The personal reasons consisted of continuing communication with friends after schools using social networking sites (such as Nasza Klasa, Facebook) and communicators (such as Gadu-Gadu).

"They go on various social networking sites, I know that Facebook is very popular, or Gadu-Gadu, they speak about it very often, sometimes during school break I hear that here and there they have posted some pictures", teacher 5, line 5 -7

Polish teachers also commented on increased awareness among parents of the importance of the Internet as an educational tool. They believed that access to the Internet is available in almost every household providing that school-aged children were part of it. They also perceived the Internet as an important medium enhancing their children's development in different domains.

"I think parents are aware now that the Internet is needed for their kids to broaden their interests and hobbies and for educational purposes", teacher 7, line 16

In addition, they believed access to the Internet whilst at school is restricted as some of the websites of interest to students were not accessible at school and they could use the Internet only during the IT lessons and at times during the break between lessons on a request basis.

Linking the findings presented in the *Internet* codebook with the ecological model of cyberbullying, Marczak (2014) suggested that the Internet can be seen as part of the macrosystem (in terms of the wider society factors), which permeates throughout all other layers of the model. Internet related technologies allow for interaction between individuals, families and schools, affect young people's development, and help them gain new skills. They use social networking sites and communicators to sustain relationships with their peers outside of the school environment and use Internet related technologies for basic or school related activities for short periods of time (such as finding information). The Internet as part of the macrosystem thus affects the mesosytem layer (in terms of different communication styles) and exosystem layer (in terms of changes to learning environment).

The *Perspicacity* codebook focuses on the participants' understanding of and beliefs around the cyberbullying phenomenon. This section is broken down into two main themes, the first showed the knowledge that teachers had on cyberbullying was acquired through reading examples of cases of cyberbullying in the press or watching TV- related documentaries, as well as from personal experience of dealing with cyberbullying incidents or observing how the colleague dealt with it.

> "There were two publicized cases in Poland when there was a movie created. I can't recall the exact details but I know that the movie was of a teenage girl from around Gdansk. This movie was made using a mobile phone whilst at school, posted on the Internet. This was connected to some sort of sexual abuse as well and I know that the girl has committed suicide after the movie had been posted online," teacher 2, line 7 - 12

Moreover, this theme showed Polish teachers were aware how and via which means cyberbullying can be perpetrated. They felt that whilst cyberbullying may be used to intimidate others and cause the victim emotional pain and distress, it can also be seen as an activity that people engage in when bored, a method of entertainment and to gain popularity amongst peers.

> "I think that young people don't do it by accident but that it's premeditated to abase the other person, to cause them to hurt, to humiliate them.", teacher 7, line 1 - 4

"I think that the society changes, the young people mature quicker, they have different interests and something that in my youth was seen as something good something that was of interest to me and my peers it's nothing to them. They are not interested by literature or films so I suspect that they want to do something in life that is interesting, different to feel adrenaline buzzing in their veins.", teacher 8, line 31 - 39

They saw cyberbullying as a social activity because communicating via social networking sites is widely popular and accepted way among the teenagers. Thus, it can be assumed that Polish school staff see cyberbullying as an issue taking place not only within students' home environment.

"Someone writes some rubbish about another person. We even had such a case here in our school.", teacher 8, line 23 - 24

The *Threat to self and well-being* codebook focused on the seriousness of cyberbullying in terms of its impact on students' health and well-being. Feeling stressed and experiencing stress-related physical health problems, feeling low in mood and/or suicidal, and engaging in self-harming behaviors were the consequences of cyber victimization mentioned by the teachers.

"I had a case when it transpired afterwards whilst speaking to her parents that the victim, the girl got so stressed about being threatened and abused over the Internet that resulted in worsening of the heart condition she had.", teacher 13, line 4-6

They also consistently felt that cyberbullying may affect the cyber-victim's emotional state (in terms of the cyber-victim feeling vulnerable, humiliated and having a low self-esteem) and school attendance. The teachers expressed an opinion that the cyber-victim may feel afraid to come to school if the perpetrator is another student from their school. Further to this they identified some of the difficulties a cyber-victim may have whilst at school such as struggling with group work tasks and coming up with various reasons for not attending classes. Although this has not been mentioned by the teachers, some students also suggested that the cyber-victim's school performance may deteriorate as they may find it difficult to concentrate. One of the teachers gave an example of students who were cyberbullied and stated that the students attempted to stop attending school at the time.

> "Some victims may try to commit suicide, they may feel so alone and without any contact with the world that they may try to commit suicide.", teacher 15, line 26 - 28

> "Such a child does not want to come to school, is scared and finds a lot of excuses of why not to come to school and attend classes, struggles for example with working with other students but it's because they don't want to have anything to do with the victim.", teacher 6, line 8 - 11

Polish participants also recognized that cyber victimization may negatively impact the victim's social life in terms of social isolation and having problems interacting with other people and therefore having difficulty sustaining friendships or making new friends.

Finally, within this codebook Polish teachers did report a factor which has not, to date, been considered in the research literature. This focused on the impact of cyberbullying on young people who perpetrate this behavior. The participants highlighted that cyberbullies face a number of consequences at school in line with the school regulations (such as having his/ her behavioral grade marked down and being banned from using a mobile phone on school's premises) as well as at home in terms of parents imposing restrictions on the young people's access to the Internet.

> "From school perspective the consequences included only lower behavior grades as by law the school cannot punish the student in another way only using the behavior grades or suspension policy.", teacher 21, line 31 – 33

> "They were forbidden to use their mobile phone at school.", teacher 22, line 20 – 21

Additionally, they also spoke about a perpetrator having some law sanctions imposed on him/her. These depending on the perpetrator's age could include a judicial review of the case, having a probation officer assigned for a period of time, and being sent to a borstal or to a young offender's institution.

"They may have a probation officer assigned to them if the case goes to court and if sentenced, they may go to the Young Offender Institution for a period of time.", teacher 3, line 35 - 36

"For cyberbullies it's usually done through the judicial system, if it's a minor then it's some kind of a borstal though it's does not fulfil the rehabilitation needs for sure, and if it's an adult than a short sentence in prison.", teacher 4, line 16 - 19

The *Readiness to act* codebook combined methods for preventing and addressing cyberbullying issues in schools and managing cyber victimization by the victim and the victim's peers using the knowledge they have. A whole school community approach was considered to be required and the need to involve pupils, staff, other schools, parents, and the wider community was highlighted. Polish teachers spoke about cyber-victims accessing support from their friends, confronting the perpetrator, retaliating, and lastly seeking support and advice from adults such as their parents, older siblings, and school staff. The decision of who would be approached as explicitly stated by Polish teachers seemed to depend on the cyber-victim's relationships with his/her parents or the atmosphere in the family home.

"Very often it is the case that the parents hear about the situation quite late in time. Well it may depend on the relationships or atmosphere at home but I think that young people are not very willing to share their problems with their parents, especially not at first and it's similar case whist sharing problems with the teachers. This depends who this teacher is and if young people have trust in them then yes it's more likely they would share their problems, however from what I know about young people, teachers and parents are the last resort they turn to when looking for help. I know this from my experience really," teacher 2, line 8 - 12

One female teacher gave an example of her son who when he was cyberbullied sought her support. She believed that this was because of the positive atmosphere of home environment and the son's perception that the parents would not blame him for his behavior and rather try to find a constructive solution to the problem he had.

"I had such a case with my own son, when I saw what was online, because he came and told me. My son is quite open with us and comes to us if things are happening and knows that even if he did something wrong he can come to us and will not be punished but that we will try together to find some sensible solution from the situation he found himself in.", teacher 7, line 7 - 10

These findings concur with the ways of coping with cyberbullying experiences as identified in the literature. Research indicate that cyber-victims tend to use technological coping strategies such as changing privacy settings (Aricak et al., 2008; Juvonen & Gross, 2008), user names (Juvonen & Gross, 2008) or email addresses (Smith et al., 2008) as a way of preventing further cyber victimization. Other active coping strategies employed by young people included confronting cyberbullies (Patchin & Hinduja, 2006; Aricak et al., 2008; Juvonen & Gross, 2008), informing parents or other adults about being cyberbullying (Slonje & Smith, 2008; Aricak et al., 2008; DeHue et al., 2008), and asking friends for advice (Slonje & Smith, 2008; Aricak et al., 2008; DeHue et al., 2008).

Polish teachers spoke about a number of measures known to them that were put in place in their school to prevent cyberbullying and to help the school staff and the students involved deal with such an incident when it takes place. They spoke about advising students in terms of preventing further cybervictimization, putting emphasis on the importance of not using whichever platform cyberbullying was taking place.

"It is difficult to ascertain who did what and as the perpetrator needs to be found by appropriate body, I would say 'don't get in touch with that person, don't respond'. That's what I would advise absolutely.", teacher 15, line 22 - 24

Teachers also spoke about how they would deal with an incident of cyberbullying. They stated that they would inform the parents, or the guardians of the students involved in such an incident. One of the teachers whilst recalling an incident she dealt with in the past, spoke about still feeling unsure whether she has made the right decision, adding that she decided to contact the students' parents about the situation that was brought to her attention.

> "I'm not sure whether I was right but I thought I needed to talk to the parents first.", teacher 7, line 33

Other teachers stated that they would either contact the police as they felt that then the perpetrator could be traced or seek further guidance from other professionals such as a school psychologist or a school pedagogue.

> "Don't even know whether there is sense to talk to the perpetrator, I would go straight to the police, they could do something about it.", teacher 6, line 2 - 4

The teachers also spoke about some measures that have been put in place at the schools where they work that increased their understanding of the cyberbullying phenomenon and the procedures they followed whilst dealing with the cyberbullying incidents. These included training events focusing on the cyberbullying phenomenon for teachers, holding special assemblies for students, during which this topic has been raised and posters placed on the school walls which included a 'what to do' guide for students if they are cyberbullied. In addition to these cyberbullying-deterrent measures teachers talked about having imposed a mobile phone ban on school premises as a way of preventing cyberbullying, which they felt made a recognizable difference.

> "There is an automatic ban on the use of mobile phones by kids. They cannot use their mobile phones whilst on school premises. They can access the school mobile phone, the parents know its number and they also can access a landline and if there is such a need they can always talk to their

parents, notify them about things. This is the way we do it in this school,"
teacher 6, line 1 - 5

The *Seen through the eyes of bystander* codebook described a cyber-victim and a cyberbully as perceived through the eyes of others. Teachers using their experience of incidents they dealt with in the past characterized the cyber-victim as quite an isolated person and outside of a peer group. One teacher gave an example of a student whose behavior has changed during the course of a school year. The teacher noticed that she [the student] was treated by her peers in a different manner. It transpired that she had been a cyber-victim and that some of her peers believed the messages that have been posted. This in turn changed the peer group's perception of their 'friend' and initiated the visible change in the relationship between the students.

> "I did not have to ask. I actually saw the difference in her [the victim's] behavior, judging from how she was at the beginning of the school year and later on. She became more private, lonely, on her own during the breaks. Before she used to be quite friendly with others....You can notice that part of the class was avoiding her, the other part kept laughing at her. Obviously some students believed that the messages were true and were just avoiding her," teacher 17, line 28 - 34

Participants also agreed on a number of negative features which characterize a cyberbully. These included the lack of consideration for the victim's feelings, lack of perspective taking, not thinking about the consequences of his/her behavior and the impact it may have on the victim, and being proud of his/her behavior and engaging in cyberbullying purposefully to make oneself feel better.

> "Well when you think about the other side of the coin, the perpetrators or the cyberbullies, people who just hurt others. I think that such characteristics or features just reinforce themselves in that person even more and they start to think 'oh I can do anything' so that there is no space for feelings such as the empathy towards another human being left, no

perspective taking, no 'how would I feel if this happened to me'. Such features are just lacking in this person. That's what I think anyway.", teacher 6, line 12 – 16

Teachers also indicated that perpetrating cyberbullying may be used as a maladaptive coping mechanism, fulfilling a need to feel in control or to attract attention, employed when the perpetrators face or have to deal with a difficult situation at home, and which in turn allows the individuals to feel in control of their lives.

"The perpetrator is a kid who has some kind of problems or issues, most likely at home and I think maybe they are just trying to become centre of their parents' attention. Maybe the parents have an alcohol problem, maybe there is a lot of arguments in the family home going on and maybe the kid is just trying to turn the parents' attention to themselves to feel they still exist.", teacher 3, line 31 - 33

Therefore, school staff could play an important role when working with students to enable them to understand the real emotional and psychological impact cyberbullying can have. As dealing with such issues in a school context required considerable tact and discretion, future research should consider how these incidents could be dealt with most effectively in the future.

The *Avoidance* codebook focused on exploring reasons why young people tend not to report being cyberbullied, more specifically on factors preventing effective problem-solving, which in turn could impact the victim's readiness to act in such circumstances. These included being afraid of parental reaction, not knowing who the best person would be to speak about a cyberbullying incident to or not believing that school staff could be of help in such matters. Teachers also felt that another deterrent factor to not reporting cyberbullying incidents is the victim's perception of the lack of the social support available to them.

"I can't see this happening. None of the students would come to speak to me about such an issue. Thinking about the students I have and their social background I don't think even one would come. It's not only that they would not tell me they would not tell it to anyone and just kept it to themselves," teacher 18, line 28 - 29

Doing nothing in response to being victimized has been previously reported though passive coping strategies are infrequently employed (Patchin & Hinduja, 2006). In terms of cyberbullying this may be more complex as current findings suggest that students are reluctant to report cyber victimization to teachers, parents or police for fear of retribution from the bully and other students. Previous research indicated that school staff were the least likely chosen adults to report cyber-victimization to (Slonje & Smith, 2008; Kowalski et al., 2008). The findings showing young people's reluctance to approach parents or teachers for support (Marczak, 2014) emphasized an interesting conundrum in the literature in this area (Slonje & Smith, 2008; Kowalski et al., 2008). In theory, positive family relationships and the ability to seek and receive support from adults should help young people deal with difficult situations. This is an area which requires significant consideration from parents, school staff and the young people themselves particularly given the fact that schools are already reporting struggling with the increase in workload in terms of the national curriculum and the lack of time to teach.

The *Support* codebook focused on suggestions made by Polish teachers which they would like to be employed within schools and their wider communities and which could further cyberbullying prevention and management. Teachers spoke about a requirement to have a designated member of school staff who deals specifically with cyberbullying incidents, such as a psychologist or a school pedagogue, and would give students information on the subject, was a clear point of call for students to report cybervictimization and who whilst would be able to give appropriate support to students would also be able to advise teachers on management of a cyberbullying incident.

"Surely the preventative measures should be put in place. And the psychologist should have some kind of plan of action prepared in case it's needed, so for example they should know who to contact first, whether it's parents or teacher," teacher 3, line 24 - 27

"I think that we [the teachers] should learn many things still. To say the truth the schools in general need someone like a psychologist or a pedagogue to be employed full-time. If that took place then we would be told what to do, what is the risk how to behave if a student reports such a problem or if we learn by accident that a student is cyberbullied. I can tell you that if a student would come to me at the moment I would try to find out what I should do as I don't have this knowledge as yet," teacher 4, line 5 – 9

Moreover, they felt that accessing outside agencies for help and support in dealing with cyberbullying incidents should be made more straightforward. They believed that other agencies, such as the police, would be better equipped in dealing with cyberbullying incidents than school staff and therefore such a liaison would be of benefit both to all involved in an incident of cyberbullying in some respect.

"I think that what is happening now should not really take place anymore. Such avoiding of accessing outside agencies' help such as even informing the police or referring a student to an outside agency for help, such as a pedagogue or a psychologist. Till now it never happened." teacher 13, line 34 – 36

Additionally, teachers highlighted the need for more information on the issue of cyberbullying and therefore they would welcome talks or workshops on the issue separately for both teachers and students. They hoped that this in turn would raise the parents' awareness of the cyberbullying phenomena as well. Finally, Polish teachers spoke at length about the lack of guidance they feel is prevalent with regard to the handling or dealing with cyberbullying incidents.

"I don't know anything about this. I don't know if the ministry [of education] deals with such issues but if it does then it's all top secret as I know absolutely nothing about such guidelines," teacher 6, line 16 - 17

The presented above results highlight difficulties faced by Polish teachers when managing cyberbullying incidents in terms of safeguarding students in the schools, the barriers encountered by staff in order to be able to carry out this function and the need to involve the wider community for successful management of cyberbullying incidents.

SUMMARY

These findings highlight that raising awareness among adults needs to continue. Adults (school staff and parents – representing exosystem and mesosystem in the ecosystemic framework) are responsible for creating environments in which young people's capacities and competencies for healthy relationships can be promoted and in which opportunities for negative peer interactions are minimized (Craig & Pepler, 2007). Adults can help young people protect themselves against cyber victimization, provide support during a cyberbullying incident, minimize the re-occurrence of cyber victimization only when it is understood and accepted that cyberbullying is not just a school staff' problem, and that parental involvement together with help from the wider society (statutory and regulatory organisations representing the macrosystem) are essential requirements of the intervention programmes.

Bronfenbrenner's (1979) theory of ecological systems provides a framework for conceptualizing cyberbullying. It states that human development is affected by several ecological systems. Bronfenbrenner's (1979) model has been adapted to explain a wide range of social problems, such as childhood obesity (Opalinski, 2006), postpartum depression (Garfield & Isacco, 2009), the multiple causes of aggressive behavior (WHO, 2002), and traditional bullying (Swearer and Espelage, 2004). Marczak (2014) proposed it can also be used to help to explain the phenomenon of cyberbullying. Micro, meso, exo, and macro systems of the model are all intertwined and are present in the young person's life from the very beginning, first of all in the family house, and then in school and wider community. Findings from this study highlight that the experience of teachers in terms of dealing with the incidents of cyberbullying is similar in terms of some teachers having had such an experience whilst others did not. Regardless of the level of experience, Polish teachers were aware of incidents involving students if not from the school they worked at then in others. Moreover, whilst some teachers were able to follow the school's anti-cyberbullying policy, others were not aware whether such policy existed within their educational establishment. They saw the need for further guidance from the policy makers on how to manage cyberbullying incidents, the need for further training events or workshops that would enhance their knowledge in this area.

CONCLUSION

Few researches have been conducted on cyberbullying prevention and intervention (Grigg, 2010), although a whole school approach is seen as imperative. Both the preventative and the management strategies should ideally combine as many ecological systems as possible to help reinforce the message that whether it is traditional school bullying or cyberbullying, such behavior in wrong and should be avoided. In accordance to the Ecological Systems Theory (Bronfenbrenner, 1979), it is of paramount importance that students, school staff, parents and the wider community work together in order to develop and implement multi-level strategies.

REFERENCES

Ang, R. P., Huan, V. S., & Florell, D. (2014). Understanding the relationship between proactive and reactive aggression, and cyberbullying across United States and Singapore adolescent samples. *Journal of Interpersonal Violence, 29*(2), 237-254. DOI: 10.1177/ 0886260513505149.

Ang, R. P., Tan, K. A., & Talib Mansor, A. (2011). Normative beliefs about aggression as a mediator of narcissistic exploitativeness and cyberbullying. *Journal of interpersonal violence, 26*(13), 2619-2634. DOI: 10.1177/0886260510388286.

Aricak, T., Siyahhan, S., Uzunhasanoglu, A., Saribeyoglu, S., Ciplak, S., Yilmaz, N., & Memmedov, C. (2008). Cyberbullying among Turkish adolescents. *CyberPsychology & Behavior, 11*(3), 253-261. doi: 10.1089/cpb.2007.0016.

Arslan, S., Savaser, S., Hallett, V., & Balci, S. (2012). Cyberbullying among primary school students in Turkey: Self-reported prevalence and associations with home and school life. *Cyberpsychology, Behavior, and Social Networking, 15*(10), 527-533. http://doi.org/10.1089/cyber. 2012.0207.

Askew, S. (1989). Aggressive behaviour in boys: to what extent is it institutionalized? In D. P. Tattum & D. A. Lane (Eds.) *Bullying in Schools*, (pp. 659-713). Stoke-on-Trent: Trentham Books.

Baldry, A. C., & Farrington, D. P. (2000). Bullies and delinquents: Personal characteristics and parental styles. *Journal of community & applied social psychology, 10*(1), 17-31. http://dx.doi.org/10.1002/(SICI)1099-1298(200001/02)10:1<17::AID-CASP526>3.0.CO;2-M.

Betts, L. R. & Spenser, K. A. (2017). "People think it's a harmless joke": young people's understanding of the impact of technology, digital vulnerability and cyberbullying in the United Kingdom, *Journal of Children and Media, 11*(1), 20-35. DOI: 10.1080/17482798.2016. 1233893.

Bonanno, R. A. & Hymel, S. (2013). Cyber bullying and internalizing difficulties: Above and beyond the impact of traditional forms of bullying, *Journal of Youth and Adolescence, 42*(5), 685-697. DOI: 10.1007/s10964-013-9937-1.

Braun, V., & Clarke, V. (2013). *Successful qualitative research: A practical guide for beginners.* Sage.

Brewer G. & Kerslake, J. (2015). Cyberbullyng, self-esteem, empathy and loneliness, *Computers in Human Behaviour, 48*(C), 255-260. https://doi. org/10.1016/j.chb.2015.01.073.

Brighi, A., Melotti, G., Guarini, A., Genta, M. L., Ortega, R., Mora-Merchán, J., Thompson, F. (2012). Self-esteem and loneliness in relation to cyberbullying in three European countries, In Q. Li, D. Cross, and P. K. Smith (Eds.), *Cyberbullying in the global playground: research from international perspectives* (pp. 32-56), Sussex, UK: Blackwell Publishing Ltd.

Bronfenbrenner, U. (1979). Contexts of child rearing: Problems and prospects. *American Psychologist*, *34*(10), 844. http://dx.doi.org/ 10.1037/0003-066X.34.10.844.

Byron, T. (2008). *Safer children in a digital world: The report of the Byron Review: Be safe, be aware, have fun.* Department for Children, School and Families, and the Department for Culture, Media and Sport. Retrieved from: https://dera.ioe.ac.uk//7332/

Cairns, R. B., Leung, M. C., Buchanan, L., & Cairns, B. D. (1995). Friendships and social networks in childhood and adolescence: Fluidity, reliability, and interrelations. *Child development*, *66*(5), 1330-1345. DOI: 10.2307/1131650.

Carter, C. (2002). Schools Ethos and the Construction of Masculine Identity: do schools create, condone and sustain aggression? *Educational Review*, *54*(1), 27-36. https://doi.org/10.1080/00131910120110857.

Chang, F. C., Lee, C. M., Chiu, C. H., Hsi, W. Y., Huang, T. F. & Pan, Y. C. (2013). Relationships among cyberbullying, school bullying, and mental health in Taiwanese adolescents, *Journal of School Health, 83*(6), 454-462. https://doi.org/10.1111/josh.12050.

Children's Society and Young Minds (2018). *Safety net: Cyberbullying's impact on young people's mental health inquiry report.* Retrieved from: https:// www.childrenssociety.org.uk/ sites/ default/ files/ social-media-cyberbullying-inquiry-full-report_0.pdf.

Craig, W. M., & Pepler, D. J. (2007). Understanding bullying: From research to practice. *Canadian Psychology*, *48*(2), 86. http://dx.doi.org/10.1037/ cp2007010.

DeHue, F., Bolman, C., & Völlink, T. (2008). Cyber-bullying: Youngsters' experiences and parental perception. *Cyberpsychology and Behavior*, 11(2), 217–223. doi:10.1089/cpb.2007.0008.

Erdur Bakera, O. & Tanrikulu, O. (2010). Psychological consequences of cyber bullying experiences among Turkish secondary school children, *Procedia Social and Behavioral Sciences*, 2(2), 2771-2776. doi:10.1016/j.sbspro.2010.03.413.

Ertmer, P. A., & Ottenbreit-Leftwich, A. T. (2010). Teacher technology change: How knowledge, confidence, beliefs, and culture intersect. *Journal of research on Technology in Education*, 42(3), 255-284. https://doi.org/10.1080/15391523.2010.10782551.

Floros, G. D., Siomos, K. E., Fisoun, V., Dafouli, E., & Geroukalis, D. (2013). Adolescent online cyberbullying in Greece: The impact of parental online security practices, bonding, and online impulsiveness. *Journal of School Health*, 83(6), 445-453.

Garfield, C. F., & Isacco, A. (2009). Urban fathers' role in maternal postpartum mental health. *Fathering: A Journal of Theory, Research, and Practice about Men as Fathers*, 7(3), 286-302. http://dx.doi.org/10.3149/fth.0703.286.

Grigg, D. W. (2010). Cyber-Aggression: Definition and Concept of Cyberbullying. *Australian Journal of Guidance and Counselling*, 20, 143-156. http://dx.doi.org/10.1375/ajgc.20.2.143.

Guan, N. C., Kanagasundram, S., Ann, Y. H., Hui, T. L., & Mun, T. K. (2016). Cyber bullying-a new social menace. *Advisory Board, Associate Editors Associations Between Low Self-Control and Editorial Board Members iii-v and Aggression Among Malaysian Male Prisoners 79-86 Information for Authors vi*, 104.

Hinduja, S., & Patchin, J. W. (2008). Cyber-bullying: An exploratory analysis of factors related to offending and victimization. Deviant Behavior, 29(2), 129–156. doi:10.1080/01639620701457816.

Hinduja, S., & Patchin J. W. (2009) *Bullying Beyond the Schoolyard: Preventing and Responding to Cyberbullying*. Thousand Oaks, CA: Sage.

Hinduja, S. & Patchin, J. W. (2010). Bullying, cyberbullying, and suicide, *Archives of Suicide Research, 14*(3), 206–221 doi: 10.1080/13811118.2010.494133.

Hinduja, S. & Patchin J. W. (2014). *Cyberbullying: identification, prevention, & response.* Cyberbullying Research Center. Retrieved from http://cyberbullying.org/Cyberbullying-Identification-Prevention-Response.pdf.

Jlang, J. (2018). *How Teens and parents navigate screen time and device distractions.* Pew Research Center. Retrieved from https://www.pew internet.org/ 2018/ 08/ 22/ how-teens-and-parents-navigate-screen-time-and-device-distractions/.

Juvonen, J., & Gross, E. F. (2008). Extending the school grounds?—Bullying experiences in cyberspace. *Journal of School health*, 78(9), 496–505. DOI: 10.1111/j.1746-1561.2008.00335.x.

Kirwil, L. (2011). *Polskie dzieci w Internecie. Zagrożenia i bezpieczeństwo - część 2. Częściowy raport z badań EU Kids Online II przeprowadzonych wśród dzieci w wieku 9-16 lat i ich rodziców. [Polish children on the Internet. Dangers and safety – part 2. Partial report of EU Kids Online II conducted among children aged 9-16 years old and their parents].* Warszawa: SWPS – EU Kids Online - PL. Retrieved from http:// www. swps. pl/ images/ stories/ zdjecia/ eukidsonline/ 1_ kirwil_raport_polska_eukidsonline_v3.pdf.

Kowalski, R. M., Giumetti, G. W., Schroeder, A. N., & Lattanner, M. R. (2014). Bullying in the digital age: A critical review and meta-analysis of cyber-bullying research among youth. *Psychological Bulletin,* 140(4), 1073–1137. doi:10.1037/a0035618.

Kowalski, R. M., & Limber, S. P. (2007). Electronic bullying among middle school students. *Journal of Adolescent Health*, 41, 22–30. doi:10.1016/ j.jadohealth.2007.08.017.

Kowalski, R. M., Limber, S. P., & Agatston, P. W. (2008). *Cyberbullying.* Malden, MA: Blackwell.

Lam, L. T., Cheng, Z., & Liu, X. (2013). Violent online games exposure and cyberbullying/victimization among adolescents. *Cyberpsychology, Behavior, and Social Networking, 16*(3), 159-165. DOI: 10.1089/cyber. 2012.0087.

Landstedt, E. & Persson, S. (2014). Bullying, cyberbullying, and mental health in young people, *Scandinavian Journal of Public Health, 42*(4), 393-399. doi: 10.1177/1403494814525004.

Li, Q. (2007). Bullying in the new playground: Research into cyber-bullying and cyber victimisation. *Australasian Journal of Educational Technology*, 23(4), 435. Retrieved from ajet.org.au/ index.php/AJET/ article/download/1245/617.

Macaulay, P. J., Betts, L. R., Stiller, J., & Kellezi, B. (2018). Perceptions and responses towards cyberbullying: A systematic review of teachers in the education system. *Aggression and violent behavior, 43*, 1-12. https://doi.org/10.1016/j.avb.2018.08.004.

Marczak, M. (2014). *An ecological model of cyberbullying based on the stakeholders' perceptions of the phenomenon.* Unpublished PhD thesis, University of Nottingham.

Marczak, M., & Coyne, I. (2015). A focus on online bullying. In A. Attrill (Ed.), *Cyberpsychology*. Oxford, UK: Oxford University Press.

Marczak, M,. & Coyne, I. (2016). English teachers and cyberbullying - a qualitative exploration of the stakeholders' perceptions and experience of the phenomenon. In M. F. Wright (Ed.), *A social-ecological approach to cyberbullying* (pp. 197-224). Hauppauge: Nova Publishing.

Ministry of Justice (2015). *Revenge Porn: be aware b4 you share.* Retrieved from https://www.gov.uk/government/publications/revenge-porn-be-aware-b4-you-share.

Mishna, F., Cook, C., Gadalla, T., Daciuk, J., & Solomon, S. (2010). Cyber bullying behaviors among middle and high school students. *American Journal of Orthopsychiatry,* 80(3), 362– 374. doi:10.1111/j.1939-0025.2010.01040.x.

Modecki, K. L., Minchin, J., Harbaugh, A. G., Guerra, N. G., & Runions, K. C. (2014). Bullying prevalence across contexts: A meta-analysis measuring cyber and traditional bullying. *Journal of Adolescent Health,* 55(5), 602–611. doi:10.1016/j.jadohealth.2014.06.007.

NSPCC (2013). *Under Pressure: Childline Review.* What's Affected Children in April 2013 to March 2014. Retrieved from https://www

.nspcc.org.uk/globalassets/documents/annual-reports/childline-review-under-pressure.pdf

Oldenburg, B., van Duijn, M., Sentse, M., Huitsing, G., van der Ploeg, R., Salmivalli, C., & Veenstra, R. (2015). Teacher characteristics and peer victimization in elementary schools: A classroom-level perspective. *Journal of Abnormal Child Psychology*, *43*(1), 33-44. DOI 10.1007/s10802-013-9847-4.

Olweus, D. & Limber, S. P. (2018). Some problems with cyberbullying research, *Current Opinion in Psychology*, *19*, 139–143. DOI: 10.1016/j.copsyc.2017.04.012.

O'Moore, M., Kirkham, C., & Smith, M. (1997). Bullying behaviour in Irish schools: a nationwide study. *Irish Journal of Psychology, 10*, 426–441. https://doi.org/10.1080/03033910.1997.10558137.

Opalinski, A. (2006). Pouring rights contracts and childhood overweight: A critical theory perspective. *Journal for Specialists in Pediatric Nursing*, *11*(4), 234-243. https://doi.org/10.1111/j.1744-6155.2006.00075.x.

Patchin, J. W., & Hinduja, S. (2006). Bullies move beyond the schoolyard a preliminary look at cyber- bullying. *Youth Violence and Juvenile Justice*, 4(2), 148–169. doi:10.1177/1541204006286288.

Patchin J. W. & Hinduja, S. (2010). Cyberbullying and self-esteem, *Journal of School Health,80*(12), 614-621. doi: 10.1111/j.1746-1561.2010. 00548.x.

Popović-Ćitić, B., Djurić, S., & Cvetković, V. (2011). The prevalence of cyberbullying among adolescents: A case study of middle schools in Serbia. *School Psychology International*, 32(4), 412–424. https://doi. org/10.1177/ 0143034311401700.

Pyżalski, J., Zdrodowska, A., Tomczyk, Ł., Abramczuk, K. (2019). *Polskie badanie EU Kids Online 2018. Najważniejsze wyniki i wnioski* [*Polish EU Kids Online research 2018. The most important results and conclusions*]. Poznań: Wydawnictwo Naukowe UAM. Retrieved from https://fundacja.orange.pl/files/user_files/EU_Kids_Online_2019_v2.p df?fbclid=IwAR2Cu36BgtbIYyBjdh2yvHEe_Ar4wHXi02xqHjX8f07d iucIrD4jxDUItRc.

Raskauskas, J., & Stoltz, A. D. (2007). Involvement in traditional and electronic bullying among adolescents. *Developmental Psychology,* 43(3), 564. doi:10.1037/0012-1649.43.3.564.

Shapka, J. D., & Law, D. M. (2013). Does one size fit all? Ethnic differences in parenting behaviors and motivations for adolescent engagement in cyberbullying. *Journal of Youth and Adolescence,* 42(5), 723-738. doi 10.1007/s10964-013-9928-2.

Schmitz, M., Hoffman, M. S., & Bickford, J. H. (2012). Identifying cyberbullying, connecting with students: The promising possibilities of teacher-student social networking. *Eastern Education Journal,* 16. Retrieved from: https://thekeep.eiu.edu/cgi/viewcontent.cgi?referer= https://www.google.com/&httpsredir=1&article=1000&context=eemed u_fac.

Schneider, S. K., O'Donnell, L., Stueve, A., & Coulter, R. W. (2012). Cyberbullying, school bullying, and psychological distress: A regional census of high school students. *American Journal of Public Health,* 102(1), 171–177. doi: 10.2105/AJPH.2011.300308.

Slonje, R., & Smith, P. K. (2008). Cyberbullying: Another main type of bullying?. *Scandinavian journal of psychology,* 49(2), 147-154. doi: 10.1111/j.1467-9450.2007.00611.x.

Smith, P. K., Mahdavi, J., Carvalho, M., Fisher, S., Russell, S. & Tippett, N. (2008). Cyberbullying: its nature and impact in secondary school pupils, *Journal of Child Psychology and Psychiatry* 49(4), 376–385. DOI: 10.1111/j.1469-7610.2007.01846.x

Spears, B. A., Taddeo, C. M., Daly, A. L., Stretton, A. & Karklins, L. T. (2015). Cyberbullying, help-seeking and mental health in young Australians: Implications for public health, *International Journal of Public Health,* 60(2), 219-226 http://dx.doi.org/10.1007/s00038-014-0642-y.

Steffgen, G., König, A., Pfetsch, J., & Melzer, A. (2011). Are cyberbullies less empathic? Adolescents' cyberbullying behavior and empathic responsiveness. *Cyberpsychology, Behavior, and Social Networking,* 14(11), 643-648. DOI: 10.1089/cyber.2010.0445.

Sutton, J. & Smith, P. K. (1999). Bullying as a group process: An adaptation of the participant role approach. *Aggressive Behaviour*, 25, 97-111. https:// doi.org/ 10.1002/ (SICI)1098-2337 (1999)25:2 <97::AID-AB3> 3.0.CO;2-7.

Swearer, S. M., & Espelage, D. L. (2004). Introduction: A Social-Ecological Framework of Bullying Among Youth. In *Bullying in American schools* (pp. 23-34). Routledge.

Tanaś, M., Kamieniecki, W., Bochenek, M., Wrońska, A., Lange, R., Fila M., Loba, B. (2017). *Nastolatki 3.0. Wyniki ogólnopolskiego badania nastolatków w szkołach*. Warszawa: NASK. (Teenagers 3.0. Results from the national research of Polish teenagers in schools). Retrieved from: https:// akademia.nask.pl/ publikacje/ Raport_ z_ badania_ Nastolatki_3_0.pdf.

Tokunaga, R. S. (2010). Following you home from school: A critical review and synthesis of research on cyber-bullying victimization. *Computers in Human Behavior*, 26(3), 277–287. doi:10.1016/j.chb.2009.11.014.

Williams, K., & Guerra, N. (2007). Prevalence and predictors of Internet bullying. *Journal of Adolescent Health*, 41, 14–21. doi:10.1016/j. jadohealth.2007.08.018.

Wolak, J., Mitchell, K. J., & Finkelhor, D. (2007). Does online harassment constitute bullying? An exploration of online harassment by known peers and online-only contacts. *Journal of Adolescent Health*, 41(6), S51–S58. doi:10.1016/j.jadohealth.2007.08.019.

World Health Organisation. (1999). *The world health report 1999: Making a difference*. Retrieved from: https://www.who.int/whr/1999/en/.

World Health Organisation. (2002). *The world health report 2002: Reducing Risks, Promoting Healthy Life*. Retrieved from: https://www. who.int/whr/2002/en/.

World Health Organisation (2014). *Health for the world's adolescents: A second chance in the second decade*. Retrieved from: http://apps. who.int/ adolescent/ second-decade/ section2/ page1/ recognizing-adolescence.html.

Ybarra, M. L. (2004). Linkages between depressive symptomatology and Internet harassment among young regular Internet users.

Cyberpsychology and Behavior, 7(2), 247–257. doi:10.1016/j. jadohealth.2007.08.019.

Ybarra, M. L., & Mitchell, K. J. (2008). How risky are social networking sites? A comparison of places online where youth sexual solicitation and harassment occurs. *Pediatrics,* 121(2), e350– e357. doi:10.1542/ peds.2007-0693.

In: Digital Technology   ISBN: 978-1-53616-438-1
Editor: Michelle F. Wright   © 2019 Nova Science Publishers, Inc.

Chapter 4

CYBERBULLYING:
CHALLENGES AND IDEAS FOR PREVENTION

Julia Barlińska[*], PhD
Faculty of Psychology, University of Warsaw, Warsaw, Poland

ABSTRACT

The aim of the chapter is to characterize the phenomenon of cyberbullying, review research on the psychological factors limiting electronic violence, and present an applicational research program - the first Polish interdisciplinary project of prevention of cyberaggression among children and adolescents – project IMPACT[1]. Cyberbullying is defined as acts of aggression or peer violence involving negative behavior towards victims using information and communication technologies, carried out by perpetrators or bystanders. Psychological recommendations for preventive measures of cyberbullying will be presented as the result of a series of 3 polish studies conducted in the project IMPACT: 1 – qualitative interviews with students and teachers (N = 100); 2 – quantitative study (N = 628 pupils) and 3 – pilot testing in 32 junior-

---

[*] Corresponding Author's E-mail: jbarlinska@psych.uw.edu.pl.
[1] The project was financed by The National Centre for Research and Development "Social Innovations" Program.

high schools regarding the effectiveness of the 10 hours program of multi-faceted cyberbullying prevention designed in the project IMPACT. Based on the integrated results of the 3 studies, key psychological inhibitors of electronic aggression have been identified in the form of social competences or the knowledge about specific areas of social functioning. These inhibitors include: (1) self-control, (2) empathy, both online and offline, (3) awareness of the regulatory function of automatisms and their influence on aggression escalation, and (4) awareness about the specificity of computer-mediated communication. The results of the studies confirm that multi-aspect activities addressing activation and development of these skills have a viable chance to be an answer to the postulated need to develop harmonious individual and social functioning within the realities of the cyberspace and be an effective tool to reduce cyberbullying.

1. INTRODUCTION

Since the dawn of civilization aggression and violence have always been present as an element of interpersonal relationships. The development of modern information and communication technologies gave humans a new digital presence. Cyberbullying and wider electronic aggression among young people have become an important social problem and one of the most dangerous cyberthreats for the mental health of young network users is cyberbullying. It is a very harmful type of interpersonal violence accomplished with the use of internet tools and a challenge for schools all over the world (Kowalski, Giumetti, Schroeder, & Lattaner, 2014; Zych, Ortega-Ruiz, & Delrey, 2015; Wright et al., 2017). Often, the acts of cyberbullying occur together with other forms of aggressive behaviors, especially with offline peer violence, intensifying the negative influence on the mental health of contemporary students (Fletcher et al., 2014). It is an extremely damaging type of interpersonal violence present in schools throughout different countries. It is also a social phenomenon requiring the development of empirically verified guidelines for intervention and prevention. This new form of violence is primarily connected to increased access to information and communication technologies for children and teenagers. It creates the possibility of abuse and socially negative behaviors, such as peer cyberbullying. Cyberbullying involves a wide range of groups and roles among students - victims, perpetrators, and bystanders. It is a problem for the school environment but it is often carried out outside of school, making it a social problem too. In most cases, cyberbullying is interconnected with school bullying and has an important negative impact on aggressive behavior at school and mental health outcomes Considering the potential of an unlimited number of bystanders, the difficulty in controlling the phenomenon by adults and the suicidal potential, the scientific verification of effective methods of counteracting this form of violence seems to be a key challenge for contemporary prevention.

1.1. The Profile of Cyberbullying Phenomenon

The problem of cyberbullying, as a new type of peer aggression, affects mostly teenagers (Smith, 2011, 2016). It is estimated that around 85% of teens, aged from 12 to 13, have some experience with cyberbullying (Kowalski et al., 2014). The data showing the scale and dissemination of this phenomenon differ significantly depending on the applied methodology, between 10% to 42% for the experience of victimization, between 3% to 23% for being the perpetrator of electronic violence (Kowalski et al., 2014), and 55% for being the witness of cyberaggression (Pfetsch, 2016). The meta-analysis of 82 studies shows that rates of perpetration are 20% and 23% for victims (Cook, Williams, Guerra, & Kim, 2010). Additionally, the problem has be characterized as a global concern (Smith, Kwak, & Toda, 2016; Wright et al., 2017). Considering the local, Polish data - one of the most recent research that took into account the measuring of electronic aggression three months prior to the study showed that 14% of students witnessed the situation when one of their school friends were harassed for a long time with the use of the Internet or a telephone/smartphone in a manner that caused suffering, and it was difficult for them to defend themselves (Pyżalski et al., 2017). Furthermore, Pyżalski and colleagues found that 8% of their sample were victims and 11% confessed to being perpetrators.

The manner of defining social problems influences the methodology of preventive and interventional practices. One of the most widely used definitions describes cyberbullying as "any behavior performed through electronic or digital media by individuals or groups that repeatedly communicates hostile or aggressive messages intended to inflict harm or discomfort on others" (Tokunaga, 2010 p. 278). This definition is liked by practitioners because of its capacity, allowing for a wide range of preventive measures. There are many different approaches, however. Some researchers emphasize the similarity of cyberbullying to traditional bullying showing the validity of the criteria used for defining the traditional peer violence (i.e., repetitiveness, intentionality, lack of balance of power). The only difference would be the social space where such acts of aggression took place - the cyberspace (Olweus, 2012). Others emphasize the uniqueness of some aspects of electronic aggression absent from traditional face-to-face violence. According to those researchers the phenomenon of cyberbullying is different from traditional peer violence because: (a) technological devices are used, (b) usually has indirect nature, (c) direct feedback for the perpetrator about the victim's response is limited, (d) there are no time and space limitations, the victim can be attacked always and everywhere, 24/7, without the possibility of escaping, (e) the audience is potentially unlimited and the roles of bystanders are more complex, and (f) it is less controlled and less noticed by adults (Smith, 2011). The third, intermediate, approach, accentuates the distinctness of mechanisms present at the source of the phenomena in traditional peer violence as well, specifically repetitiveness, intentionality, and lack of balance of power; cyberbullying acts derive more from the characteristics of technology than psychological factors or the ones being the interactive effect, including the sensation of anonymity, rapid dissemination of electronic content, ability to copyability of the electronic acts, and longevity of internet traces or effects of computer-mediated-communication (Dooley, Pyżalski, & Cross, 2009; Pyżalski, 2011; Barlińska, Szuster, & Winiewski, 2013, 2018).

Cyberbullying has many forms with different behaviors and occurs at various frequencies (Smith, 2016; Wright et al., 2017). Detailed characteristics of the most popular forms of cyberbullying in a group of Polish teenagers were revealed in a study spanning 3 months in the project IMPACT (Plichta, Pyżalski, Szuster, Barlińska, Wójcik, Kowalewicz,

2017). The first stage of the study used qualitative methods - 105 interviews were conducted with students ($N = 55$) and teachers ($N = 45$) of junior-high school in Poland. The content analysis of the interviews showed the most popular forms of peer cyberbullying among teenagers. The next stage was a quantitative research in order to empirically verify the scope of those phenomena. The research had an auditorial and online character. The subjects were 628 students (48% were boys and 52% were girls) from 11 middle schools from different regions of Poland (Małopolska, central Poland, Wielkopolska). A shortlist of the most popular displays of cyberbullying (Top 5) along with the frequencies and the place of the offense are shown in the Table 1.

Preparing effective solutions to counteract cyberbullying requires considering both universal characteristics and specific forms of cyberbullying. It is also necessary to concentrate on the specifics of teenager development. The teenage years are a crucial development period marked by a lot of changes that occur for the most part as a result of social interactions - presently more and more in cyberspace. The challenges of growing up mean that teenagers are particularly susceptible to anti-social behaviors in cyberspace. It is favored by a high level of egocentrism and limited ability of decentration (Piaget & Inhelder, 1962) and reflection about the consequences of their behavior (Hoffmann, 2000), moral relativism and testing of moral rules (Kohlberg, 1976), and not ended formation of personal identity (Erikson, 1968).

Certain aspects of lack of social, psychological, and health adjustment are identified as sources and consequences of online aggression and peer cyberbullying. A Polish study with 628 students confirmed the importance of cyberbullying experiences for lowering the life satisfaction of victims and perpetrators (Szuster et al., 2017). Happiness and life satisfaction are important elements of well-being and are also important factors for producing internal motivation and beneficial for building social relationships. A low level of well-being might be a factor contributing to depression risk - a phenomenon recently on the rise among Polish teenagers. It shows a negative potential and a devastating character of such experiences for the well-being of teenagers. Other correlates of cyberbullying are also a reason for concern. Among others, they include criminal activities, problems at school, use of psychoactive substances, depression, norm breaking (Ybarra & Mitchell, 2007), positive attitude towards cyberbullying and identification with norms conducive to cyberbullying (Pyżalski, 2011), psychosomatic problems, depression, anxiety, lowered self-esteem (Ybarra, Mitchel, & Lenhart, 2010), and suicidal thoughts and attempts (Hinduja & Patchin, 2008, Alavi et al., 2017). Cyberbullying is a serious problem for the public health sector. The list of its negative correlates is the proof of importance of this problem and the need to introduce effective countermeasures.

**Table 1. Forms of cyberbullying, their frequency
and the place in ranking**

Forms of electronic aggression	%	Place in ranking
1. I have called other people names in a chatroom	28	1
2. I commented posts in internet forums in order to ridicule/annoy/scare another person	17	2
3. I showed on the Internet/sent to my friends a photo of another person I had made in an unpleasant situation for such person	16	3
4. I intentionally excluded/did not allow to enter a person to my "friend list" on the internet to annoy him/her.	16	3
5. I added comments to other peoples' profiles in portals like Instagram or Facebook in order to annoy them	13	4

Source: Plichta, Pyżalski, Szuster, Barlińska, Wójcik, Kowalewicz, 2017.

Cyberbullying concerns a wide range of roles among pupils - victims, perpetrators, and bystanders. It is, therefore, a problem of the whole school, and, outside school, a social problem. It is worth mentioning that, according to some studies, cyberbullying is seen as more grievous than direct violence, because of the presence of numerous witnesses of an act of cyberbullying (Slonje & Smith, 2008; Barlińska et al., 2013). Bystanders to cyberbullying are rarely fully neutral (Garandeau & Cillessen, 2006; Macháčková, Dědková, Ševčíková, & Černá, 2016), engaging in cyberbullying as a consequence of a rash unreflective action, joining the bully in fear of being rejected by their peer group, by clicking the "Like" button in social media services, and expressing their approval of the behavior of the perpetrator (Macháčková et al., 2013, 2015; Bastiaensens et al., 2014; Pfetsch, 2016). The works of a Scandinavian pioneer of research on the role of the bystander in peer bullying Christina Sallmivalli (1996) show that between 20% to 30% of students join the harassing of the victim and thus reassert victimization. Other studies show a similar proportion of passive witnesses, that do not do anything in reaction to someone's harm (Gini, 2008; Barlińska et al., 2013, 2018). In total, prevalence rates for cyberbystanders range from 20% to 55% (Pfetsch, 2016), which are higher rates than 20% for cyberbullies and 23% for cybervictims (Cook et al., 2010). Prosocial behaviors designed to help the victim are unfortunately the rarest. Prosocial behaviors reduce the repetition of violence and stimulate helping behavior (Barlińska et al., 2013, 2018; Macháčková, Dedkova, Sevcikova, & Cerna, 2013, 2018). The structure of reactions of cyberbystanders encompass a wider range of factors, including: (a) individual factors, i.e., empathy, (b) the role of situational context, i.e., the number of witnesses, and (c) social factors, i.e., relations of different quality between the participants and the role of proximity (Barlińska, Szuster, & Winiewski, 2013, 2015; DeSmet, Bastiaensens, Van Cleemput, & Poels, 2016; Song & Oh, 2018; Macháčková, Dedkova, Sevcikova, & Cerna, 2013, 2018). It is necessary to concentrate on preventive measures for bystanders of cyberbullying as they are the most numerous group participating in the act. Such preventive measures have the potential to reduce the process of escalation of cyberviolence and is validated by an increasing number of studies (Barlińska et al., 2018; Macháčková et al., 2018, Pfetsch, 2016).

To sum up, the studies performed during the last dozen years helped to distinguish a number of conditions that are important for the etiology of cyberbullying and for the effective reduction of its escalation. The most important are universality of the occurrence, the existence of serious individual and social consequences, the necessity to concentrate on triad approach and the specific character of all three roles - victims, perpetrators, and bystanders - to cyberbullying with a special consideration given to bystanding.

1.2. The Factors That Limit Cyberbullying

Because of a specific character of symptoms, cyberbullying requires different methods of effective preventive treatment and intervention than in the case of traditional violence (Ttofi & Farrington, 2011). During the development of research on cyberbullying the goals of empiric verification shifted from the description and characterization of the phenomenon to testing specific educational-preventive programs. A number of intervention programs on how to specifically tackle cyberbullying have been developed alongside programs on traditional bullying (i.e., Menesini et al., 2012; Williford et al., 2013), some exclusively target cyberbullying (e.g., Ortega-Ruiz et al., 2012; Pieschl & Porsch, 2013; Schultze-Krumbholz, et al., 2014), and some include bystander or peer support elements proven to be effective in reducing victimization from cyberbullying on the global level (Menesini et al., 2012; Palladino et al., 2012; Salmivalli et al., 2011). This last stage of research would not be possible without identifying the factors that modify the phenomenon of cyberbullying. Among them, the most important factors are social and psychological (Livingstone, Haddon, Görzig, & Ólafsson, 2011; Ttofi & Farrington, 2011, Barlińska, Szuster, & Winiewski, 2018). Additionally, the experiences derived from trying to limit other internet threats, i.e., the access to dangerous content with the use of software only, clearly show that there is the need to address the "human factor" by teaching teenagers to think over the content accessible on the internet and their behavior (Livingstone et al., 2011). Nevertheless, one particular area that remains largely unknown is exploring which specific factors and how effectively activated increase bystanders' intervention in cyberbullying – thinking both in terms of effective factors and successful ethos of activating such factors. It is crucially important not only to identify the factors reducing the perpetration of cyberbullying but also to construct a space for positive communication, the culture of respect, and helping others in difficult online situations (Smith, 2011). It justifies the need to build social competences and fortify positive behaviors online as an alternative to cyberbullying.

The results of many studies show the significance of social competences important for preventing cyberbullying. Factors like empathy, perspective taking, prosocial norms, self-control, and self-efficacy in preventing violence increase the probability of reacting in a way that is helpful to the victims of cyberbullying (Machackova, Dedkova, Sevcikova, & Cerna, 2013; Barlińka, Szuster, & Winiewski, 2013, 2015; DeSmet et al., 2016). This justifies treating the training of social competences as one of the key components for the program of cyberbullying prevention.

In the Polish project – IMPACT, based on the integrated results of qualitative and quantitative studies, key psychological inhibitors of electronic aggression have been identified in the form of social competences or the knowledge about specific areas of social functioning (Barlińska, Lalak, & Szuster, 2018, Barlińska, Plichta, Pyżalski, & Szuster, 2018; Barlińka, Szuster, & Winiewski, 2018; Kozubal, Szuster, & Barlińska, 2019). These inhibitors include: (1) self-control and its symptoms (e.g., suppressing, distancing, postponing, "cooling down" online contacts), (2) empathy, both online and offline, (3) awareness of the regulatory function of automatisms and their influence on aggression escalation, and (4) awareness about the specificity of mediated communication. The basic characteristics of those factors and premises for preventive treatment are described below.

1.2.1. Self-Control

Self-control is a complex, multidimensional set of cognitive competences comprising the ability to suppress emotions and behaviors, delaying gratification, and maintain control (Baumeister, Bratslavsky, Muraven, & Tice, 1998; Mischel, Shoda, & Rodriguez, 1989; Mischel & Ayduk, 2004). The relationships between the ability of self-control in the early stages of development and more effective social functioning in adult life were found. The examples of those relationships are building more stable and satisfying interpersonal relationships, smaller number of conflicts with law, lower tendency to commit misdemeanors, and lower level of aggression (Mischel, Shoda, & Rodriguez, 1989). Self-control belongs to a group of social competences that can be developed and perfected. Studies on the effect of self-control training confirm its influence on concentration effectiveness, cognitive, and school and academic abilities (Peng & Miller, 2016; Diamond & Lee, 2011), as well as improved social functioning, which is crucially important for reducing cyberbullying (Kozubal, Szuster, & Barlińska, 2019).

The reason to choose self-control as the factor of preventive measures is also the results of qualitative and quantitative studies conducted in the framework of project IMPACT (e.g., negative correlations of self-control level with cyberbullying experiences). Self-control reduces aggression and increases chances for effective delaying and suppressing, which reduces impulsive reactions (with aggression also) and allows to stimulate proper emotion regulation (Szuster et al., 2017).

1.2.2. Empathy

Empathy is the ability to see, recognize, and sense the emotional states of other people (De Vignemont & Singer, 2006). Empathy is also one of the most documented psychological factors that effectively reduce different displays of aggression (Jolliffe & Farrington, 2004). The results of certain studies show that activating empathy for perpetrator, victim and bystander reduces traditional bullying and cyberbullying (Macaula & Boulton, 2017). Data focused on cyberbystanding points to empathy as one possible protective factor against negative online behavior (as a cyberbully or passive cyberbystander) (Barlińska et al,, 2013, 2015; Desmet et al., 2016) and also as one that increases the probability of prosocial online behavior (e.g., supporting the victim; Pfetsch et al., 2014; Macháčková et al., 2015; Macaula & Boulton, 2017). The basic method of activating empathy (and the most adequate for the conditions of computer-mediated communication (Kiesler, Siegel, & McGuire, 1984) is perspective tacking (Davis, 1996). Empathy enhances sensitivity to the needs of others, which makes it the essential element of cyberbullying prevention. The most advanced mechanisms, i.e., the role and perspective taking, allow us to anticipate the consequences of our actions for other people. Contrary to genetically determined affective empathy (Matthews et al., 1981; Rushton et al., 1986; Zahn-Waxler et al., 1992), the cognitive one is driven primarily by environmental factors, such as parental or school influence (Baron-Cohen, 2014). Modelling, inducing and perspective-taking are often mentioned as parenting techniques facilitating the development of cognitive empathy (Hoffman, 2006). They are also basic techniques implemented in school programs.

1.2.3. Automatisms

The automatic character of behavior regulation is more and more appreciated in present thinking about the functioning of a person online and offline (Carr, 2010; Ledzińska & Postek, 2017). Automatisms, as processes that do not engage conscious attention and cognitive effort, can guarantee an effective functioning in a more and more complex reality, where the speed of reaction counts. On the other hand, information overflow hinders the process of decision-making (Ledzińska & Postek, 2017). This carries a risk of wrong choices, especially in more complex situations, e.g., social relationships online, often leading to incorrect behavior and impulsive decisions such as reinforcing cyberbullying behavior of a bystander (Kozubal, Szuster, Barlińska, 2019). Increasingly often the role of electronic tools (e.g., certain characteristics of computer software, the composition of internet communication, and the abundance of information present in the network) is shown to enhance automatic regulation and significantly reduce the possibilities of reflexive regulation (Ledzińska & Postek, 2017). It increases the probability of reacting with aggression.

Also the results of qualitative studies of the IMPACT project confirmed the dominance of automatic regulation among adolescents when functioning online in the form of: preference of basic, expressive and easily accessible stimuli, dominance of attributes of external appearance in social perception, unreflective copying the behaviors of peers, impulsive engagement in electronic violence (most often as a result of a conflict), and problems with articulating and expressing certain thoughts, including the reasons for personal behavior or experienced emotions and using labels without understanding their content and meaning (Szuster et al., 2017). This "negative" consequence of brain plasticity in the form of neural adjustment reaction to the specificity of electronic tools and intensification of cyberbullying have not yet been taken into consideration in Polish preventive-educational endeavors geared towards reducing electronic violence and it needs to be addressed.

1.2.4. The Unique Character of Online Communication

The data show that computer-mediated communication creates specific conditions conductive towards thoughtless actions that indirectly enhance cyberbullying (Barlińska, Szuster, & Winiewski, 2018; Boyd, 2007; Kiesler et al., 1984; Smith, 2016). The most susceptible group are teenagers. The researchers analyzing the phenomenon of cyberviolence pay particular attention to the unique character of cyberbullying characterized by permanent accessibility of the victim, anonymity, the presence of countless spectators, and cockpit effect (Walrave & Heirman, 2009; Barlińska, Szuster, & Winiewski, 2013; Kozubal, Szuster, & Barlińska, 2019). Activation of reflection on the specificity of computed -mediated communication and focusing on its influence on the process of cyberbullying can reduce online aggression. The model of effective communication based on the nonviolent communication concept created by Marshall Rosenberg was adapted to cyberspace conditions as an alternative to undesirable behaviors of teens online. This method to reduce aggression in relationships also in the online context was confirmed by numerous studies (Rosenberg, 2003; Cox & Dannahy, 2005; Barlińska et al., 2017).

To sum up, the results of studies conducted in the IMPACT project determined a number of factors and strategies with the greatest probability to reduce cyberbullying including: (a) self-control practices, (b) activation of empathy – perspective taking in online communication, (c) being conscious of psychological automatisms that enhance aggression in computer-mediated communication, and (d) being aware of the unique character of online environment and its influence on the behavior of youth (Pyżalski et al., 2017; Szuster et al., 2017). The conclusions of the studies were transformed into activities in the form of exercises, demonstration of different effects, and regularities, as well as activation methods. They became the basis of an innovative Polish program of cyberbullying prevention conducted as part of project IMPACT.

2. PROJECT IMPACT - DESCRIPTION OF THE FIRST POLISH INTERDISCIPLINARY PROGRAM FOR CYBERBULLYING PREVENTION

The reviews and meta-analyses concentrated on the effectiveness of limiting electronic aggression show the importance of two premises: the importance of systemic solutions engaging a wide group of stakeholders (e.g., children, teenagers, parents, school, internet service providers, state institutions; Livingstone et al., 2011) and the need to design interdisciplinary solutions, uniting psychological-pedagogical and technological aspect (Ttofi & Farrington, 2011).

Among specific educational-preventive approaches contained in the idea of designing multi aspect solutions it is worth to distinguish the approach that integrates: (a) positive prevention that should be interpreted as increasing constructive and creative propositions of online activities being an alternative for aggressive and risky behavior online, (b) actions that increase consciousness, knowledge and practical skills of students and their teachers concerning responsibility and accountability for the actions performed online, in the context of protection from cyberbullying, and (c) social competences training that are a natural buffer for the perilous behavior online (Pyżalski, 2011; Barlińska et al., 2013, 2018, Szuster et al., 2017; Fundacja Praesterno Fundacja Dajemy Dzieciom Siłę, 2018; Kzoubal, Szuster, & Barlińska, 2019). Integration of those guidelines (important from the perspective of reducing cyberbullying) was introduced in the IMPACT project. Its goal was to create the first Polish interdisciplinary program for teenage cyberbullying prevention (Pyżalski et al., 2017).

The program, is the effect of synergy cooperation of an interdisciplinary team of experts of psychology (Wydział Psychologii UW - Faculty of Psychology, Warsaw University), pedagogy and public health (Instytut

Medycyny Pracy w Łodzi - Institute of Occupational Medicine in Łódź) and technical sciences (Wydział Elektroniki i Technik Informacyjnych Politechniki Warszawskiej - Faculty of Electronics and Information Technology, Warsaw University of Technology) as well as non-governmental organizations with experience in deploying prevention programs (Fundacja Dajemy Dzieciom Siłę - Empowering Children Foundation and Fundacja Praesterno - Praesterno Foundation). The program was financed by The National Centre for Research and Development (Social Innovations program) and is directed towards students (recipients) and teachers (organizers) (Pyżalski et al., 2017).

The program was constructed using the new recommendations concerning the creation of scientifically validated evidence based intervention programs in accordance with the standards created by the Society of Prevention Research (SPR; Gottfredson et al., 2015). Because of it, the program is an important addition to the prevention of electronic aggression currently available in Poland, which lacks the solutions of an interdisciplinary team of researchers. Currently available preventive propositions in Poland that concern electronic aggression among teenagers are scarce, short in duration, and not in accordance with SPR standards. They do not address a number of factors limiting cyberbullying described in this chapter.

The results of a two-year, interdisciplinary research program of three institutions with different specialization are complex for the prevention of electronic aggression with the aim to: a) develop and strengthen social competences that can limit aggressive behavior (Department of Psychology, Warsaw University); b) reduce factors contributing to cyber-victimization and cyber-perpetration as well as the behaviors of witnesses that amplify electronic aggression and the modification of undesirable behavior in order to increase the intensity of constructive and creative actions online (Institute of Occupational Medicine in Łódź); c) increase the safety of students online by applying best standards of - base line of school internet security - containing indications concerning the organizational and technical solutions that can be used to prevent becoming a perpetrator or a victim of electronic aggression (Faculty of Electronics and Information Technology, Warsaw University of Technology).

The program developed different tools and methods (their effectiveness has been verified) of working with students, i.e., elements of workshop activities and social competences training, scripts for classroom work, multimedia resources, resources to activate certain psychological aspects, such as empathy, social norms, and e-learning courses, films, and audio recordings. The program contains elements designed to increase awareness of cyberthreats and technical aspects of internet security as well as activities correcting undesirable behavior and building new skills (Barlińska et al., 2017). Thanks to integrated multi-aspect activities, those skills have a viable chance to be an answer to the postulated need to develop e-soft social competences. Those competences are the basis of harmonious individual and social functioning within the realities of contemporary state of information-communication technologies.

2.1. Methodology of the IMPACT Project

The program was created as a result of activities divided into two stages: the research and pilot phase. The first phase was the research stage of the project which comprised review, evaluation, and modification of the existing activities towards prevention of destructive online functioning of middle school teenagers with respect to their effectiveness at featured levels. The goal was to identify the verified premises in order to prepare an integrated prevention program. This stage also consisted of qualitative, quantitative, and experimental studies to prepare key indicators of change (important from the point of view of electronic aggression) and their operationalization in form of a questionnaire and experimental tools for its measurement on the three levels described above.

The final effect of the first stage was a 10-hour pilot version of an integrated, multi-aspect program of preventive-educational activities (the basis for it were the results of research phase studies) and a research tool (a set of tests) to evaluate the program in its pilot phase. The entirety of the program is balanced in terms of pedagogical and psychological activities as well as internet security. Each of the 10 lessons has a separate script containing a general description of the unit, the necessary resources, a detailed description of the lesson, a substantive validation showing the lesson in the context of studies' results, and bibliography and additional sources for the teacher. Moreover, the additional multimedia content is connected to the lessons within the task. The program is an interactive and engaging educational proposition. The content of those materials is composed of multimedia presentations used to illustrate and animate the exercises, a series of short educational movies, mobile apps, and a prototype of an introductory software platform for the program. A manual for teachers was also prepared. The final choice of 10 lessons are listed below in Table 2.

Different forms of learning were created to improve social competences. These included exercises, demonstration of different effects, and regularities, as well as activation methods. Four lessons out of 10 were aimed to acquaint the students with the issues of psychological automatisms that increase aggression in computer based mediated contact, self-control, empathy, and perspective tacking, as well as the unique character of online environment and its influence on the behavior of teenagers. These lessons focused on the theme of "the robot that is in each of us" (Fundacja Praesterno, Fundacja Dajemy Dzieciom Siłę, 2018).

The second stage implemented the pilot version of the program on trial basis (Fundacja Praesterno - Praesterno Foundation). The pilot version of the program was introduced in 30 schools from different voivodeships (provinces) and 22 towns by a group of trained professionals - teachers from a chosen school for the period of 1 semester. The lessons were performed in stages which allowed for monitoring and correcting the program after each pilot implementation. In each school one class had the IMPACT project implemented (experimental group) and another class was randomly picked as control group. In the control group the program was not implemented. The study was conducted in pre- post-test model with the participation of 1040 students - 546 in classes with the program and 494 in control classes. The pre-test was enrolled in both classes (program and control) in each school before the beginning of the program and post-test was given after the end of the program in the program (experimental) class.

Table 2. 10 lessons of the IMPACT program

Lesson 1. Me in the digital world	The first lesson of the cycle is to build a space for reflection on the functioning of teenagers in the online world.
Lesson 2. Privacy and security	The second lesson focuses on increasing students' knowledge, practical skills, and awareness in the field of information security and privacy online.
Lesson 3. Robot in me. About automatisms	The third lesson shows the student how automatic, unconscious processes and reactions can affect functioning online and communication with others.
Lesson 4. How can you control a robot? Self-control	The fourth lesson builds the awareness about the potential to monitor some automatic regulations and effectively control one's behavior also in cyberbullying incidences.
Lesson 5. What no robot can do. Emotions, empathy and perspective taking of another person	The fifth lesson focuses on activating empathy in the triad: the perpetrator, the victim, and the witness.
Lesson 6. When the robot mediates in the conversation ... The specificity of online communication	The sixth lesson aims to raise the awareness that digital space intensifies automatic, unconscious processes, fostering the appearance of negative and hurtful behaviors in cyberbullying acts.
Lesson 7. How not to hurt others in the classroom? - basics of knowledge about bullying and cyberbullying	The lesson concerns the recognition of a wide range of online and offline activities that may constitute online peer violence.
Lesson 8. Responsible and effective actions in case of cyberbullying - the perspective of victims, bystanders and perpetrators	The eighth lesson concentrates on deepening the understanding, adopting the perspective of all actors of the cyberbullying phenomenon (witnesses, victims and perpetrators) and discussing the response options in case of cyberbullying.
Lesson 9. The bright side of the Internet - how to use the web proactively and pro-socially	The ninth lesson focuses on developing a creative culture of positive, innovative use of information and communication technologies (ICT) and digital literalization that can help reduce negative experiences and reduce the risk of engaging in risky situations.
Lesson 10. Investigation on the Web - Where is Ewa?	The last lesson is an integration of knowledge from all previously presented topics presented in the form of a game where the student, becomes an "online detective."

Source: Fundacja Praesterno, Fundacja Dajemy Dzieciom Siłę 2018.

One of the key methods of psychological verification of the effectiveness of the program was the measurement of students' reaction to a set of simulated chat conversations containing cyberbullying situation dialogues. The students were given 5 pairs of chat conversations with the dialogues containing unpleasant statements or descriptions of hurtful activities towards a specific person belonging to a circle of friends using the chat. The chats contained 5 of the most common (according to the results from the first stage of the study) forms of cyberbullying: flaming, mocking comments, publication and distribution of compromising protos, and outing, mean comments of someone's profile in social media (one of them in the subject pair in pre-test and post-test). It allowed not only to evaluate the general effectiveness of the project but also to identify the forms of cyberbullying, where the performed activities produced the biggest change.

The students could choose one from the three ways to react:

1. giving a like (reinforcing cyberbullying, joining the cyberbully)
2. deleting the conversation or not doing anything (neutral reaction)
3. reporting the situation to an administrator (prosocial behavior, defending the cybervictim).

In all final results of the program group, in comparison to the preliminary results, the percentage of students reinforcing cyberbullying was lower, in favor of neutral and defending reactions. Not all results were statistically significant though. Substantial differences were found for reacting to publication and distribution of compromising photos, outing, and mocking comments. In the case of the first two forms (distribution of compromising photos and outing), program group students opposed cyberbullying by reporting the conversation to an administrator substantially more often. In the case of mocking comments, a higher percentage of students would delete the conversation. The effectiveness of the program for those forms can be explained by a higher willingness of students to react towards cyberbullying acts with a higher victimizing potential. Based on the results it was suggested that participation in the program increases the willingness of students to oppose cyberbullying (Fundacja Praesterno, Fundacja Dajemy Dzieciom Siłę; 2018).

The assessment of attractivity and adequacy of the methods of the program for the age group 12-16 years was conducted alongside the main evaluation of the effectiveness of the program. Thirty teachers and 528 students participated in this part of the evaluation. The final versions of all 10 lessons that constituted the pilot version of the program were positively evaluated by the teachers. 74% to 100% (depending on the lesson) of the teachers positively answered the question if the goals and effects of the lessons were achieved. The choice of didactic methods to the presented content was appraised even higher. Specifically, 90% to 100% of teachers considered them adequate. All exercises in the program and additional didactic materials underwent a careful evaluation as well. Each exercise and material were evaluated by the students. They were giving grades from 1 to 5 (where 5 means the highest grade). The grades were high, between 3.70 to 4.93, depending on the lesson (Fundacja Praesterno, Fundacja Dajemy Dzieciom Siłę; 2018). The Table below presents the average grade of the lessons addressing the subject of psychological cyberviolence modifiers - as described in the chapters above.

Table 3. Average lesson grades (on the scale from 1 to 5)

Lesson 3. Robot inside me. About automatisms.	4.10
Lesson 4. How can a robot be controlled? Self-control.	4.21
Lesson 5. Things no robot can do. Emotions, empathy and perspective taking.	4.13
Lesson 6. When a robot mediates the conversation. The unique character of online communication.	4.33

The results of this pilot stage were used to prepare the final version of the program and to create tools for its implementation - methodical textbook, final versions of films and apps and e-learning course for teachers.

Those tools are now available to teachers in Poland as part of a free, educational offer for schools.

CONCLUSION

Cyberbullying is a social phenomenon, whose scale, number of forms and consequences require the preparation of empirically verified guidelines concerning intervention and prevention. It is important to create tools with the scientifically proven effectivity to react efficiently towards social problems of such importance. The IMPACT project described in this chapter is a proposition of such a solution. Its methodology might be the inspiration for other countries, where such programs have not yet been implemented, especially in Eastern Europe.

REFERENCES

Alavi N, Reshetukha T, Prost E, Antoniak K, Patel C, Sajid S, et al., (2017). Relationship between bullying and suicidal behaviour in youth presenting to the emergency department. *J Can Acad Child Adolesc Psychiatry*, 26:70–7.

Barlińska, J., Szuster, A., Winiewski, M. (2013). Cyberbullying among adolescent bystanders: role of the communication medium, form of violence, and empathy. *Journal of Community and Applied Social Psychology, 23,* 37-51. doi:10.1002/casp.2137 14.

Barlińska, J., Szuster, A., Winiewski, M. (2015). The role of short- and long-term cognitive empathy activation in preventing cyberbystander reinforcing cyberbullying behaviour. *Cyberpsychology, Behavior, and Social Networking.* doi: 10.1089/cyber.2014.0412.

Barlińska, J., Plichta, P., Pyżalski, J., Szuster, A., Wójcik, S., Kowalewicz, T. (2017) *Metodologia ewaluacji ćwiczeń i narzędzi.* [*Methodology for evaluating exercises and tools*]. Unpublished report on the implementation of the IMPACT program - Interdisciplinary Model of Counteracting Aggression and Technological Cyberbullying financed from the resources of National Center for Research and Development Social Innovation.]

Barlińska, J., Szuster, A., Winiewski, M. (2018). Cyberbullying Among Adolescent Bystanders: Role of Affective versus Cognitive Empathy in Increasing Prosocial Cyberbystander Behavior. *Frontiers in Psychology-Educational Psychology.* doi.org/10.3389/fpsyg.2018.00 799.

Baumeister, R., Bratslavsky, E., Muraven, M., Tice, D. M. (1998). Ego Depletion: Is the Active Self a Limited Resource? *Personality processes and individual differences. 74(5):*1252-65.

Boyd, D. (2007). Why youth (heart) social network sites: the role of networked publics in teenage social life. In: D. Buckingham (Ed.), *McArthur Foundation on Digital Learning – youth, identity and digital media volume.* Cambridge: MIT Press, p. 119–142.

Carr, N. (2010). *The Shallows: What the Internet Is Doing to Our Brains.* N.Y., London: W. W. Norton & Company.

Cook, C. R., Williams, K. R., Guerra, N. G. and Kim, T. E. (2010). Variability in the prevalence of bullying and victimization: A cross-national and methodological analysis. In *Handbook of bullying in schools: an international perspective,* eds S. Jimerson, S. M. Swearer and D. L. Espelage (New York & London: Routledge) 347–362.

Cox, E., Dannahy, P. (2005). The value of openness in e-relationships: Using nonviolent communication to guide online coaching and mentoring. *International Journal of Evidence Based Coaching and Mentoring*, 3(1), 39–51.

Davis, M. H. (1996). *Empathy: a Social-Psychological Approach.* Boulder, CO: Westview Press.

De Vignemont, F., Singer, T. (2006). The empathic brain: How, when and why? *Trends in Cognitive Sciences, 10,* (10), 435–441.

DeSmet, A., Bastiaensens, S., Van Cleemput, K., and Poels, K. (2016). Deciding whether to look after them, to like it, or leave it: A multidimensional analysis of predictors of positive.... *Comp. in Human Behavior, 57,* 398 – 415 doi: 10.1016/j.chb.2015.12.051.

Diamond, A., Lee, K. (2011). Interventions shown to aid executive function development in children 4 to 12 years old. *Science*, 333 (6045), 959‒64. DOI: 10.1126/science.1204529.

Dooley, J. J., Pyżalski, J., Cross, D. (2009). Cyberbullying versus face-to-facebullying: a theoretical and conceptual review. *Journal of Psychology, 217,* (4), 182-188.

Erikson, E. H. (1968). *Identity: Youth and Crisis.* New York: W. W. Norton.

Fletcher, A., Fitzgerald, Yau, N., Jones, R., Allen, E., Viner, R. M., and Bonell, C. (2014). Brief report: Cyberbullying perpetration and its associations with socio-demographics, aggressive behaviour at school, and mental health outcomes. *J. of Adolescence,* 37(8):1393-8. doi: 10.1016/j.adolescence.2014.10.005.

Fundacja Praesterno, Fundacja Dajemy Dzieciom Siłę (2018). *Program IMPACT Interdyscyplinarny Model Przeciwdziałania Agresji I Cyberprzemocy Technologicznej Raport ewaluacyjny]* [*IMPACT Program Interdisciplinary Model of Counteracting Aggression and Technological Cyberbullying. Evaluation Report.* Unpublished report on the implementation of the IMPACT program - Interdisciplinary Model of Counteracting Aggression and Technological Cyberbullying financed from the resources of National Center for Research and Development Social Innovation.

Garandeau, C. F., & Cillessen, A. H. N. (2006). From indirect aggression to invisible aggression: A conceptual view on bullying and peer group manipulation. *Aggression and Violent Behaviour, 11,* 612-625.

Gini, G., Albiero, P., Benelli, B., & Altoe, G. (2008). Determinants of adolescents' active defending and passive bystanding behavior in bullying. *Journal of adolescence,* 31, (1), 93-105.

Gottfredson, Cook, Gardner, Gorman-Smith, Howe, Sandler, Zafft (2015). Standards of Evidence for Efficacy, Effectiveness, and Scale-up. *Research in Prevention Science: Next Generation Prevention Science.* Doi: 10.1007/s11121-015-0555-x.

Hinduja, S., Patchin, J. W. (2008). Cyberbullying: An exploratory analysis of factors related to offending and victimization. *Deviant Behavior,* 29(2), 129–156.

Hoffman, M. L. (2000). *Empathy and moral development. Implication for caring and justice.* Cambridge: Cambridge University Press.

Jolliffe, D., Farrington, D. P. (2004). Empathy and offending. A systematic review and metaanalysis. *Aggression and Violent Behavior, 9*, 441–476.

Kiesler, S., Siegel, J., McGuire, T. W. (1984). Social psychological aspects of computer mediated communications. *American Psychology*, 39: 1123–1134.

Kohlberg, L. (1976). Moral stages and moralization. The cognitive-developmental approach. In: T. Lickona (Ed.). *Moral Development and Behavior*. New York: Holt, Rinehart and Winston, p. 31–53.

Kowalski, R. M., Giumetti, G. W., Schroeder, A. N., and Lattaner, M. R. (2014). Bullying in the digital age: a critical review and meta-analysis of cyberbullying research among youth. *Psychol. Bull.* 140, 1073–1137. doi:10.1037/a0035618.Kozubal, M., Szuster, A., Barlińska, J. (2019). Cyberbystanders, empathy and social norms. *Studia Psychologica, 61(2)*, 120-131. doi: 10.21909/sp.2019.02.777.

Ledzińska, M., Postek, S. (2017). From metaphorical information overflow and overload to real stress: theoretical background, empirical findings and applications, *European Management Journal, 35, 785-793*.

Livingstone, S., Haddon, L., Görzig, A., Ólafsson, K. (2011). *Risks and safety on the internet: The perspective of. European children. Full Findings*. LSE, London: EU Kids Online.

Macaula P., Boulton, M. J. (2017). *Adolescent bystander responses to offline and online bullying: The role of bullying severity and empathy*. Conference: 22nd Annual CyberPsychology, CyberTherapy & Social Networking Conference, At University of Wolverhampton.

Macháčková, H., Dedkova, L., Sevcikova, A., Cerna, A. (2013). Bystanders' Support of Cyberbullied Schoolmates. *Journal of Community & Applied Social Psychology, 23*(1), 25–36.

Macháčková, H., Dedkova, L., Sevcikova, A., Cerna, A. (2016). Empathic responses by cyberbystanders: The importance of proximity. *Journal of Youth Studies, 19, 6,* 793-804. ISSN 1367-6261. doi:10.1080/ 13676261.2015.1112882.

Macháčková, H., Dedkova, L., Sevcikova, A., Cerna, A. (2018). Bystanders' supportive and passive responses to cyberaggression. *Journal of School*

Violence, 17,1, 99-110, ISSN 1538-8220, doi:10. 1080/15388220.2016. 1222499.

Mischel, W., Shoda Y., Rodriguez MI. (1989). Delay of gratification in children. *Science, 244(4907)*, 933–938.

Mischel, W., & Ayduk, O. (2004). Willpower in a cognitive-affective processing system: The dynamics of delay of gratification. In R. F. Baumeister & K. D. Vohs (Eds.), *Handbook of Self-Regulation: Research, Theory, and Applications*. New York, NY: Guildford Press.

Olweus, D. (2012). Cyberbullying: An overrated phenomenon? *European Journal of Developmental Psychology, 5*, 520-538.

Peng, P. Miller, A. C. (2016). Does attention training work? A selective meta-analysis to explore the effects of attention training and moderator. *Learning and Individual Differences*, 45. doi:10.1016%2Fj.lindif. 2015.11.012.

Peter, J. R., Macaulay, P. and Boulton, M. J. (2017). Adolescent bystander responses to offline and online bullying: The role of bullying severity and empathy. *Conference: 22nd Annual CyberPsychology, Cyber Therapy & Social Networking Conference*, At University of Wolverhampton.

Pfetsch, J. (2016). Who is who in Cyberbullying? Conceptual and Empirical Perspectives on Bystanders in Cyberbullying. In *A Social-Ecological Approach to Cyberbullying*, ed M. F. Wright (Hauppauge: NY: Nova Publishing), ch 9, 121-150.

Piaget, J., Inhelder, B., (1962). *The Psychology of the Child.* New York: Basic Books.

Plichta, P., Pyżalski, J., Szuster, A., Barlińska, J., Wójcik, S., Kowalewicz, T. (2017). *Raport z badań ilościowych projektu IMPACT. [Quantitive research report of the project IMPACT]*. Unpublished report on the implementation of the IMPACT program - Interdisciplinary Model of Counteracting Aggression and Technological Cyberbullying financed from the resources of National Center for Research and Development Social Innovation.

Pyżalski, J. (2011). Electronic aggression among adolescents: An old house with a new facade (or even a number of houses). In: C. Hällgren, E.

Dunkels, G-M. Franberg (red.), *Youth culture and net culture: Online social practices,* Hershey, PA, IGI Global.

Pyżalski, J., Szuster, A., Barlińska, J., Plichta, P., Wójcik, S., Kowalewicz, T. (2017). *Program IMPACT Interdyscyplinarny model przeciwdziałania agresji i technologicznemu cyberprzemocy. Raport z fazy badawczej.* [*IMPACT Program Interdisciplinary Model of Counteracting Aggression and Technological Cyberbullying. Report from the research phase*].Unpublished report on the implementation of the IMPACT program - Interdisciplinary Model of Counteracting Aggression and Technological Cyberbullying financed from the resources of National Center for Research and Development Social Innovation.

Rosenberg, M. B. (2003). *Nonviolent Communication: A Language of Life* (2nd ed.). Encinitas, CA: PuddleDancer Press. p. 220. ISBN 978-1-892005-03-8.

Salmivalli, C., Lagerspetz, K., Bjorkqvist, K., Osterman, K., Kaukiainen, A. (1996). Bullying as a group process: Participant roles and their relations to social status within the group. *Aggressive Behavior, 22,* 1–15.

Slojne, R., and Smith, P. K. (2008). Cyberbullying: Another main type of bullying? *Scan. J. of Psych.* 49 (2), 147–154. doi:10.1111/j.1467-9450. 2007.00611.x.

Smith, P. K. (2011). Bullying in schools: Thirty years of research. In: C.P. Monks, I. Coyne (Ed.). *Bullying in different contexts* p. 36–60. Cambridge: Cambridge University Press.

Smith, P. K., (2016). Bullying: Definition, Types, Causes, Consequences and Intervention. *Soc. and Pers. Psych. Compass* 10/9, 519–532. doi 10.1111/spc3.12266.

Smith, P. K., Kwak, K., and Toda, Y. (2016). *School bullying in different cultures: Eastern and western perspectives.* Cambridge, MA: Cambridge University Press.

Song, J., and Oh, I. (2018). Factors influencing bystanders' behavioral reactions in cyberbullying situations. *Comp. in Human Behavior 78,* 273-282. doi: 10.1016/j.chb.2017.10.008.

Steffgen, G., König, A. (2009). Cyber bullying: The role of traditional bullying and empathy. In: B. Sapeo, L. Haddon, E. Mante-Meijer, L. Fortunati, T. Turk, E. Loos (Eds.). *The good, the bad and the challenging. Conference Proceedings*, vol. II,. Brussels, Belgium: Cost office, 1041–1047.

Szuster, A., Barlińska, J., Plichta, P., Pyżalski, J., Wójcik, S., Kowalewicz, T. (2017). *Diagnoza potrzeb w zakresie interdyscyplinarnych podstaw programu profilaktyki*. [*Diagnosis of needs in the field of interdisciplinary foundations of the prevention program*]. Unpublished report on the implementation of the IMPACT program - Interdisciplinary Model of Counteracting Aggression and Technological Cyberbullying financed from the resources of National Center for Research and Development Social Innovation.

Tokunaga, R. S. (2010). Following you home from school: A critical review and synthesis of research on cyberbullying victimization. *Comp. in Human Behavior, 26*, 277-287. doi:10.1016/j.chb.2009. 11.014.

Ttofi, M. M., and Farrington, D. P. (2011). Effectiveness of school-based programs to reduce bullying: A systematic and metanalytic review. *J. of Exp. Criminology, 7*, 27–56. doi 10.1007/s11292-010-9109-1.

Twemlow, S. W., Fonagy, P., Sacco, F. C., Gies, M. L., Hess, D. (2001). Improving the social and intellectual climate in elementary schools by addressing the bully-victim- bystander power struggles. In: J. Cohen (Ed.). *Caring classrooms, intelligent schools: The social emotional education of young children*. New York: Teachers College Press, 162-182.

Walrave, M., Heirman, W. (2009). Skutki cyberbullyingu – oskarżenie czy obrona technologii? *Dziecko krzywdzone. Teoria. Badania. Praktyka, 1*(26), 27–46. [The effects of cyberbullying - prosecution or defense of technology? *Child abused. Theory. Research. Practice, 1* (26), 27–46.]

Wright, M., Yanagida, T., Aoyama, I., Ševčíková, A., Hana Macháčková, H., Dědková, L. et al., (2016). Differences in Severity and Emotions for Public and Private Face-to-Face and Cyber Victimization Across Six Countries. Journal of Cross-Cultural Psychology, Thousand Oaks:

SAGE Publications, 2017, vol. 48, No 8, p. 1216-1229. ISSN 0022-0221. doi:10.1177/0022022116675413.

Ybarra, M. L., Mitchell, K. J., Lenhart, A. (2010). Cyberbullying research in United States. In: J. A. Mora-Merchan, T. Jager, T. (Eds.). *Cyberbullying: A Cross-national comparison.* Landau: Verlag Empirische Padagogik.

Ybarra, M. L., Mitchell, K. J. (2007). Prevalence and frequency of Internet harassement instigation: implications for adolescent health. *Journal of Adolescent Health, 41*(2), 189–195.

Zych, I., Ortega-Ruiz, R., and DelRey, R. (2015). Systematic review of theoretical studies on bullying and cyberbullying: facts, knowledge, prevention and intervention. *Aggressive Violent Behaviour.* 23,1–21. doi:10.1016/j.avb.2015.10.001.

In: Digital Technology   ISBN: 978-1-53616-438-1
Editor: Michelle F. Wright   © 2019 Nova Science Publishers, Inc.

Chapter 5

SEXTING:
A NEW WAY TO EXPLORE SEXUALITY

Mónica Ojeda[1], MD, Rosario Del Rey[1,], Phd,*
Rosario Ortega-Ruiz[2], Phd and José A. Casas[2], Phd
[1]Department of Educational and Developmental Psychology,
Universidad de Sevilla, Seville, Spain
[2]Department of Psychology, Universidad de Córdoba, Córdoba, Spain

ABSTRACT

Sexting is a recent phenomenon which is being increasingly accepted
as normal and has become another way for adolescents to express and
explore their sexuality. In recent years, sexting has attracted considerable
media attention and the concern of researchers, families, and schools in
response to the possible risks involved. However, no definitive conclusions
have been reached over either its definition as a concept or its possible
consequences. In this chapter, we will discuss what exactly this
phenomenon consists of.

In this chapter, after discussing the concept of sexting and taking into
account all its definitions (from the most restrictive to the most

---

[*] Corresponding Author's E-mail: delrey@us.es

comprehensive), we will explain how frequently this practice occurs in each of its commonest forms: sending, receiving, and third-party forwarding of messages. In addition, we will describe the importance of peer context and gender differences in this phenomenon, as well as commenting on the potential risks of sexting and showing the possible consequences for adolescents of getting involved in this practice. Finally, we will highlight the importance of education in encouraging healthy practices in intimate communication between adolescents.

Keywords: sexting, adolescence, sexuality, social networks, internet

INTRODUCTION

The digital environment has opened up myriad possibilities and advantages in the social life of all people, but particularly of adolescents. Approximately 77% of all young Europeans between the age of 13 and 16 use social networks (Livingstone et al., 2011), and for this reason, the environmental influences on a young person's development have already become part of an ecological techno-subsystem where, in addition to the influence of contexts which have been studied previously (Bronfenbrenner 1979), the focus is on the way they interact with digital communication, information and leisure technologies in immediate or direct environments (Johnson, 2010). We are therefore currently witnessing new digital advances which certainly have a positive impact on the daily lives of adolescents, but which have also exposed them to additional risks which may inhibit their socio-emotional development (Englander & McCoy 2017).

One of the areas which has changed radically with the advent of Information and Communication Technologies - ICT - is the expression of sexuality. Adolescence is a period marked by growing sexual-erotic curiosity, the search for identity, the development of social interaction skills, and the questioning of normative limits (Chalfen, 2009; Ling, 2004). As a result, sexting has become yet another way by which adolescents can express and explore their sexuality. However, there is no general consensus in the scientific literature about what this phenomenon specifically refers to - when researchers analyze this practice they often start from different definitions;

there is no agreement over whether it constitutes risk behavior for adolescents or not. In this chapter, we will delve deeper into each of these questions.

TOWARDS A MORE ACCURATE CONCEPT OF SEXTING

The term 'sexting' was coined from the combination of "sex" and "texting" and came into vogue at the beginning of the 21st century as a new way of expressing and exploring sexuality (Davidson, 2015). The definition varies depending mainly on the kind of behavior it refers to; it can mean active sexting, in other words, creating, sending, or third-party forwarding of sexual material; it also includes passive sexting, either receiving content directly from the creator or receiving material forwarded by others. The definitions also vary depending on the sexual content it refers to, ranging from text messages to images or videos, and depending on the degree of explicitness of the sexual content, whether it is suggestive or explicit (Barrense-Dias et al., 2017). In addition, although sexting is most commonly linked to mobile phones, it can occur not only via text messages or multimedia, but also via email, social networks and live streaming through a webcam (Schubert & Wurf, 2014). However, since mobile devices currently have a huge range of applications, most definitions usually refer to these, although it must be said that this is not a key factor in the definitions of sexting.

Sexting, in one of its more restrictive definitions, can be defined as sending sexually explicit images (Choi, Van Ouytsel, & Temple, 2016; Marume, Maradzika, & January, 2018; Wolak, Finkelhor, & Mitchell, 2012; Ybarra & Mitchell, 2014). It can also be defined as sending, receiving, and third-party forwarding of sexually suggestive or explicit images, videos, or text messages (Mitchell et al., 2011; Villacampa, 2017), which is one of the broadest, most complex definitions. Strassberg et al. (2013) state that some authors find restrictive definitions - for instance, those which focus only on explicit material - not informative enough, and therefore, perhaps the most accurate definitions are the more complex ones, which reflect a wide range of behavioral traits, types of content, and degree of explicitness of the sexual content. In this way, both active and passive sexting behavior can be analyzed in greater detail.

Although sexting is a constantly evolving concept, we need to establish a clear, validated, and universal definition, which can lay the foundation for our knowledge of this construct (Barrense-Dias et al., 2017). Nevertheless, until scientific consensus over the definition of this phenomenon is reached, the definition referred to in each study must be specified in detail and special attention paid to the concept it is based on, so as to clarify what kind of sexting behavior the findings refer to.

HOW COMMON IS SEXTING?

Although sexting is not restricted to young people, there is growing concern among families, educators, and the media over young people's participation in it and the effect it can have on their well-being, and this has led to sexting being studied in this particular population (Anastassiou 2017). The estimation of how many adolescents are involved in sexting varies, mainly, according to the definition used and, therefore, the specific behavior they refer to. The following paragraphs show the rates of involvement found over the last few years, depending on whether the researchers refer to the behavior of sending, receiving, or third-party forwarding of sexual content.

According to the studies which define sexting as sending sexual content, the involvement rates range between 4% and 31%. In particular, one study carried out in 2012 showed that 28% of adolescents had sent a nude photograph of themselves via text messages or email (Temple et al., 2012). In 2013, a study found that 21.2% of the adolescents had sent suggestive or explicit sexual photos and 24.8% had sent texts with suggestive sexual content (Peskin et al., 2013). In 2014, a study found that 11.9% of the adolescents between 10 and 19 years old had sent a sexually suggestive image (Klettke, Hallford, & Mellor 2014). In 2017, Strassberg, Cann, and Velarde stated that the percentage of males sending sexually explicit images was 15.8% compared to 13.6% for females. Also, in 2017, Woodward,

Evans, and Brooks reported that 31% of the respondents in their study admitted to sending sexual content. Finally, in a study carried out in 2018, it was found that between 4% and 16% had sent sexual content (Burén & Lunde, 2018), and a recent meta-analysis showed an average prevalence of sending sexual content of 14.8%. In addition, the possibility of sending content without consent was 12% (Madigan et al., 2018).

The studies which refer to receiving sexting-related content present figures ranging between 7.1% and 49%. In 2012, Mitchell et al. found that 7.1% of the participants had received this type of content. Another study in 2013 found that 31% of the adolescents in the study had received suggestive or explicit sexual pictures and 31.5% had received text messages with suggestive sexual content (Peskin et al., 2013). In 2014, Klettke and his team found that a slightly higher percentage (11.9%) of the adolescents, aged between 10 and 19 years, had received some kind of sexual or suggestive image. In 2017, Woodward, Evans, and Brooks reported that 49% of the respondents had received images containing nudity, and Strassberg, Cann, and Velarde (2017) found that the percentage for those who has received this type of content was 40.5% in males compared with 30.6% in females. Finally, in a study in 2018, it was found that between 20 and 32% had received sexual content (Burén & Lunde 2018), and a recent meta-analysis showed that the average prevalence of reception of sexual content was 27.4%. In addition, the possibility of receiving content without consent was 8.4% (Madigan et al., 2018).

Although most research refers to sending and/or receiving in its definition of sexting, some studies also include the third-party forwarding of sexual content. In the studies which refer to third-party forwarding of content of this type, figures ranging between 2.3% and 25% have been found. In one study in 2015, it was reported that 1 in 10 students had sent explicit photos of other people (Patrick et al., 2015). In addition, although most of these studies were cross-sectional (Smith, Thompson, & Davidson 2014), a longitudinal study was carried in 2017 which found that the rate of third-party forwarding of sexual content was over 25% (Strassberg, Cann, & Velarde 2017).

It has been pointed out that there is considerable variability in the prevalence of sexting depending on sociodemographic variables (Olivari & Confalonieri 2017). It seems that, in general, rates increase as the young people get older and progress into adolescence (Madigan et al., 2018) and sexting generally occurs more between desired and real sexual and/or romantic partners (Wood et al., 2015). Furthermore, although most of the young people using sexting do so with people they know personally, almost one in three young people share photos with recipients they only know through Internet (Ybarra & Mitchell, 2014). In regards the gender of those involved, a wide range of studies show a varying prevalence of participation. Some have found that girls are more likely to share sexual images than boys (Reyns et al., 2013; Ybarra & Mitchell, 2014), while others show that boys participate to a greater extent (Gómez & Ayala, 2014; West et al., 2014). Other studies have found no gender differences in the rates of sending and receiving sexual messages or images (Campbell & Park 2014; Lenhart, 2009; Rice et al., 2012; Vanden Abeele et al., 2014). However, it appears that boys forward and ask for sexual images and messages more than girls, and girls recognize that they are more frequently asked to send sexual content (Norman, 2017).

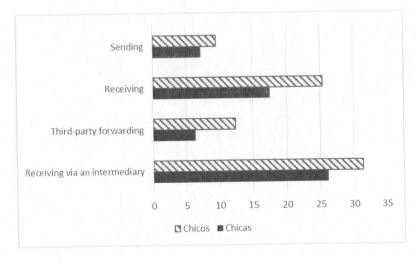

Figure 1. Percentage of boys and girls involved in sexting behavior.

In our study, which involved 3417 Spanish schoolchildren (48.3% girls), aged between 11 and 19 years old (M = 13.70, SD = 1.32), 8.4% of the students admitted to having sent sexual content, 21.6% had received it directly from the creator of the sexual content, 9.5% had forwarded sexual material from other people, and 28.8% had received sexual content from other people through an intermediary. Significant differences were also found in terms of the gender of those involved, with boys participating most in all the behavior we analyzed (see Figure 1).

INFLUENCE OF PEER CONTEXT
AND GENDER DIFFERENCES

Despite the fact that sexting, with its relatively low rates of involvement, cannot be considered a normative practice, it has been found that the exchange of sexual content is becoming increasingly normalized among adolescents. This belief influences adolescents' perception of this practice and, in turn, fuels the motivation to participate in it without regard for strategies that could protect them against its possible consequences. Similarly, studies have shown that sexting is not a gender-neutral phenomenon and is subject to the same power relations and gender stereotypes which exist in real life, which is an important factor to take into account when analyzing sexting.

The Peer Context

The generalized belief that sexting is commonly used as a strategy among adolescents to establish intimate relationships influences the perception that adolescents have about the normalization of sexting. Despite the fact that the exchange of sexual content is becoming increasingly normalized among adolescents and young people (Stanley et al., 2018), it cannot yet be considered a normative practice (Van Ouytsel et al., 2015).

However, the perception that this behavior has become common has in turn influenced the views that adolescents have about the normalization of sexting (Lippman & Campbell, 2014). This leads to erroneous beliefs about other adolescents' behavior which fuels the normalization of the exchange of sexual content through the Internet, affecting in turn the individual behavior of those involved, justifying it and allowing it to increase (Wood et al., 2015). In this way, peer norms play a crucial role when adolescents post sexual photos of themselves on the Internet (Baumgartner et al., 2015). In fact, the results of studies indicate that adolescents' wish to participate in sexting is associated with positive attitudes towards this practice and the extent to which they perceive that their peers approve of it (Van Ouytsel et al., 2017). In this case, the subjective norm in adolescents is one of the strongest predictors of their sexual intent (Walrave et al., 2015). It has also been found that the adolescents agree that messages from their group of friends and the media influence their predisposition to sexting by suggesting that it is a normal practice (Davidson, 2015). Thus, subjective norms, the intentions underlying this behavior and the expectations of sexting are predictors of participation in this phenomenon (Weisskirch & Delevi, 2011; Strassberg et al., 2013).

The reasons why young people participate in sexting is also a key factor in them getting involved in this practice. However, it seems that, on many occasions, adolescents downplay their reasons for doing so and some have never given a thought to why they participate in sexting (Villacampa, 2017), which could be due, to a great extent, to the current normalization of this phenomenon. Although the motivation varies widely, peer pressure or coercion appear to be among the key causal factors in the logic of participation in sexting, especially in girls. This peer pressure can even lead to involuntary sending of sexual content (Klettke, Hallford, & Mellor 2014). In fact, peer support and peer pressure have been shown to constitute the most influential motivating factor, and they affect shared sexting of images both of oneself and of other people (Lee, Moak, & Walker, 2016). The main reasons why adolescents take part in sexting behavior therefore include social pressure, their perception of sexting as an integral part of romantic relationships, as a tool for simply having fun, and as a tool for self-presentation or even revenge (Kopecký, 2015). Other reasons cited are that it is considered cool/sexy, the desire to initiate sexual activity, to attract attention or to have fun (Henderson, 2011), as well as boredom, as a form of self-control, accidentally, or involuntarily (Kopecký, 2012), or as an act of hedonism (Parker et al., 2013).

Within the peer context, the desire for popularity has also been shown to play a relevant role. This factor is one of the best predictors of the use of virtual social networks (Utz, Tanis, & Vermeulen 2012). As commented above, adolescence is a stage marked by growing curiosity about sexuality, the search for identity, the development of social interaction skills, and the questioning of normative limits (Chalfen, 2009; Ling, 2004). Attitudes towards sexting and participation in sexting are therefore closely related to an adolescent's urge to increase their popularity (Gewirtz-Meydan, Mitchell, & Rothman 2018). Peer norms play a crucial role in adolescents posting sexual pictures of themselves on the Internet (Baumgartner et al., 2015). Adolescents who feel a greater need for popularity are more likely to publish such photos of themselves (Vanden Abeele et al., 2014). In this way, it has been found that the peer context, in particular the overwhelming motivation to gain popularity, significantly affects adolescents' online behavior, since it is the ideal environment in which to present themselves to a wider audience. In fact, adolescents striving for popularity may consider posting sexual photos of themselves as a key strategy for becoming more popular with their peers (Baumgartner et al., 2015).

Gender Differences

For both boys and girls alike, sexting can serve as an invitation to participate in sexual activities (Wurtele & Miller-Perrin, 2014). However, other research has confirmed that sexting is not a gender-neutral activity and is influenced by gender stereotypes and inequalities (Walker, Sanci, & Temple-Smith 2011). This dynamic is particularly noticeable in sexting, not only in the specific motivation which encourages adolescents to take part in it, but also in the roles that the young people involved assume and the outcomes which occur after the content is posted.

In particular, boys are usually seen as those who request sexual content, while girls are responsible for setting the limits and ensuring they are adhered to (Symons et al., 2018). When sexual content is posted, girls also suffer more negative consequences than boys. In fact, boys not only suffer fewer negative consequences but even obtain positive outcomes (Speno, 2016). For this reason, although the desire for popularity seems to be a predictor of involvement in sexting similarly for both girls and boys – in other words, girls, too, seek acceptance and popularity through sexually permissive behavior (Vanden Abeele et al., 2014), they do not obtain the same results. By taking part in sexting, boys boost their social prestige and gain popularity in their peer group. However, on the contrary, in most cases, girls not only do not gain popularity, but they are also frequently insulted and rejected, and suffer negative feelings after sexting (Burén & Lunde 2018; Temple & Choi, 2014). This shows that although the desire for popularity influences both genders, there may be a need for different theoretical models to account for the behavior of boys and girls (Vanden Abeele et al., 2014).

This fact evidences the double sexual standards prevalent in sexting, since it is the girls whose reputation is usually harmed and who suffer most of the consequences and negative impact of this phenomenon (Wood et al., 2015). In general, therefore, girls are usually the worst affected: boys are admired and their popularity increases, while sexually active girls are criticized, shamed, and despised (Ringrose et al., 2012). One of the reasons why this occurs is that the images or videos in which a naked or semi-nude female body appears are likely to lead to disapproving accusations of sexual promiscuity, which does not happen in images or videos where male bodies appear. In addition, young people in general tend to ignore men's actions and hold girls and women responsible for risking online abuse (Salter, 2016).

Therefore, although there is a lack of consensus and possible gender neutrality in the rates of involvement in sexting, it has been proven that this phenomenon is subject to the same social gender relations which govern relationships in real life. It is therefore necessary to add the gender perspective to our understanding of sexting if we are to make an effective analysis of the current state of this issue (Symons et al., 2018).

THE POSSIBLE CONSEQUENCES OF SEXTING

Sexting is a phenomenon which worries parents and teachers alike and is one of the issues which most concerns society about the dangers and risks of young people using the Internet (Willard, 2007). The flames have been fanned by the media (Brito, 2012) to such an extent that it has become a subject of scientific study due to the possible negative consequences which have been spread by the media and which society as a whole generally considers alarming (Klettke, Hallford, & Mellor, 2014). This may be why the literature has focused more on the consequences of this phenomenon, and on its abstinence and prohibition, rather than on accepting it as a new form of online relationships and acting to prevent its possible negative effects (Döring, 2014).

In general, it has been claimed that sexting creates conflict over privacy and the protection of personal content, as well as social, moral, and ethical disputes (Schubert & Wurf, 2014). Despite the fact that in the past people used to exchange images and sexual messages without the need for digital media, new technologies and the Internet have made it more accessible and have broadened the range of its consequences (Van Ouytsel, Walrave & Van Gool, 2014). Nevertheless, there is currently no consensus in the scientific literature over the importance of considering sexting as risk behavior (Souza & Alves, 2018).

Some studies defend adolescents' freedom of sexual expression on the Internet, arguing that the risks of this behavior do not lie in the fact of sharing the file itself, but in its possible further diffusion on the Internet and the speed at which this can happen, which can greatly increase the potential audience (Livingstone & Görzig, 2014). When the sexual content is spread without consent, it can negatively influence the victim's reputation, and affect them on an academic, physical, and psychological level (Van Ouytsel et al., 2015). Other authors consider it necessary to act against any type of online behavior that has potential risks, and that the behavior of sexting itself may have negative consequences. In particular, it appears that some young people who participate in sexting experience peer pressure, with the consequent emotional difficulties that this may entail (Van Ouytsel et al., 2015). In addition, some studies have revealed that sexting can affect the physical and psychological health of the young people involved, leading to symptoms of depression, aggression, or problems with sexual behavior, among others, and even, in some cases, to suicidal ideation (Jasso-Medrano, Lopez-Rosales, & Gámez-Guadix, 2018; Strasburger, Jordan, & Donnerstein, 2012).

Similarly, although sexting is often seen currently as a means for adolescents to explore their sexual identity, it can also lead to involvement with other more extreme types of behavior, such as grooming, pornography, harassment, cyberbullying or extortion, or even blackmail involving sexual abuse in exchange for not spreading the intimate content (Cooper et al., 2016; Kopecký, 2015; Strassberg et al., 2013; Olivari & Confalonieri, 2017).

SEXTING AND SEXUAL EDUCATION

Although there is no general consensus over whether sexting constitutes risk behavior or not (Souza & Alves, 2018), it has been shown that banning this practice and the use of fear and abstinence strategies are ineffective in avoiding the possible consequences that can derive from sexting (Strassberg, Cann, & Velarde, 2017). In general, the literature and educational campaigns have focused more on analyzing sexting as a problem and promoting these strategies, rather than accepting consensual sexting as a means of intimate sexual communication which fits in with contemporary forms of communication (Strassberg, Cann, & Velarde, 2017; Döring, 2014). Focusing on abstinence and fear strategies in sexting, without proposing alternative approaches, can simply make young people more interested in it (Gómez & Ayala, 2014). For this reason, it appears that, regardless of the categorization of sexting as a risk behavior or not, most studies recommend that we take steps to counter the behavior involved in sexting in order to prevent any potentially negative consequences.

In general, it seems that in order to act to prevent the possible consequences of this phenomenon, schools play a fundamental role in the protection of young people (Theodore, 2011). Indeed, although the rates of involvement in sexting in schools are lower than those in other contexts, sexting also takes place during school hours (Schubert & Wurf, 2014). In fact, teachers themselves support the idea that schools can and should play an essential role in educating pupils about ICT use (Mura, Bernardi, & Diamantini, 2014). Therefore, given the possible consequences involved in this phenomenon and the difficulties faced by the teachers who work with young people on a daily basis (McEachern, McEachern-Ciattoni, & Martin, 2012), education and prevention at school plays a key role (Kopecký, 2012). In addition, school counsellors, school psychologists, and educators in general are in a unique position where they can address sexting proactively in schools by implementing specific educational programs of prevention (Bhat, 2018).

Despite this, little research has been carried out to date which can serve as a reference point for schools and institutions on what action they should take to make prevention and interventions in this area effective. Although this area is still in its infancy and few studies have been carried out, the scientific literature has provided us with strategies to help prevent the consequences of sexting by following a plan of action based on the findings in these studies (Döring, 2014). Among the strategies recommended are encouraging control over one's personal image (Diliberto & Mattey, 2009) and sexual ethics to make informed ethical decisions, creating opportunities to listen to adolescents' points of view (Walker, Sanci, & Temple-Smith, 2011), sex education (Strasburger, Jordan, & Donnerstein, 2012), resistance to peer pressure (Van Ouytsel et al., 2015) and educating onlookers (Powell & Henry, 2014). In addition, it is especially important to train professionals (Ahern & Mechling, 2013) and implement programs which focus on denormalization and safety strategies, without resorting to abstinence or fear tactics (Albury, Hasinoff, & Senft, 2017; Dobson & Ringrose, 2016; Wurtele & Miller-Perrin, 2014). Furthermore, not only should we act by implementing the strategies proposed in the scientific literature, but it is also essential to evaluate their effectiveness and adapt the action taken to the demands of the context where it occurs, in order to improve educational practice and develop evidence-based procedures (Livingstone & Smith, 2014).

Given the need for guidance about effective means of prevention, we are currently carrying out a systematic review to find out what steps are being taken in schools to address sexting, as well as the relevant lines of action to take effective preventive measures in the adolescent population. In all, 92 articles have been included in this review. We found that although the number of studies peaked in 2014, there has been less scientific research in recent years. However, given the need to intervene in sexting, we expect this figure to rise. In addition, most studies come from the USA; since sexting is clearly influenced by contextual and cultural factors, studies from other geographical areas need to be encouraged so as to check if any differences exist between countries.

Regarding specific lines of action, 7.6% of articles recommend acting on sexting, without identifying any key aspects; 84.8% propose acting on this phenomenon and include strategic issues for prevention and/or effective intervention; and 7.6% of the studies suggest taking specific action on sexting. In the same way, almost all the research refers to the importance of prevention and the key role of schools in implementing it (85.9%).

The strategies identified as fundamental aspects to address in sexting were categorized, and this produced 15 key lines of action for preventing and acting against this practice:

1. Developing specific programs on sexting, including face-to-face sessions and/or using IT, which deal specifically with training and awareness-raising in this phenomenon, including both proactive and reactive activities.
2. Promoting the safe, healthy use of technology, in particular on internet and social networks, through activities aimed at promoting safe online behavior, with a special focus on digital privacy, control over the use of private data, and digital rights and obligations.

3. Carrying out a specific analysis to raise awareness of the risks and consequences associated with sexting. However, this must be done in combination with other steps, as on its own, it may not be fully effective.

4. Including the subject of sexting in sex education programs: sexting is now a part of intimate communication, and as such, should be included in programs which address sex education, both in face-to-face sessions and through IT.

5. Providing training for professionals: continuous training should be provided for those who work with children and young people to improve their professional skills and strengthen the educational response to real-life situations with students.

6. Promoting sexual ethics: developing skills to enable young people to establish ethical intimate relationships, based on consent rather than coercion or pressure.

7. Raising awareness of gender roles and stereotypes: promoting knowledge of the cultural values, gender roles and stereotypes which are involved in social relationships, and discussing the norms involved in heteronormative femininity and masculinity.

8. Drawing up regulations and putting protocols into practice: designing codes of practice for schools and clear protocols of action which will enable the educational community to know how to act.

9. Promoting consistency among the different agents involved: involving the whole educational community, as well as any other institution or agents in society, to promote the consistency and stability of these initiatives.

10. Working on the risk factors associated with peer groups: designing activities which address the key role of peer groups and onlookers, with a focus on areas such as social prestige, the need for popularity, peer pressure and critical attitudes.

11. Working from the adolescents' own ideas and experiences: the activities need to be analysed and adapted to their perceptions and experiences. This can be done either in mixed groups or groups divided according to gender.

12. Improving the atmosphere in schools: fostering a positive atmosphere, loving relationships and respect.

13. Taking steps specially directed at vulnerable groups: encouraging diversity and carrying out activities which are adapted to groups which are potentially more likely to be harmed, such as LGBTQ+, racial / ethnic minorities and victims of bullying, among others.

14. Applying disciplinary or legal measures: setting up clear punishments for aggressive behavior, recognising criminal offences which may be committed when sexual content is shared without consent.

15. Including sexting in preventive programs for other associated risks: the topic of sexting can be included in both digital and face-to-face activities which deal with the associated risks of Internet use.

As well as these lines of action, a number of studies have shown that the strategies used to address sexting should avoid the use of fear tactics and should encourage greater awareness and critical thinking. They also recommend making a critical assessment of, firstly, the phenomenon of sexting, in order to establish a baseline from which to shape the plan of action to the context in which it is set, and, secondly, the steps taken, in order to measure how effective it is. However, despite the different approaches put forward in the scientific literature, in only one article was the action assessed to measure its effectiveness. It is therefore vital to continue deepening our knowledge about the nature of this phenomenon and try to build up a list of recommended strategies where the practical steps are based on real-life evidence. In other words, we should work with initiatives which have been evaluated and shown to be suitable and which will allow us to address the consequences of sexting effectively.

CONCLUSION

Sexting has developed into a new way in which adolescents can explore their sexuality. This has occurred as a result of the nature of contemporary of society, which is constantly interconnected via the digital world. However, the concept of sexting is still continually evolving and new facets are continually being discovered. The literature we have reviewed stresses the need to establish a scientific consensus over the definition of sexting in order to lay solid foundations for this construct. However, in the meantime, researchers must specify in detail which definition they are referring to in each study, and readers must pay particular attention in this regard, so that they can know what kind of sexting behavior the findings are referring to.

Although the prevalence of sexting varies mainly depending on the type of behavior referred to in the definition used, it should probably not be considered as a normative practice. However, it has been found that the exchange of sexual content is becoming increasingly normalized among adolescents. This belief fuels the perception adolescents have about it and, in turn, feeds the motivation to participate in it without a thought for any strategies which might allow them to counter its possible consequences. Similarly, according to several studies, sexting is not a gender-neutral phenomenon and is exposed to the same power relations and gender stereotypes which occur in normal life, which further highlights the importance of taking these dynamics into account when analysing sexting.

In addition, there is a growing concern among families, teachers and society over Internet use by young people in general, and in particular, the dangers and risks involved in sexting. However, no general consensus has been reached in the scientific literature about the importance of considering sexting as risk behavior. Some authors defend the view that adolescents should be given the freedom to express their sexuality through the Internet, while others consider that we must act when faced with any kind of online behavior which may involve potential risks. However, regardless of whether sexting is categorised as risk behavior or not, most studies do recommend that action be taken against the kinds of behavior involved in sexting in order to prevent possible negative consequences.

In general, however, it seems that schools can play a fundamental role in acting to prevent the potentially negative consequences of sexting. Despite this, up to now, there has been very little research which could act as a reference point for schools and institutions on what steps they should take to make prevention and intervention in this area effective. Although this field is still in its infancy and few studies have been carried out, the scientific literature has provided us with strategies to help prevent the consequences of sexting by following a plan of action based on the findings in these studies.

It is therefore crucial to continue deepening our knowledge of the nature of sexting and to put into practice the strategies recommended in the studies in order to prevent the potential negative consequences involved and to evaluate its effectiveness in designing evidence-based action plans which could enable us to address this phenomenon effectively.

REFERENCES

Ahern, N. R., and Mechling, B. 2013. "Sexting: Serious Problems for Youth." *Journal of Psychosocial Nursing and Mental Health Services* 51 (7): 22–30.

Albury, K., Hasinoff, A. A., and Senft, T. 2017. "From Media Abstinence to Media Production: Sexting, Young People and Education." In *The Palgrave Handbook of Sexuality Education*, 527–45. London: Palgrave Macmillan UK. https://doi.org/10.1057/978-1-137-40033-8_26.

Anastassiou, A. 2017. "Sexting and Young People: A Review of the Qualitative Literature." *The Qualitative Report* 22 (8): 2231–39.

Barrense-Dias, Y., Berchtold, A., Suris, J. C., and Akre, C. 2017. "Sexting and the Definition Issue." *Journal of Adolescent Health* 61 (5): 544–54. https://doi.org/https://doi.org/10.1016/j.jadohealth.2017.05.009.

Baumgartner, S. E., Sumter, S. R., Peter, J., and Valkenburg, P. M. 2015. "Sexual Self-Presentation on Social Network Sites: Who Does It and How Is It Perceived?" *Computers in Human Behavior* 50 (September). Pergamon: 91–100. https://doi.org/10.1016/J.CHB.2015.03.061.

Bhat, C. S. 2018. "Proactive Cyberbullying and Sexting Prevention in Australia and the USA." *Journal of Psychologists and Counsellors in Schools* 28 (1): 120–30. https://doi.org/https://doi.org/10.1017/jgc.2017.8.

Brito, P. Q. 2012. "Tweens' Characterization of Digital Technologies." *Computers & Education* 59 (2). Pergamon: 580–93. https://doi.org/10. 1016/J.COMPEDU.2012.03.005.

Bronfenbrenner, U. 1979. *The Ecology of Human Development: Experiments by Nature and Design.* Harvard University Press.

Burén, J., and Lunde, C. 2018. "Sexting among Adolescents: A Nuanced and Gendered Online Challenge for Young People." *Computers in Human Behavior* 85: 210–17.

Campbell, S. W., and Park, Y. J. 2014. "Predictors of Mobile Sexting among Teens: Toward a New Explanatory Framework." *Mobile Media & Communication* 20 (1): 20–39. https://doi.org/https://doi.org/10.1177/ 2050157913502645.

Chalfen, R. 2009. "It's Only a Picture: Sexting, 'smutty' Snapshots and Felony Charges." *Visual Studies* 24 (3): 258–68. https://doi.org/10. 1080/14725860903309203.

Choi, H., Van Ouytsel, J., and Temple, J. R. 2016. "Association between Sexting and Sexual Coercion among Female Adolescents." *Journal of Adolescence* 53 (December). Academic Press: 164–68. https://doi.org/ 10.1016/J.adolescence.2016.10.005.

Cooper, K., Quayle, E., Jonsson, L., and Svedin, C. G. 2016. "Adolescents and Self-Taken Sexual Images: A Review of the Literature." *Computers in Human Behavior* 55: 706–16.

Davidson, J. 2015. *Sexting : Gender and Teens.* Springer.

Diliberto, G. M., and Mattey, E. 2009. "Sexting: Just How Much of a Danger Is It and What Can School Nurses Do About It?" *NASN School Nurse* 24 (6): 262–67.

Dobson, A. S., and Ringrose, J. 2016. "Sext Education: Pedagogies of Sex, Gender and Shame in the Schoolyards of *Tagged* and *Exposed.*" *Sex Education* 16 (1): 8–21. https://doi.org/10.1080/14681811.2015. 1050486.

Döring, N. 2014. "Consensual Sexting among Adolescents: Risk Prevention through Abstinence Education or Safer Sexting?" *Cyberpsychology: Journal of Psychosocial Research on Cyberspace* 8 (1). https://doi.org/ https://doi.org/10.5817/CP2014-1-9.

Englander, E. K., and McCoy, M. 2017. "Pressured Sexting and Revenge Porn in a Sample of Massachusetts Adolescents." *International Journal of Technoethics (IJT)* 8 (2): 16–25.

Gewirtz-Meydan, A., Mitchell, K. J., and Rothman, E. F. 2018. "What Do Kids Think about Sexting?" *Computers in Human Behavior* 86: 256–65. https://doi.org/https://doi.org/10.1016/j.chb.2018.04.007.

Gómez, L. C., and Ayala, E. S. 2014. "Psychological Aspects, Attitudes and Behaviour Related to the Practice of Sexting: A Systematic Review of the Existent Literature." *Procedia-Social and Behavioral Sciences* 132: 114–20.

Henderson, L. 2011. "Sexting and Sexual Relationships Among Teens and Young Adults." *McNair Scholars Research Journal* 7 (1).

Jasso-Medrano, J. L., Lopez-Rosales, F., and Gámez-Guadix, M.. 2018. "Assessing the Links of Sexting, Cybervictimization, Depression, and Suicidal Ideation Among University Students." *Archives of Suicide Research* 22 (1): 153–64. https://doi.org/10.1080/13811118.2017.1304304.

Johnson, G. M. 2010. "Internet Use and Child Development: Validation of the Ecological Techno-Subsystem." *Journal of Educational Technology & Society* 13 (1). International Forum of Educational Technology & Society: 176–85. https://doi.org/10.2307/jeductechsoci.13.1.176.

Klettke, B, Hallford, D. J., and Mellor, D. J. 2014. "Sexting Prevalence and Correlates: A Systematic Literature Review." *Clinical Psychology Review* 34 (1): 44–53.

Kopecký, K. 2012. "Sexting among Czech Preadolescents and Adolescents." *Academia.Edu.*

———. 2015. "Sexting Among Slovak Pubescents and Adolescent Children." *Procedia - Social and Behavioral Sciences* 203 (August): 244–50. https://doi.org/10.1016/j.sbspro.2015.08.289.

Lee, C. H., Moak, S., and Walker, J. T. 2016. "Effects of Self-Control, Social Control, and Social Learning on Sexting Behavior Among South Korean Youths." *Youth & Society* 48 (2). SAGE Publications: 242–64. https://doi.org/10.1177/0044118X13490762.

Lenhart, A. 2009. "Teens and Sexting: How and Why Minor Teens Are Sending Sexually Suggestive Nude or Nearly Nude Images via Text Messaging."

Ling, R. 2004. *The Mobile Connection: The Cell Phone's Impact on Society.* San Francisco: Morgan Kaufmann.

Lippman, J. R., and Campbell, S. W. 2014. "Damned If You Do, Damned If You Don't...If You're a Girl: Relational and Normative Contexts of Adolescent Sexting in the United States." *Journal of Children and Media* 8 (4): 371–86. https://doi.org/10.1080/17482798.2014.923009.

Livingstone, S., and Görzig, A. 2014. "When Adolescents Receive Sexual Messages on the Internet: {Explaining} Experiences of Risk and Harm." *Computers in Human Behavior* 33: 8–15. https://doi.org/10.1016/j.chb.2013.12.021.

Livingstone, S., and Smith, P. K. 2014. "Annual Research Review: Harms Experienced by Child Users of Online and Mobile Technologies: The Nature, Prevalence and Management of Sexual and Aggressive Risks in the Digital Age." *Journal of Child Psychology and Psychiatry* 55 (6): 635–54. https://doi.org/10.1111/jcpp.12197.

Livingstone, S., Haddon, L., Görzig, A., and Ólafsson, K. 2011. "Risks and Safety on the Internet: The Perspective of European Children: Full Findings and Policy Implications from the EU Kids Online Survey of 9-16 Year Olds and Their Parents in 25 Countries." London, UK: EU Kids Online.

Madigan, S., Ly, A., Rash, C. L., Van Ouytsel, J., and Temple, J. R. 2018. "Prevalence of Multiple Forms of Sexting Behavior Among Youth." *JAMA Pediatrics* 172 (4): 327–35. https://doi.org/10.1001/jamapediatrics.2017.5314.

Marume, A., Maradzika, J., and January, J. 2018. "Adolescent Sexting and Risky Sexual Behaviours in Zimbabwe: A Cross-Sectional Study." *Sexuality & Culture*, February. Springer US, 1–11. https://doi.org/10.1007/s12119-018-9508-4.

McEachern, A. G., McEachern-Ciattoni, R. T., and Martin, F. 2012. "Sexting: New Challenges for Schools and Professional School Counselors." *Journal of School Counseling* 10 (20): 1–28.

Mitchell, K. J., Finkelhor, D., Jones, L. M., and Wolak, J. 2011. "Prevalence and Characteristics of Youth Sexting: A National Study." *PEDIATRICS* 129 (1): 13–20. https://doi.org/10.1542/peds.2011-1730.

Mura, G., Bernardi, M., and Diamantini, D. 2014. "Diffusion of ICT Related Problems among Students: The Teachers' Experience." *Bordón. Revista de Pedagogía* 66 (3): 105–20.

Norman, J. M. 2017. "Implications of Parenting Behaviour and Adolescent Attachment for Understanding Adolescent Sexting." University of Windsor.

Olivari, M. G., and Confalonieri, E. 2017. "Adolescenti e Sexting: Una Review Della Letteratura." *Maltrattamento e Abuso All'infanzia* 2: 119–40. ["Adolescents and Sexting: A Review of Literature." *Child Maltreatment and Abuse* 2: 119–40].

Parker, T. S., Blackburn, K. M., Perry, M. S., and Hawks, J. M. 2013. "Sexting as an Intervention: Relationship Satisfaction and Motivation Considerations." *The American Journal of Family Therapy* 41 (1): 1–12. https://doi.org/10.1080/01926187.2011.635134.

Patrick, K, Heywood, W., Pitts, M. K., and Mitchell, A. 2015. "Demographic and Behavioural Correlates of Six Sexting Behaviours among Australian Secondary School Students." *Sexual Health* 12 (6): 480–87.

Peskin, M. F., Markham, C. M., Addy, R. C., Shegog, R., Thiel, M., and Tortolero, S. R. 2013. "Prevalence and Patterns of Sexting Among Ethnic Minority Urban High School Students." *Cyberpsychology, Behavior, and Social Networking* 16 (6). Mary Ann Liebert, Inc. 140 Huguenot Street, 3rd Floor New Rochelle, NY 10801 USA: 454–59. https://doi.org/10.1089/cyber.2012.0452.

Powell, A., and Henry, N. 2014. "Blurred Lines? Responding to 'sexting'and Gender-Based Violence among Young People." *Children Australia* 39 (2): 119–24.

Reyns, B. W., Burek, M. W., Henson, B., and Fisher, B. S. 2013. "The Unintended Consequences of Digital Technology: Exploring the Relationship between Sexting and Cybervictimization." *Journal of*

Crime and Justice 36 (1). TF: 1–17. https://doi.org/10.1080/0735648X. 2011.641816.

Rice, E., Rhoades, H., Winetrobe, H., Sanchez, M., Montoya, J., Plant, A., and Kordic, T. 2012. "Sexually Explicit Cell Phone Messaging Associated with Sexual Risk among Adolescents." *Pediatrics* 130 (4): 667–673. https://doi.org/10.1542/peds.2012-0021.

Ringrose, J., Gill, R., Livingstone, S., and Harvey, L. 2012. "A Qualitative Study of Children, Young People and'sexting': A Report Prepared for the NSPCC." London, UK.

Salter, M. 2016. "Privates in the Online Public: Sex(Ting) and Reputation on Social Media." *New Media & Society* 18 (11). SAGE PublicationsSage UK: London, England: 2723–39. https://doi.org/ 10.1177/1461444815604133.

Schubert, A., and Wurf, G. 2014. "Adolescent Sexting in Schools: Criminalisation, Policy Imperatives, and Duty of Care." *Issues in Educational Research* 24 (2): 190–211.

Smith, P K, Thompson, F., and Davidson, J. 2014. "Cyber Safety for Adolescent Girls: Bullying, Harassment, Sexting, Pornography, and Solicitation." *Current Opinion in Obstetrics and Gynecology* 26 (5): 360–65.

Souza, F., and Alves, R. 2018. "A Prática Cultural Do Sexting Entre Adolescentes: Notas Para a Delimitação Do Objeto de Estudo." *Acta Comportamentalia: Revista Latina de Análisis Del Comportamiento* 26 (1). ["The Cultural Practice of Sexting Among Adolescents: Notes for the Delimitation of the Object of Study." *Acta Comportamentalia: Latin Journal of Behavior Analysis* 26 (1)].

Speno, A. G. 2016. "Adolescent Sexting: An Examination of the Psychosocial Contributions to the Creation and Sharing of Sexual Images." University of Missouri (Columbia). https://search. proquest.com/openview/6b503e067bafa6b4cb69f8d4418ff4ec/1?pq-origsite=gscholar&cbl=18750&diss=y.

Stanley, N., Barter, C., Wood, M., Aghtaie, N., Larkins, C., Lanau, A., and Överlien, C. 2018. "Pornography, Sexual Coercion and Abuse and Sexting in Young People's Intimate Relationships: A European Study."

Journal of Interpersonal Violence 33 (19): 2919–44. https://doi.org/ 10.1177/0886260516633204.

Strasburger, V. C., Jordan, A. B., and Donnerstein, E. 2012. "Children, Adolescents, and the Media:: Health Effects." *Pediatric Clinics* 59 (3): 533–87.

Strassberg, D. S., Cann, D., and Velarde, V. 2017. "Sexting by High School Students." *Archives of Sexual Behavior* 46 (6). Springer US: 1667–72. https://doi.org/10.1007/s10508-016-0926-9.

Strassberg, D. S., McKinnon, R. K., Sustaíta, M. A., and Rullo, J. 2013. "Sexting by High School Students: An Exploratory and Descriptive Study." *Archives of Sexual Behavior* 42 (1): 15–21. https://doi.org/10. 1007/s10508-012-9969-8.

Symons, K, Ponnet, K., Walrave, M., and Heirman, W. 2018. "Sexting Scripts in Adolescent Relationships: Is Sexting Becoming the Norm?" *New Media & Society* 20 (10): 3836–57. https://doi.org/https://doi.org/ 10.1177/1461444818761869.

Temple, J. R., and Choi, H. 2014. "Longitudinal Association between Teen Sexting and Sexual Behavior." *Pediatrics* 134 (5): 1287–92. https://doi.org/doi:10.1542/peds.2014-1974.

Temple, J. R., Paul, J. A., Van Den Berg, P., Le, V. D., McElhany, A., and Temple, B. W. 2012. "Teen Sexting and Its Association with Sexual Behaviors." *Archives of Pediatrics and Adolescent Medicine* 166 (9): 828–33.

Theodore, S. 2011. "Integrated Response to Sexting: Utilization of Parents and Schools in Deterrence." *Journal of Contemporary Health Law and Policy* 27: 365.

Utz, S., Tanis, M., and Vermeulen, I. 2012. "It Is All About Being Popular: The Effects of Need for Popularity on Social Network Site Use." *Cyberpsychology, Behavior, and Social Networking* 15 (1). Mary Ann Liebert, Inc. New Rochelle, NY 10801 USA : 37–42. https://doi.org/10. 1089/cyber.2010.0651.

Vanden Abeele, M., Campbell, S. W., Eggermont, S., and Roe, K. 2014. "Sexting, Mobile Porn Use, and Peer Group Dynamics: Boys' and Girls' Self-Perceived Popularity, Need for Popularity, and Perceived Peer

Pressure." *Media Psychology* 17 (1). Taylor & Francis: 6–33. https://doi.org/10.1080/15213269.2013.801725.

Van Ouytsel, J., Ponnet, K., Walrave, M., and d'Haenens, L. 2017. "Adolescent Sexting from a Social Learning Perspective." *Telematics and Informatics* 34 (1). Pergamon: 287–98. https://doi.org/10.1016/J.TELE.2016.05.009.

Van Ouytsel, J., Walrave, M., and Van Gool, E. 2014. "Sexting: Between Thrill and Fear—How Schools Can Respond." *The Clearing House: A Journal of Educational Strategies, Issues and Ideas* 87 (5). Routledge: 204–12. https://doi.org/10.1080/00098655.2014.918532.

Van Ouytsel, J., Walrave, M., Ponnet, K., and Heirman, W. 2015. "The Association Between Adolescent Sexting, Psychosocial Difficulties, and Risk Behavior." *The Journal of School Nursing* 31 (1): 54–69. https://doi.org/10.1177/1059840514541964.

Villacampa, C. 2017. "Teen Sexting: Prevalence, Characteristics and Legal Treatment." *International Journal of Law, Crime and Justice* 49 (June): 10–21. https://doi.org/10.1016/j.ijlcj.2017.01.002.

Walker, S, Sanci, L., and Temple-Smith, M. 2011. "Sexting and Young People: Experts' Views." *Youth Studies Australia* 30 (4): 8–16.

Walrave, M., Ponnet, K., Van Ouytsel, J., Van Gool, E., Heirman, W., and Verbeek, A. 2015. "Whether or Not to Engage in Sexting: Explaining Adolescent Sexting Behaviour by Applying the Prototype Willingness Model." *Telematics and Informatics* 32 (4). Elsevier Ltd: 796–808. https://doi.org/10.1016/j.tele.2015.03.008.

Weisskirch, R. S., and Delevi, R. 2011. "'Sexting' and Adult Romantic Attachment." *Computers in Human Behavior* 27 (5): 1697–1701.

West, J. H., Lister, C. E., Hall, P. C., Crookston, B. T., Snow, P. R., Zvietcovich, M. E., and West, R. P. 2014. "Sexting among Peruvian Adolescents." *BMC Public Health* 14 (1): 811. https://doi.org/10.1186/1471-2458-14-811.

Willard, N. E. 2007. *Cyber-Safe Kids, Cyber-Savvy Teens : Helping Young People Learn to Use the Internet Safely and Responsibly.* John Wiley & Sons.

Wolak, J., Finkelhor, D., and Mitchell, K. J. 2012. "How Often Are Teens Arrested for Sexting? Data from a National Sample of Police Cases." *Pediatrics* 129 (1). American Academy of Pediatrics: 4–12. https://doi. org/10.1542/peds.2011-2242.

Wood, M., Barter, C., Stanley, N., Aghtaie, N., and Larkins, C. 2015. "Images across Europe: The Sending and Receiving of Sexual Images and Associations with Interpersonal Violence in Young People's Relationships." *Children and Youth Services Review* 59: 149–60. https://doi.org/https://doi.org/10.1016/j.childyouth.2015.11.005.

Woodward, V. H., Evans, M., and Brooks, M. 2017. "Social and Psychological Factors of Rural Youth Sexting: An Examination of Gender-Specific Models." *Deviant Behavior* 38 (4): 461–76. https://doi.org/10.1080/01639625.2016.1197020.

Wurtele, S. K., and Miller-Perrin, C. 2014. "Preventing Technology-initiated Sexual Victimization of Youth: A Developmental Perspective." In *Sex Education: Attitude of Adolescents, Cultural Differences and Schools' Challenges*, edited by M.C. Kenny, 147–175. New York: Nova.

Ybarra, M. L., and Mitchell, K. J. 2014. "'Sexting' and Its Relation to Sexual Activity and Sexual Risk Behavior in a National Survey of Adolescents." *Journal of Adolescent Health* 55 (6): 757–64. https://doi.org/https://doi.org/10.1016/j.jadohealth.2014.07.012.

In: Digital Technology　　　　　　ISBN: 978-1-53616-438-1
Editor: Michelle F. Wright　　　　© 2019 Nova Science Publishers, Inc.

Chapter 6

SOCIAL MEDIA, ONLINE COMMUNITIES, CONNECTION AND COPING: CONTEXTUAL CONSIDERATIONS WITHIN THE DEVELOPMENTAL PERIOD OF EMERGING ADULTHOOD

Samantha L. Gray, PhD, Lindsey Lockridge and Ryan Peleaux*

College of Applied Behavioral Sciences,
University of Indianapolis, Indianapolis, IN, US

ABSTRACT

Social media and online communities regularly bring millions of people together in various ways, and are used for a wide range of reasons. Often, individuals build social networks where they can connect with like-minded friends or communities. Research has demonstrated that these social spaces have the potential to serve as effective sources of connection

---
* Corresponding Author's E-mail: graysl@uindy.edu.

and coping resources (e.g., among those without direct interpersonal support). However, research has also demonstrated the ability of these spaces to become unhealthy sources of connection and coping, potentially resulting in significant psychological distress. A review of general trends on social media engagement, online communities, and how they may be used as tools for connection and coping will be examined in this chapter. Example contextual content discussed include: memes, self-deprecating humor, anonymous thread discussions, and echo chambers. To that end, this chapter aims to provide a brief review of the potentially positive and negative aspects of social media as a source of connection and coping. Developmental considerations are provided as an initial anchor for this chapter, and are incorporated throughout the paper.

TECHNOLOGY, THEORY, AND EMERGING ADULTHOOD

Social Media Overview and Developmental Considerations

For digital natives, or young people who have only known a world where the internet and access to social technologies have essentially always existed, the tasks associated with moving throughout the lifespan have not inherently changed. Rather, digital natives meet their psychosocial developmental tasks in context of the external environment and social lives in which they know. A great deal of research supports the notion that developmental tasks historically associated with adolescence (e.g., identity development and separation-individuation) have shifted into a period known as '*emerging* adulthood.' However, because the tasks of exploring ones identity (identity development) and becoming more autonomous while maintaining emotional closeness to loved ones (separation-individuation) have not changed, digital natives experience their development in the spaces in which they live. This interaction between development and technology has become an inherent part of the digital native's lifestyle. Currently, digital natives are comprised of two generations: Y and Z. Generation Y, better known as the 'Millennial' generation, is largely composed of individuals born anywhere from 1981 to 1996 (Howe & Strauss, 2004; Pew Research Center, 2018). Generation Z is then largely comprised of individuals born from 1997 to present (Dimock, 2019). It is important to note that there is variation among researchers and within the mass media regarding birth years and associated age ranges for the various generations (Törőcsik, Szűcs, & Kehl, 2014). However, even accounting for those variations in years, these generations both currently include individuals whose age places them within the psychosocial developmental period of emerging adulthood (18-25). Therefore, when considering the experiences of digital natives (i.e., Millennials and Gen Z), it can be helpful to simultaneously consider the role identity development and individuation play as a developmental underpinning for online engagement.

It has been suggested that the process of separating and individuating from one's parents is a process that can disrupt a young person's self-view, such that a new desire to socially integrate with their peer group becomes more desirable than continuing to be integrated with their parents (Koepke & Denissen, 2012). The developmental literature in this area widely supports the notion that young people shift their connections from parents to peers, and use those peer groups for comparison and connection in an attempt to strengthen their developing identities. These developmental tasks are not specific to any particular generational cohort, although whichever generation is currently within the period of emerging adulthood may serve as a point of critical examination as they transition from adolescence to adulthood. Rather, each generational cohort is tasked with meeting their developmental milestones in context of the current sociocultural climate and experience.

Although demonstrated to not be the period of 'storm and stress' researchers once believed it to be as related to separating from parents, the functionalist theoretical groundwork related to conflict and revolt in this transitional period is likely still applicable in understanding sociocultural youthful movements (Eisenstadt, 2017). One facet of this theory proposes that young people form groups which band them together, in essence, providing a social crutch for transitioning from the highly personal familial affiliations they have known, to the "impersonal, bureaucratic world" they have not known (Goertzel, 1972). The theory further postulates that as young adults emerge into the world around them, they are learning to cope with the non-familial world by creating more meaningful interactions with the outside world. Thus, it can be argued that young people are tasked with creating more affective solidarity through connection with their generational peer group to cope with the superficialities faced in society at large.

This task of infusing more meaningful, personal relationships with an arguably superficial external world is not an easy one – especially in context of the impersonal social elements inherent to a digital world. Along with this desire to connect more deeply with their peer group, is the idea that young adults now have the ability to consider more complex issues such as their own personal beliefs and values. As young people wade through these important issues, it makes sense that we see these individuals turn to each other for validation and exploration of their thoughts and feelings. This book chapter provides some contextual illustrations of how young adults use social media as a platform for that validation and exploration. In this way, social technologies have become a conduit for connection and coping.

Due to advancements in technology over the past few decades, younger generations do not only occupy physical spaces. Digital natives are generations who occupy and thrive in virtual spaces as well. The Pew Research Center (2018) reports that approximately 83% of individuals aged 18-29 use social media on a regular basis. Outcome research on the impact of social media has been mixed, such that this increased level of social media consumption has been linked to both beneficial and problematic outcomes. The ability to engage and connect within an online social platform allows users an opportunity to participate in civic discussions, assess public opinion, unite friends, build relationships, and cope with various difficulties (Bers, 2010; DeAndrea, Ellison, LaRose, Steinfield, & Fiore, 2012; Schmalz, Colistra, & Evans, 2015). And among youth in the Generation Z cohort specifically, it is suggested that they prefer connecting with their peers online, and disclose more personal issues on social media than off (Palley, 2012; Taylor & Keeter, 2010). For both Millennials and Generation Z youth, this type of engagement may precipitate psychological vulnerabilities that serve as a catalyst for poor emotional and behavioral outcomes. Beyond type or level of engagement, research has generally supported the notion that high consumption (e.g., spending significantly more time using various forms of technology than an average peer user) is associated with poor mental health outcomes (Allam, 2010; Amichai-Hamburger & Ben-Artzi, 2009; Morrison & Gore, 2010).

It is clear that Millenials and Generation Z youth have grown-up with social media, and use it as a primary tool for connection. In many ways, finding an online space for connection and coping therefore appears to be quite developmentally appropriate and normative. Given how reinforcing and gratifying social media can be in the lives of young people, this platform has essentially become a new playground for consumption of social needs. Overall, the goal for young adults then becomes establishing a method for avoiding the potential negative outcomes associated with social media consumption, while reaping the many positive benefits associated with connection and coping. One way Millennials and the Generation Z cohort accomplish this is through their use of humor and support in online settings.

CONNECTION AND COPING: CONTEXTUAL AREAS OF INTEREST

Humor and Solidarity

Since the mid-1990s, researchers have questioned how online discussion would compare to face-to-face conversation; and in particular, how humor can be adequately conveyed without the ability to hear vocal intonation or see body language. As Nancy Baym (1995) noted, discussion groups about soap operas at the time were full of humor and camaraderie despite lacking these features. This finding has been supported by other research on other online communities as well (Carter, 2005; Massanari, 2013). In the absence of being able to observe facial reactions while online, "emoticons" (i.e., punctuation based icons emoticon) or "emojis" are commonly used to express emotion. Research suggests that using such tools for computer-mediated communication has significant benefit, and increases the accuracy of online communication (Derks, Fischer, & Lo, 2008; Lo, 2008). Beyond emoticons, the Graphic Interchange Format (GIF) image – a silent, looping moving picture – originated from emojis in the early 2010s, but has since transformed into a unique blend of communication, humor, and art (Eppink, 2014). These images are commonly used to convey an emotional response in the absence of a facial reaction.

The widespread use of GIF reaction images today represents an important aspect of Millennial humor and communication, and many of the images themselves are considered memes. The participatory nature of creating, editing, and spreading these GIFs could be called an art form in itself, in a way that the use of emojis never reached. The hesitance of many to give this phenomenon of responding with GIFs, or memes, any sort of formal acknowledgement parallels the opinion of the general public during the rise of Dadaism in the early twentieth century (Hopkins, 2004; Hoins, 2016). Dadaism began as a reaction to World War I, which shook Europe's confidence in intellectual and rational thought, and artists responded with nonsense and irreverence - a symbolic rejection of capitalist society and the bourgeois (Trachtman, 2006). At the time of its popularity, it was hardly considered an art movement, much less anything respectable, and only in hindsight have historians recognized its intimate reflection of the era from which it arose (Hoins, 2016). The subculture of Millennials participating in absurdist humor and experiencing pangs of disillusionment could be considered a new wave of Dadaism. Similar to other generational cohorts, Millennials have a developmentally normative need and desire to connect and bond with others who may have shared feelings and experiences of the world around them. Given the expansive role of social media in their lives, it is not surprising that many young people would use such platforms to connect and bond (Szablewicz, 2014; Hoins, 2016; Lu & Fan, 2018). In many ways, Internet humor, memes, and YouTube have become coping skills for young people worldwide. These platforms not only serve to connect, but can also serve as tools for sarcastic response to criticism. For example, Millennials responded to an assertion that they cannot afford home ownership as a result of buying too much avocado toast by turning the claim into a sardonic meme about their financial struggles (Calfas, 2017; see KnowYourMeme, 2019). In these instances, using humor through memes can be understood as an attempt to assert a degree of control over a disparaging narrative being purported.

The rise and widespread use of memes in the last decade or so has done more than just provide social media users with an alternative way of communicating in the absence of vocal intonation and facial expression. Memes have become a way for strangers to identify with one another and develop a sense of agency in a world of rising housing prices, a difficult job market, and higher expectations of success (Szablewicz, 2014; Lu & Fan, 2018). Limor Shifman (2014, p. 41), a leading researcher on memes and Internet humor, has defined a meme as "a) a group of digital items sharing common characteristics of content, form, and/or stance, which b) were created with awareness of each other, and c) were circulated, imitated, and/or transformed via the Internet by many users." Shifman notes its difference from a viral phenomenon in that a meme is changed as it moves from one person to another. Participating in the alteration or creation of memes may add another layer of experience for young people who use them as a source of meaningful expression.

Viral content, on the other hand, is spread without any editing and looks the same no matter where it is found or who posts it (Shifman, 2011; Shifman, 2014). Memes are a product of the "Web 2.0" culture, or "participatory culture," in which users have shifted from being passive consumers of static content, to becoming the producers and collaborators of this content (Blank & Reisdorf, 2012). As such, a single meme can exist in dozens of forms, personalized and continuously spread. While almost all of them are intended to be humorous, some require various levels of "meme literacy" to understand their humor (Shifman, 2014). Due to the highly contextual nature of certain "genres" of memes, subcultures have developed alongside them and serve as a way to identify group members (Lu & Fan, 2018; Shifman, 2014).

It may seem strange that identities have developed from – or perhaps alongside – a derivative of the viral video, and even more so if one's understanding of Internet content consists primarily of cat videos and song parodies, but nearly every post-90s young adult has grown up online. Now that the children of the Internet explosion have become adults, research has been examining how exactly this has impacted this age group. What researchers are finding is that, globally, individuals whose formative years took place between the mid-90s and mid-2000s are experiencing a similar level of psychological malaise (Johnson, 2017; Lu and Fan, 2018; Szablewicz, 2014). As a result, they have used what they are most familiar with – the Internet – to connect with others who feel similarly about offline society and have naturally formed communities where they can feel empowered and understood. This appears to be true across almost all first-world countries, from the United States (US) to China and Japan, who have "Sang" and "Satori" cultures, respectively (Nae, 2017; Pinkett, 2018). Regardless of the name, Millennials may use internet humor in an attempt to cope with uncertain economic conditions and previous generations' values and milestone expectations (e.g., getting married, having a baby, buying a home etc.; Johnson, 2017; Lu & Fan, 2018; Nae, 2017; Pinkett, 2018; Szablewicz, 2014).

How could such pessimistic humor be good *or* funny, especially when self-presentation and humor theorists state that individuals seek self-enhancement? As reported by Pinkett for Voxburner (2018, para. 4), by bringing "a lightness to help them [Millennials] get through the day, but it also assures them that they are not the only ones feeling this way." Likewise, research showing similar benefits to the psychological wellbeing of Millennials, despite the humor being based in self-deprecation, nihilism, and a pessimistic outlook, has been coming to light in recent years (Lu & Fan, 2018). These memes allow Millennials a sense of belonging in a world that seems bent on pushing them out. Despite the anonymity granted by the Internet, users feel that it is more acceptable for them to be their authentic selves within these groups. Their ability to contribute to within these online spaces through the creation of memes, potentially gaining Internet fame, has allowed them to create new avenues for upward mobility, albeit ones that older generations do not understand (Lu & Fan, 2018). It is possible that this departure from creating something that their parents may understand could also be another demonstration of the separation-individuation process normally observed among young people carving out their own sense of agency. This agency is especially important to the young adults who feel that upward mobility offline is nearly impossible to achieve. Additionally, this social capital has the potentially protective benefit of being funny, since humor is believed to offset stress, reduce interpersonal conflict, improve relationships, and support psychological health in general (Dyck & Holtzman, 2013; Maiolino & Kuiper, 2014).

Not all types of humor have the same protective benefits. Self-deprecating humor has previously been tied to higher rates of depression and lower rates of life satisfaction (Frewen et al., 2008; Dyck & Holtzman, 2013). However, the use of self-deprecating humor among certain groups online has a more complicated relationship with psychological wellbeing. This type of humor has become a form of identity for many young people and fosters a sense of belonging with others who feels similarly about themselves and society (Szablewicz, 2014). Jokes that attack one's ability (or lack thereof) to succeed in life also serve as both criticism toward society and a form of self-defense against high expectations (Lu & Fan, 2018). Of course, the risk of this type of humor is that the individual begins to believe in his lower self-worth. Presently, the relationship between self-deprecating online humor, the maintenance of self-identity, group belongingness, and emotional support still requires more study. It is also unclear if the decreased psychological wellbeing for this population is due to the societal factors that led them to find other "gloomy" individuals, or vice versa.

Online Support Communities

One significant feature of social media platforms that has helped young people connect and bond online are various groups, communities, and forums. Joining or 'following' specific online groups may help create safe spaces where individuals feel more comfortable exploring topics, expressing opinions, or receiving social support. In this regard, these groups may become safe spaces where young people's online interactions are enriched through positive experiences, thus reinforcing their desire to engage or access these spaces. Some individuals utilize social media communities specifically to obtain or share advice. This type of information sharing is commonly found in 'threads,' or a long chain of replies under a topic, remark, or question initially posed by one user. These groups and the threads within them are often populated by people who carry an interest in the forum's central topic. In a study on health-related online forums, Tanis (2008) noted that people joining these sites will encounter a greater number people with experience and interest in this same topic than if they simply engaged with their offline social circle. It was further reported that as forums are accessed by more people than one's immediate social circle, the information within these posts and threads will come from more diverse sources, enabling new members to gain advice that is potentially more useful. He explains that some of these users within the community will probably have first-hand experience, making them valuable sources of information to those seeking advice. While these people may not be healthcare professionals, gaining information from people with whom they can compare their own situation can bring them certainty and help them cope with their situation (Tannis, 2008).

Collin and colleagues (2011) present numerous considerations regarding participation in online social networks. For example, they report that new members often migrate to social networks to express themselves and gain a sense of identity. Particularly for young people, freedom from the regulation they experience in their offline life enables them to express themselves in ways they otherwise might not. These platforms may enable individuals the ability to establish and reinforce their identities in terms of their political views, ethnicity, culture, or sexuality. The opportunity to do this is an important asset in the times of peoples' lives when they're becoming independent from their families and looking for new connection (Collin et al., 2011).

Individuals may seek out online communities not only for advice and information but also for a sense of social support. The online open forum context allows people to express themselves freely, solicit help from others and obtain the support of their peers, as well as lower the stigma of seeking help. This format may be useful for isolated individuals, who may be more willing or able to engage with people online than with people offline (D'Agostino et al., 2017). Whether individuals are isolated socially or geographically, online groups may help young people stay connected. Pendry and Salvatore (2015) report that individuals can utilize online communities and interactions to make up for lack of offline relationships, enabling them to feel genuinely together instead of 'alone together.' They further discuss that this ability to stay connected and establish group identification can directly influence one's health in positive ways, especially if the group's main focus is one that is highly stigmatizing and prevents face-to-face interactions. Social group memberships can, for example, help one manage and reduce depressive symptoms, since online groups are more attractive for people who have difficulty initiating face-to-face interactions (Pendry & Salvatore, 2015). Groups centered around highly-stigmatizing issues prompt the formation of communities that are caring, supportive, and promote a feeling of social belonging. Research even suggests that the presence and degree of identification with an online forum and the other members within it can predict a stigmatized member's satisfaction with life (Pendry & Salvatore, 2015).

The popularity of online support groups extends into the field of mental health. In situations when mental health is of primary concern, some people may gravitate towards online forums for this subject instead of seeking formal professional services. Easily accessible online groups may be more attractive than formal mental health services, where rising copays and inadequate insurance coverage may create a significant barrier to help, or the individual may perceive a loss of autonomy through coercion and hospitalization. Additionally, online support group topics range widely, covering issues including depression, suicide, self-harm, eating disorders, and anxiety (Townsend et al., 2012). The sheer variety of accessible online support groups make them an attractive choice over formal mental health services.

For people engaging in high-risk behaviors, such as substance abuse, the anonymity present in these groups may be highly desirable. On the social networking platform Reddit, individuals can create a throw-away account specifically for a single post, enabling additional layers of anonymity (D'Agostino et al., 2012). Members in online forums are able to maintain anonymity as they either lurk and review useful posts or topics or interact with other members, while social media networks like Twitter and Facebook typically encourage users to provide their name and an identifying photo, therefore losing the advantages that anonymity provides to stigmatized users (Pendry & Salvatore, 2015). Online support groups and forums often fulfill their purpose of lending a sense of support to participants, though their efficacy in reducing symptoms is not adequately researched and the presence of multiple individuals providing potentially asynchronous information can be a disadvantage when individuals are in a crisis (Townsend et al., 2012). Regardless, examination of an opiate support group on Reddit by D'Agostino and colleagues (2012) revealed that very few of the comments contained bad or harmful information.

It has also been suggested that participation in online communities, and the establishment of a group identity is associated with greater participation in civic activities related to the groups' topics (Pendry & Salvatore, 2015). Specifically, this work suggested that there is correlation between online engagement and offline actions, like civic and political engagement. The more people use online discussion forums, the more they may be empowered become active in the forum's topic offline. With the ultimate goal of online community participation being coping and connection, any outcomes which may materialize in offline activities are of additional benefit. To that end, while online communities foster connection through virtual means, they also have the ability to encourage creation and maintenance of these relational opportunities through offline means as well. This may help individuals solidify social support through direct interpersonal interaction (Pendry & Salvatore, 2015). In this regard, the benefits of online interaction extend beyond their immediate context.

While it is clear that online communities can offer a degree of positive outcomes as individuals attempt to cope and connect with others, not all will experience such outcomes. There are other aspects of online communities which can make them aversive, toxic, and even hostile to new members, or foster negative behaviors in existing members. These include the potential for the creation of echo chambers, cyberbullying and flaming; and even one aspect that can otherwise be beneficial: the anonymity provided by online forums.

As mentioned before, the anonymity present in the online context allows for a sense of freedom to be honest and open in their various posts (D'Agostino et al., 2012). However, this very same veil of anonymity that prompts users to express themselves, can lead to toxic disinhibition, which encourages negative behavior (Lapidot-Lefler & Barak, 2012). In addition to anonymity, disinhibition also results from the lack of eye-contact within online interaction, especially when combined with non-disclosure of personal data and invisibility (Lapidot-Lefler & Barak, 2012). Eye-contact plays a key role in facilitating typical interpersonal interactions, enabling intimacy, emotional communication, and moderation of interaction, and research supports that a lack of eye-contact has a greater influence on the presence of toxic disinhibition than simple anonymity (Lapidot-Lefler & Barak, 2012). This toxic online disinhibition can perpetuate behaviors an overall negative environment within the online community (Lapidot-Lefler & Barak, 2012).

Aggression and bullying researcher Dan Olweus' work outlining the relationship between indirect and direct models of bullying continues to be as a model to help further examine the various layers of bullying (Schenk & Fremouw, 2012; Smith, 2019). These models demonstrate that cyberbullying can occur when individuals participate in aggressive behaviors via indirect pathways (i.e., online settings). Cyberbullying has been positively associated with the development of various types and severity levels of psychological distress, including suicidal ideation for some young people. (Moore, Nakano, Enomoto & Suda, 2012; Sabella, Patchin, & Hinduja, 2013; Wang et al., 2019). While cyberbullying is appropriately viewed as a problematic, Sabella and colleagues (2013) caution against making causal claims regarding cyberbullying and suicidal ideation or behaviors. It is also important to note that incidents of cyberbullying are not reserved for children and adolescents as studies have examined these effects in adult populations (Barlett & Chamberlin, 2017; Schenk & Fremouw, 2012; Wang et al., 2019).

Although adults, including young adults, are arguably better able to defend themselves against such forms of cyberbullying or better manage such occurrences, all online community users may be potentially affected by these negative experiences. One form of cyberbullying is 'flaming,' and encompasses a number of online behaviors (Watts, Wagner, Velasquez, & Behrens, 2017). Alonzo and Aiken (2004) explain that flames are typically motivated by hostile intentions, and incorporate the use of profanity, obscenities and insults against a person or entity. Usually resulting in negative emotions such as anger and disbelief in their targets, unaddressed issues of flaming can lead to legal action such as lawsuits.

Amid the potential for cyberbullying, one way in which individuals may attempt to avoid negative experiences is to unite with those who support their pre-existing opinions and beliefs. This strategy can effectively establish the creation of an echo chamber where contrary opinions and beliefs are not typically incorporated into online discussions (Hayat & Samuel-Azran, 2017). In an online context, the phenomenon of echo chambers has a more serious effect on participants in that they steer each other in the direction of more polarized and extreme beliefs (Karlsen et al., 2017). As young people work to solidify their own sense of identity, it may be comforting to participate in online communities which allow clusters of individuals to bond together over perceived or real shared experiences (Hogg & Rinella, 2018). While a certain level of comfort and shared experience is typically ideal for engagement, disagreements and opposing opinions still make up a significant part of online communities.

The internet affords users opportunities not only to interact with like-minded individuals, but also to converse with those holding opposing or different views (Karlsen et al., 2017). Even though users can often be exposed to others' opposing viewpoints and contradicting information, this does not mean that their beliefs or opinions change, and often become even more solidified in their original views, at least in the short term. Regarding echo chambers, Karlsen and colleagues note that extended exposure to opposing opinions may lead debating individuals to change their beliefs over long periods of time (Karlsen et al., 2017). Regarding identity development, a similar pattern is noted where initially being exposed to opposing views may encourage individuals to strengthen their rigidity around their identity. However, extended exposure to opposing views may be related more malleable perspectives – especially when humor, levity, or a degree of comfort can be infused into the experience (Habib, 2008).

This review demonstrates just a few of the complexities and contextual issues surrounding social media, online communities, and connecting & coping in a digital world. Although the potential negative outcomes of social technology use need to be considered, it appears that social media and online communities can serve in beneficial ways for young people who are looking for a source of connection. They can encourage members to engage in offline social interaction and civic engagement, help them cope with mental health and other difficulties, and explore various aspects of their identity, beliefs, or values. Elements of comfort, levity and/or humor, which appear to be especially important when interacting with opposing viewpoints, may be a unique facet of social technology which permits individuals a safe space for exploration. As emerging adulthood can be a time of uncertainty and developmentally appropriate exploration, the use of social technologies as a conduit for connection and coping may be more normative for current digital natives than previous generations.

REFERENCES

Allam, M. (2010). Excessive internet use and depression: Cause-effect bias? *Journal of Psychopathology, 43(5),* 334.

Alonzo, M., & Aiken, M. (2004). *Flaming in electronic communication. Decision Support Systems, 36(3),* 205–213.

Amichai-Hamburter, Y. & Ben-Artzi, E. (2009). Depression through technology. *New Scientist, 204(2739),* 28-29.

Arnett, J. J. (2007). Suffering, selfish, slackers? Myths and reality about emerging adults. *Journal of youth and adolescence, 36*(1), 23-29.

Barlett, C. P., & Chamberlin, K. (2017). Examining cyberbullying across the lifespan. *Computers in Human Behavior, 71,* 444-449.

Baym, N. K. (1995). The performance of humor in computer-mediated communication. *Journal of Computer-Mediated Communication, 1(2).*

Bers, M. (2010). Beyond computer literacy: Supporting youth's positive development through technology. *New Directions for Youth Development, 2010(*128), 13-23.

Blank, G. & Reisdorf, B. C. (2012). The participatory web. *Information, Communication & Society, 15(4)*, 537-554.

Calfas, J. (2017). Millionaire to Millennials: Stop Buying Avocado Toast If You Want to Buy a Home. *Money*. Retrieved from http://money. com/money/4778942/avocados-millennials-home-buying/.

Carter, D. (2005). Living in virtual communities: An ethnography of human relationships in cyberspace. *Information, Communication & Society, 8(2)*, 148-167.

Collin, P., Rahilly, K., Richardson, I., & Third, A. (2011). *The benefits of social networking services.*

D'Agostino, A. R., Optican, A. R., Sowles, S. J., Krauss, M. J., Escobar Lee, K., & Cavazos-Rehg, P. A. (2017). Social networking online to recover from opioid use disorder: A study of community interactions. *Drug and Alcohol Dependence, 181*, 5–10.

DeAndrea, D. C., Ellison, N. B., LaRose, R., Steinfield, C., & Fiore, A. (2012). Serious social media: On the use of social media for improving students' adjustment to college. *The Internet and higher education, 15*(1), 15-23.

Derks, D., Fischer, A. H., & Bos, A. E. (2008). The role of emotion in computer-mediated communication: A review. *Computers in human behavior, 24*(3), 766-785.

Dimock, M. (2019). *Defining generations: Where Millennials end and Generation Z begins.* Pew Research Center. Retrieved from https:// www. pewresearch. org/ fact-tank/ 2019/ 01/ 17/ where- millennials-end-and-generation-z-begins/.

Dyck, K. T. H., & Holtzman, S. (2013). Understanding humor styles and well-being: The importance of social relationships and gender. *Personality and Individual Differences, 55(1), 53-58.*

Eppink, J. (2014). A brief history of the GIF (so far). *Journal of Visual Culture, 13(3)*, 298-306.

Frewen, P. A., Brinker, J., Martin, R. A., & Dozois, D. J. A. (2008). Humor styles and personality-vulnerability to depression. *Humor – International Journal of Humor Research, 21(2).*

Habib, R. (2008). Humor and disagreement: Identity construction and cross-cultural enrichment. *Journal of Pragmatics, 40*(6), 1117-1145.

Hayat, T., & Samuel-Azran, T. (2017). "You too, Second Screeners?" Second Screeners' Echo Chambers During the 2016 US Elections Primaries. *Journal of Broadcasting & Electronic Media, 61*(2), 291-308.

Hoins, M. (2016). "Neo-Dadaism": Absurdist Humor and the Millennial Generation. *Medium.* Retrieved from https://medium.com/@meganhoins/ neo- dadaism- absurdist- humor- and- the- millennial-generation-f27a39bcf321.

Hopkins, D. (2004). Dada and Surrealism: *A very short introduction.* New York: Oxford University Press.

Howe, N., & Strauss, W. (2004). *Millennials rising: The next great generation.* New York: Vintage.

Johnson, A. (2017). *Adulting is Hard: Anxiety and Insecurity in the Millennial Generation's Coming of Age Process.*

Karlsen, R., Steen-Johnsen, K., Wollebæk, D., & Enjolras, B. (2017). *Echo chamber and trench warfare dynamics in online debates. European Journal of Communication, 32(3), 257–273.*

KnowYourMeme. (2019). Avocado Toast. *KnowYourMeme.* Retrieved from https://knowyourmeme.com/memes/avocado-toast.

Koepke, S., & Denissen, J. J. A. (2012). Dynamics of identity development and separation-individuation in parent-child relationships during adolescence and emerging adulthood - A conceptual integration. *Developmental Review, 32*(1), 67-88.

Lapidot-Lefler, N., & Barak, A. (2012). *Effects of anonymity, invisibility, and lack of eye-contact on toxic online disinhibition. Computers in Human Behavior,* 28(2), 434–443.

Lo, S. K. (2008). The nonverbal communication functions of emoticons in computer-mediated communication. *CyberPsychology & Behavior, 11*(5), 595-597.

Lu, M., & Fan, H. (2018). I sang, therefore I am! Uses and gratifications of self-mocking memes and the effects on psychological well-being. *International Journal of Cyber Behavior, Psychology and Learning, 8(2)*, 35-50.

Maiolino, N., & Kuiper, N. (2014). Integrating humor and positive psychology approaches to psychological well-being. *Europe's Journal of Psychology, 10(3)*, 557-570.

Massanari, A. L. (2013). Playful participatory culture: Learning from Reddit. *Selected Papers of Internet Research, 14*.

Moore, M. J., Nakano, T., Enomoto, A., & Suda, T. (2012). *Anonymity and roles associated with aggressive posts in an online forum. Computers in Human Behavior, 28(3), 861–867.*

Morrison, C. & Gore, H. (2010). The relationship between excessive internet use and depression: A questionnaire-based study of 1,319 young people and adults. *Psychopathology, 43,* 121-126.

Nae, N. (2017). The more they change, they more they stay the same: Japanese Millennials and their attitudes toward work and family. *Euromentor Journal Studies about Education, 8(7)*, 53-70.

Palley, W. (2012). *Gen Z: Digital in their DNA*. New York, NY: Thompson.

Pendry, L. F., & Salvatore, J. (2015). Individual and social benefits of online discussion forums. *Computers in Human Behavior, 50*, 211–220.

Pinkett, J. (2018). Trend Alert: Sang Culture. *Voxburner*. Retrieved from https://www.voxburner.com/blog-source/2018/05/29/sang-culture.

Sabella, R. A., Patchin, J. W., & Hinduja, S. (2013). Cyberbullying myths and realities. *Computers in Human behavior, 29(6)*, 2703-2711.

Schenk, A. M., & Fremouw, W. J. (2012). Prevalence, psychological impact, and coping of cyberbully victims among college students. *Journal of school violence, 11(1)*, 21-37.

Schmalz, D. L., Colistra, C. M., & Evans, K. E. (2015). Social media sites as a means of coping with a threatened social identity. *Leisure Sciences, 37(1)*, 20-38.

Shifman, L. (2011). An anatomy of a Youtube meme. *New Media & Society, 14(2)*, 187-203.

Shifman, L. (2014). *Memes in Digital Culture*. Cambridge, MA: The MIT Press.

Smith, P. K. (2019). Research on Cyberbullying: Strengths and Limitations. In *Narratives in Research and Interventions on Cyberbullying among Young People* (pp. 9-27). Springer, Cham.

Szablewicz, M. (2014). The "losers" of China's Internet: Memes as "structures of feeling" for disillusioned young netizens. *China Information, 28(2)*, 259-275.

Tanis, M. (2008). *Health-Related On-Line Forums: What's the Big Attraction?* Journal of Health Communication, 13(7), 698–714.

Taylor, P., & Keeter, S. (Eds.). (2010). *Millennials: A portrait of generation next*. Washington, DC: Pew Research Center.

Törőcsik, M., Szűcs, K., & Kehl, D. (2014). How Generations Think: Research on Generation Z. *Acta universitatis Sapientiae, communicatio, 1*(1), 23-45.

Townsend, L., Gearing, R. E., & Polyanskaya, O. (2012). Influence of health beliefs and stigma on choosing internet support groups over formal mental health services. *Psychiatric Services, 63*(4):370-6.

Trachtman, Paul. (2006). A Brief History of Dada. *Smithsonian Magazine*. Retrieved from https://www.smithsonianmag.com/arts-culture/dada-115169154/.

Wang, W., Xie, X., Wang, X., Lei, L., Hu, Q., & Jiang, S. (2019). Cyberbullying and depression among chinese college students: A moderated mediation model of social anxiety and neuroticism. *Journal of Affective Disorders, 256*, 54-61.

In: Digital Technology   ISBN: 978-1-53616-438-1
Editor: Michelle F. Wright   © 2019 Nova Science Publishers, Inc.

Chapter 7

NEGATIVE ISSUES RELATED TO SMARTPHONE AND SOCIAL MEDIA USE AND ABUSE

William Stanley Pendergrass[*], *DSc*
American Public University System, Charles Town, WV, US

ABSTRACT

The smartphone has become a valuable tool for modern society. Smartphones combine what used to be separate devices into one: telephone, computer, camera, recorder, etc. Since its introduction in 2007, in the form of the iPhone, it is viewed by most as the must-have device in our lives. While it does make modern communication easier, it does not come without negative effects. More and more people are beginning to recognize that there are some serious social issues which come with prolonged smartphone use and abuse. Some users find that they cannot put the device away and leave it alone. The use of many apps such as Facebook and Instagram bring some individuals to have emotional distress feelings as they compare their lives to those of their friends. It facilitates cyberbullying, cyber shaming, and phone snubbing or phubbing. This

---

[*] Corresponding Author's E-mail: William.pendergrass@mycampus.apus.edu.

chapter will focus on some of these negative issues and what might be done to address them in our daily lives.

INTRODUCTION

Over ten years ago, the smartphone was first introduced by Apple in the form of the iPhone. Apple co-founder, Steve Jobs introduced it as "a wide-screen iPod with touch controls, a phone and an internet communicator" (Merchant, 2017, p. 162). Downloadable smartphone applications or apps did not exist. The only ones available were the ones the iPhone was installed with. The Apple App Store itself did not even exist. It would come a year later, begrudgingly over Steve Jobs objections. The smartphone was a novelty, hardly anyone owned one. Think about that world and now, think about how far we've journeyed from that world today.

Fast forward to today and consider the range of smartphones and apps available now. We are nowhere remotely near the initial concept of the iPhone. Today, nearly every person owns a smartphone and nearly everyone is interconnected with the world at large. People today can download any app, send pictures and friend requests to Facebook, read Tweets from the hundreds if not thousands of those they are following on Twitter, check email, surf the Internet, and so on and so on and so on. The world of the smartphone touches all parts of the globe, seemingly connecting everyone, yet, instead of expanding our universe and giving everyone more time to focus on personal teaks and goals, it seems to have contracted existence to a world behind a screen, only.

People have become so enamored with their digital universes that they frequently ignore the real universe around them (Chotpitayasunondh & Douglas, 2016). Social interchanges over ten years ago were much more personal. People talked, they went out to meet friends, they shopped in malls, and were aware of their surroundings. Yet today, it seems like the personal interaction has become subservient to the digital interaction. Why are people so interactive with their smartphones and not with the person sitting across the table from them? What is the psychological draw and why is it there? What are the harms associated with smartphone and app use? This chapter addresses these questions.

RESEARCH METHODOLOGY

This research effort is a continuation of a research project focusing on Internet trends and culture. Over a period of nine years, information on various aspects of the Internet and interactions with it were collected and categorized. The large amount of secondary data and numerous data thread correlations to be collected proved to be its own unique problem. Therefore, a case study methodology was selected as the method for data analysis. Yin (2009) proposed that "case studies are the preferred method [of analysis] when (a) "how" or "why" questions are being posed, (b) the investigator has little control over events, and (c) the focus is on a contemporary phenomenon within a real-life context" (Yin, 2009, p. 2).

Yin defined three principles of data collection: 1) use multiple, different sources of evidence, 2) create a database of collected material, and 3) maintain a chain of evidence (Yin, 2009, pp. 114 - 124). Multiple sources of evidence were collected in the form of news articles, Twitter posts, Facebook posts, research documents, books, and other types of secondary data. An expansive database of material, including timelines of events and sources, served as the chain of support. This data was then separated into categories or bins. In his book, *Case Study Research: Design and Methods*, Yin (2009) discusses a 1929 study which benefited from using descriptive bins to sort through a huge amount of collected data. In their landmark book, *Middletown: A Study in Modern American Culture*, Lynd and Lynd (1929) defined a number of descriptive bins so that a huge amount of seemingly unrelated data taken from numerous sources in a small Midwestern city could be anonymized to create an idea of an "average" American city. Much in the same way, a timeline of events related to Internet searches was created to show trends of relation to Internet use and issues which relate to that use, specifically those which were related to smartphone and smartphone app use and abuse and their effects on users.

THE SMARTPHONE

"The smartphone first arrived [in 2007] in the form of the iPhone" (Morris, 2017, p. 1). "Sometime around 2011 or 2012, it suddenly became very easy to predict what people would be doing in public places: Most would be looking down at their phones" (Twenge, 2017a, p. 1). The period of time is specific because that was when the number of people who owned a smartphone reached 50% of the population. (Twenge, 2017b, p. 1)

> When Apple's smartphone went on sale on June 29, 2007, the world was dominated by flip phones and Blackberrys with tiny keyboards. People carried iPods for music, Palm Pilots for calendars, and compact cameras for photography. Putting all those things into a rectangle that fit in your pocked seemed crazy. Doing it without a keyboard was even crazier. (Kelly & Regan, 2017, p. 1)

As the amount of smartphones grew and the prices, sometimes linked to communication pay plans, became more affordable for more and more, the smartphone eventually surpassed all other versions of electronic communication. It became ubiquitous in modern life, so much so that it is considered odd now to not have and use a smartphone, i.e., using a flip-phone or Blackberry. The smartphone has changed the way we interact with each other as well as communicate.

> This is the new normal: Instead of calling someone, you text them. Instead of getting together for dinner with friends to tell them about your recent vacation, you post the pictures to Facebook. It's convenient, but it cuts out some of the face-to-face interactions that, as social animals, we crave. (Twenge, 2017a, p. 1)

NEGATIVE ISSUES

Addiction

People check their smartphones about 150 times a day on average (Stern, 2013). A person's smartphone is a hard thing to put down, stay down, and stay away. There is always something to check, a Social Media friend request to agree to, a Tweet that needs to be delivered to your followers, and a Snapchat Streak to maintain. It is a 24 hour a day, 365 day a year demander of your attention. It would seem to be an easy thing to do, to just set the device down and walk away and stay away, yet for a good many users, that is asking way too much. Why is that? Why do so many people find it so difficult to put their phone away and pay attention to the world around them?

The smartphone is the instrument for many an app and many times it's a Social Media app that is first in line. Social Media employs numerous means to capture your attention and keep it. Much like operating a Slot machine, there is an action (checking your smart phone constantly) and a reward (receiving Facebook "Likes," LinkedIn recommendations, Snapchat Streaks or Instagram hearts for example). That Slot machine is operating to provide the player with an intermittent variable reward. Social Media also tricks your brain into continued and sometimes continuous interaction, losing track of time, reality, and others around you.

"Is it enjoyment or addiction?" (Morgans, 2017, p. 1) "As an experience evolves, it becomes an irresistible weaponized version of the experience it once was. In 2004, Facebook was fun; in 2016, it's addictive" (Alter, 2017, p. 5). A 2013 study found that those "who spent more time on Facebook had higher levels of activity in the nucleus accumbens – the brain's reward center" (Mariani, 2016, p. 88).

Human behavior is driven in part by a succession of reflexive cost-benefit calculations that determine whether an act will be performed once, twice, a hundred times, or not at all. When the benefits overwhelm the costs, it's hard not to perform the act over and over again, particularly when it strikes just the right neurological notes. (Alter, 2017, p. 5)

A video game designer came up with a model which he used to design software which would hook the user into continued interaction. It's called the Hook Model (Eyal, 2014). There are four steps: 1) Trigger, 2) Action, 3) Variable Reward, and 4) Investment. The Trigger is the start of the model, either internal or external. "Habit-forming products start by alerting users with external triggers like an email, a Web site link, or the app icon on a phone" (Eyal, 2014, p. 7). The Action is the behavior done in anticipation of a reward. "Companies leverage two basic pulleys of human behavior to increase the likelihood of an action occurring: the ease of performing and action and the psychological motivation to do it" (Eyal, 2014, p. 8). The Variable Reward creates intrigue. "Introducing variability [to an action] multiplies the effect, creating a focused state, which suppresses the areas of the brain associated with judgement and reason while activating the parts associated with wanting and desire" (Eyal, 2014, pp. 8-9). Finally, "the [I]nvestment implies an action that improves the serviced for the next go-around" (Eyal, 2014, p. 10).

> If you want to maximize addictiveness, all tech designers need to do is link a user's action (like pulling a lever) with a *variable reward*. You pull a lever and immediately receive either an enticing reward (a match, a prize!) or nothing. Addictiveness is maximized when the rate of reward is most variable. [emphasis original] (Harris, 2016, p. 1)

Actions like liking a Facebook page, approving a Friend request, starting a Snapchat Streak, are all examples of investing in a Social Media account.

One study asked frequent smartphone users to put their smartphones face down on a table and walk away from them. The participants noted they grew more and more anxious over time (Chever, Rosen, Carrier, & Chavez, 2014). "With constant connection comes new anxieties of disconnection, a kind of panic" (Turkle, 2011, p. 16). Another explanation for the draw of the smartphone is the Fear Of Missing Out or FOMO. FOMO is "a pervasive apprehension that others might be having rewarding experiences from which one is absent" and "a desire to stay continually connected with what others are doing" (Przybylski, Murayama, DeHaan, & Gladwell, 2013, p. 1841).

However, that continual connection has its price. In a recent study of adolescents, higher use of social media was triggered by different emotions; in boys it was by feelings of anxiety and in girls it was depression (Oberst, Wegmann, Stodt, Brand, & Chamarro, 2016).

> Our neurochemical response to every ping and ring tone seems to be the one elicited by the "seeking" drive, a deep motivation of the human psyche. Connectivity becomes a craving; when we receive a text or an e-mail, our nervous system responds by giving us a shot of dopamine. We are stimulated by connectivity itself. We learn to require it, even as it depletes us. (Turkle, 2011, p. 227)

While the brain derives pleasure from the continual reward of electronic communications, that is not the only draw within these devices. The websites and apps themselves are also setup to create the demand. They are designed to facilitate the almost constant interaction that draws in the complete attention of the user. Why? There's money to be made in what has been coined "the attention economy."

> "The attention economy" is a relatively new term. It describes the supply and demand of a person's attention, which is the commodity traded on the internet. The business model is simple: The more attention a platform can pull, the more effective its advertising space becomes, allowing it to charge advertisers more. (Morgans, 2017, p. 1)

This draw of the user's attention is engineered into the software and into the app. These are deliberate actions which not only demand attention but deliver it as well.

> You know when you open Instagram or Twitter and it takes a few moments to load updates? That's no accident. Again, the expectation is part of what makes intermittent variable rewards so addictive. This is because, without that three-second delay, Instagram wouldn't feel variable. There's no sense of will I win? because you'd know instantly. So the delay isn't the app loading. It's the cogs spinning on the slot machine. (Morgans, 2017, p. 1)

Rewards engineered into the software of apps create a powerful draw on a person's attention, thus increasing the amount of time spent on a device which in turn boosts the value of the app to advertisers and furthers profits to the app makers. People are addicted to their smartphones because the brain tells them what they are doing is important, so important that the rest of the world around them just fades away. They are also addicted to their smartphones because the propensity towards addiction has been hard wired into the device.

Snapchat is one of the most popular websites for young adults, and intentionally so. "If you're fourteen, Snapchat's user interface is intuitive; if you're twenty-two, it's intriguing; if you're over thirty-five, it's impenetrable. This encourages old people to self-deport" (Marantz, A., 2018, p. 1). Snapchat has become so ubiquitous in adolescents' lives that even the minutest disruption in the familiarity of the application could cause meltdowns in users' lives.

So Snapchat's the most popular messaging service for teenagers. And they invented this feature called 'streaks,' which shows the number of days in a row that you've sent a message back and forth with someone. So, now you could say, 'Well, what's the big deal here?' Well, the problem is that kids feel like, 'Well, now I don't want to lose my streak.' But it turns out that kids actually—when they go on vacation—are so stressed about their streak that they actually give their password to, like, five other kids to keep their streaks going on their behalf. And so you could ask when these features are being designed, are they designed to most help people live their life? Or are they being designed because they're best at hooking people into using the product? (Cooper, 2017, p. 1; Michael, 2017, p. 1)

One example reinforcing the importance of Snapchat in teens lives came when the company significantly updated their software for the first time since its introduction in 2011. "The company split the app into two sections, consolidating friend content on the left side, media content on the right, and installing a slew of other design changes" (Lorenz, 2018, p. 1). What resulted was a huge uproar from millions of Snapchat users, the majority being teens and adolescents. Hundreds if not thousands of Snapchat Streaks were lost.

Most Snapchat users had never lived through a major redesign of their most-favored app. Most will not have remembered the 2008 Facebook redesign which angered so many of its users (Beaumont, 2008). This example would be lost on most Snapchat users who consider Facebook an app for old people only and favored Snapchat for its seeming exclusiveness (Sweney, 2018). Snapchat altered their app yet again in April of 2018 which further frustrated users and resulted in a drop in their stock price (La Monica, 2018).

Emotional Distress

Studies have shown that the interconnected world that smartphones have propelled us into, does not make us feel better, it makes us feel worse (Angeluci & Huang, 2015; Primack et al., 2017;). A recent review (Mercado, Holland, Leemis, Stone, & Wang, 2017) of trends from the National Electronic Injury Surveillance System – All Injury Program (NEISS-AIP) - found that while trends for self-harm among boys showed no significant increase from 2001 to 2015, trends for females increased 8.4% yearly from 2009 to 2015. While there may be no direct correlation between self-harming trends in adolescent girls from that time period and smartphone use, it coincides with the rise in smartphone use, from its introduction by Apple in 2007 to its increased use by over half of the American public around 2011-2012 (Pendergrass, 2017). Other studies (Twenge, Joiner, Rogers & Martin, 2018; Mojtabai, Olfson, & Han, 2016) have made similar correlations between smartphone use around 2011-2012 and increased rates of depression and suicide among adolescents.

A study of college students asked them to rate their moods five times each day. It found that the more the students used Facebook, the less happy they reported they were. "However, feeling unhappy didn't lead to more Facebook use, which suggests that Facebook was causing unhappiness, not vice versa" (Twenge, 2017a, p. 1). Another study found that "people who visited social media platforms most frequently, 58 visits per week or more, had more than three times the odds of perceived social isolation than those who visited fewer than nine times per week" (Hobson, 2017, p. 1).

> Psychologically, however, [the generation who grew up in a world where there was always an iPhone, or the iGen] are more vulnerable than Millennials were: Rates of teen depression and suicide have skyrocketed since 2011. It's not an exaggeration to describe iGen as being on the brink of the worst mental-health crisis in decades. Much of this deterioration can be traced to their phones. (Twenge, 2017b, p. 1)

Cyberbullying

Olweus (1994) introduced the definition of bullying currently in use. In order for an act to be considered bullying, the act must be intentional, based on an imbalance of power and repeated (Levy et al., 2012; Olweus, 1994) Intentionality is the opposite of random or accidental actions which could harm someone. An imbalance of power does not only refer to physical strength, it represents the differences between victims and perpetrators in regard to the perpetrators' position, intelligence, or popularity. Finally, repetition means that the harmful intentional actions reoccur over some period of time (Levy et al., 2012).

Cyberbullying is bullying, using the above definition, but it also incorporates "information and communication technologies (ICTs) or other types of Internet technologies" (Levy et al., 2012, p. 5). Many children often are provided smartphones so that their parents can keep in touch with them in case of an emergency or for daily communications. These electronic devices not only have become the electronic means of conversation, depending on the model and the number and type of apps used, they are physical indicators of status and social standing. Services such as texting as well as apps such as Facebook, Twitter, Instagram and Vine allow for the free flow of communication among today's youth. In addition, conversation apps such as ask.fm, Kik, and Voxer allow for users to post anonymously or through a username, often creating a perfect avenue for anonymous cyberbullying (Alvarez, 2013). Therefore, in all cyberbullying experiences, the identity of the bully may or may not be known by the victim. The constant proliferation and evolution of smartphone apps can often leave parents clueless to their children's true online presence.

[C]yberbullying experts said cellphone messaging applications are proliferating so quickly that it is increasingly difficult for parents to keep pace with their children's complex digital lives. "It's a whole new culture, and the thing is that as adults, we don't know anything about it because it's changing every single day," said Denise Marzullo, the chief executive of Mental Health America of Northeast Florida in Jacksonville, who works with the schools there on bullying issues. No sooner has a parent deciphered Facebook or Twitter or Instagram than his or her children have migrated to the latest frontier. "It's all of these small ones where all this is happening," Ms. Marzullo said. (Alvarez, 2013, p. 1)

Cyberbullying can occur through electronically-mediated communication at school; however cyberbullying behaviors commonly occur outside of school as well (Tokunaga, 2010). Cyberbullying is also dependent on the age and social group affected. Behaviors an adult might consider cyberbullying are seen by teenagers only as "Drama" (boyd, 2014). Drama is "social and interpersonal; involves relational conflict; reciprocal; gendered; and, often performed for, in, and magnified by *networked publics*" [emphasis original] (Marwick & boyd, 2011, p. 5).

Adolescents between the ages of 12 to 14 appear to be the most vulnerable to cyberbullying victimization (Tokunga, 2010). This coincides with the ages of those vulnerable to offline bullying. Cyberbullying is more prevalent in middle school than high school and is most likely to occur when starting middle school or starting at a new school (Espelage & Horne, 2008; Pellegrini, 2002).

Cyberbullying increases the risk of suicide in victims. A recent Dutch meta-analysis of 34 studies of 284,375 people focused on the effects of bullying and suicidal thoughts along with an analysis of 9 studies of 70,102 people that focused on the relationship between bullying victims and suicide attempts aged between 9 and 21 years of age, the researchers found that those who are bullied were more than twice as likely to have suicidal thoughts as those who had not been bullied. Additionally, bullying victims were two and a half times more likely to attempt to commit suicide. (Sonaware, 2014).

Cybershaming

The concept of trolling includes a wide range of intentional activities. "Trolling is a spectrum of behaviors. Some trolling is incredibly aggressive and meets the legal threshold for harassment. Other forms of trolling, i.e., Rickrolling [a bait and switch technique which substitutes a disguised hyperlink to a video of the 1987 Rick Astley song "Never Gonna Give You Up"] are comparatively innocuous. Some trolling is persistent, continuing for weeks or even months, and some is ephemeral, occurring once and then never again" (Phillips, 2015, p. 23).

Cybershaming is a form of trolling that incorporates the episodic use of cyberbullying to draw out and identify an individual in order to highlight the incorrect behavior or attitude from that of the audience (Licht, 2016). "An audience is a prerequisite for shame, even if that audience is imagined," and shame "aims to hold individuals to the group standard" (Jacquet, 2015, p. 9). "Shaming… is a form of punishment, and like all punishment, it is used to enforce norms" (Jacquet, 2015, p. 13).

> Shame is not only a feeling. It's also a tool – a delicate and sometimes dangerous one – that we can put to use to help solve serious problems. Shaming is a nonviolent form of resistance that anyone can use, and unlike guilt, it can be used to influence the way groups behave – shame can scale. But shaming requires the attention of the audience, and attention is a zero-sum game. (Jacquet, 2015, p. 26)

Cybershaming is shaming via electronic means, just as cyberbullying is bullying via electronic means (Levy et al., 2012). Cybershaming is meant to enforce the social norms of the community, be they delineated or perceived.

"[It] can slither through the grate of bad behavior because of its intention to get vengeance or to punish. It is common to think that a perpetrator deserves to be shamed and humiliated" (Warner, 2013, p. 1). Cybershaming collectively draws the attention of the audience to a perceived outlier position, action, or intention.

Phubbing

A recent study examined the impact of smartphones on our relationships. It found that people, whose partners were more frequently distracted by their phones, were less satisfied with their relationships, and thus were more likely to feel depressed about it (Roberts & David, 2016). The word phubbing, a portmanteau of two words: Phone and snubbing, was created in 2013 to help sell printed Dictionaries in Australia (Brockington, 2013; Roberts, 2016; Roberts & David, 2016). While the word most likely did not help Australian Dictionary sales, the term actually took hold and flourished, more than likely because of the growing ubiquity of smartphone use and abuse, and the phenomenon that people immediately recognized around them.

Eventually, the term expanded to include other aspects of the snubbing. "In January [2014], the Journal Computers in Human Behavior published an article on 'partner phubbing,' or 'p-phubbing' for short. And in May [2014], Oxford Dictionaries announced that an entry for phubbing would be included in their latest online update" (Zimmer, 2016, p. 1). P-phubbing merely indicates a close relationship between the Phubber and the phubbee. "Partner phubbing...can be best understood as the extent to which an individual uses or is distracted by his or her cell phone while in the company of his or her relationship partner" (Roberts, 2016, p. 63).

The abuse of smart phones has placed people at the risk of impaired social interactions. When it comes to smartphones, tablets and other mobile delights, many of the adults have the unfortunate tendency to behave like children: prodding and poling their shiny toys to the exclusion of anyone and anything else. People would rather communicate via text instead of talking face-to-face. (Ugar & Koc, 2015, p. 1023)

A recent study found that Internet addiction was positively related to phubbing activity. (Karadag et al., 20151). "It is therefore reasonable to suggest that problematic Internet use would be associated with problematic smartphone use, which in turn may predict phubbing behavior" (Chotpitayasunondh & Douglas, 2016, p. 10). The Displacement Hypothesis has also been used to explain another reason for the draw of the smartphone's universe (Valkenburg & Peter, 2007). "The 'Displacement Hypothesis' suggests that time spent on smartphones displaces (or reduces) more meaningful interactions with your lover, weakening the relationship" (Roberts, 2016b, p. 1). Negative consequences of heavy use of Social Networking Sites include a decrease in real-life social participations and academic achievement as well as relationship problems (Kuss & Griffiths, 2011).

Phubbing and p-phubbing are seemingly unnoticed by the person with the smartphone in their hand, totally oblivious to the world around them, intent on accessing every app, every text, every Facebook post, and Instagram communication. While for the other person, without a smartphone, without the electronic distraction just inches away from their face, the snub is real and the emotions it continually brings are hurtful (Chotpitayasunondh & Douglas, 2016). Feeling rejected and ignored in favor of a bit of electronic Tweet or text creates and maintains real negativity and pain (Oberst, Wegmann, Stodt, Brand & Chamarro, 2016). It would be seemingly easy to acknowledge and reverse. However, it may not be that easy to just put the smartphone down and leave it down. There are forces both internal and external which make it harder and harder to "just stop." Both inside the mind and manufactured into the devices are powerful draws to the smartphone users' attentions.

CONCLUSION

Social media applications, used on smartphones, and connect users with worldwide instantaneous communication opportunities. Designers, developers, advertisers, marketers, etc. of smartphones and apps often intentionally design programs for continuous appeal, anticipation, response, and thrill. Many times, these very factors can be associated with adverse effects, including relationship issues, addiction, and emotional distress. Awareness of a users' own response to application designers' intended responses can help to minimize the adverse effects of social media use. While the apps, alone do not cause all adverse effects, they can exacerbate adverse responses and results in some groups, most notably the youngest and most vulnerable among us.

Are smartphones and the apps which they load a problem for the entire public? Of course not. But for some who find their smartphone more and more of an issue in their lives, the interaction between the user and the smartphone can crowd out interactions with fellow human beings. Just as in any situation where a certain activity can cause unwanted or unforeseen consequences, smartphone use and abuse should be addressed with more extreme cases seeking further help. Smartphones are not going away, nor should they. But with responsible use, they can remain the useful tools of an interconnected society.

REFERENCES

Alter, A. (2017). *Irresistible: The Rise of Addictive Technology and the Business of Keeping Us Hooked*. New York: Penguin Press.

Alvarez, L. (2013, September 13). Girl's suicide points to rise in apps used by cyberbullies. *The New York Times*. Retrieved from http://www. nytimes. com/ 2013/ 09/ 14/ us/ suicide- of- girl- after- bullying- raises-worries-onweb-sites.html?_r=1&.

Angeluci, A. & Huang, G. (2015). Rethinking media displacement: the tensions between mobile media and face-to-face interaction. *Porto Alegre*, 22(4), 173-190.

Beaumont, C. (2008, September 12). Facebook faces backlash over design changes. *The Telegraph*. Retrieved from http:// www.telegraph.co.uk/ technology/ 3358414/ Facebook- faces- backlash- over- design-changes.html.

Boyd, D. (2014). *It's Complicated: The Social Lives of Networked Teens.* New Haven, CT: Yale University Press.

Brockington, T. (2013, October 9). How McCann invented the word 'Phubbing' for Macquarie Dictionary 'A Word is Born' campaign. *Campaign Brief.* Retrieved from http://www.campaignbrief.com/ 2013/10/mccann-australia-documents-how.html.

Cheever, N., Rosen, L., Carrier, L. & Chavez, A. (2014, August). Out of sight is not out of mind: The impact of restricting wireless mobile device use on anxiety levels among low, moderate and high users. *Computers in Human Behavior, 37,* 290-297.

Chotpitayasunondh, V. & Douglas, K. (2016, May 13). How "phubbing" becomes the norm: The antecedents and consequences of snubbing via smartphone. *Computers in Human Behavior, 63,* 9-18.

Cooper, A. (2017, April 9). What is "brain hacking"? Tech insiders on why you should care. *CBS News.* Retrieved from https:// www.cbsnews.com/ news/brain-hacking-tech-insiders-60-minutes/.

Espelage, D. & Horne, A. (2008). School violence and bullying prevention: from research based explanations to empirically based solutions. In Brown, S. & Lent, R. (Eds.) *Handbook of Counseling Psychology, 4th Edition.* Hoboken, NJ: John Wiley and Sons.

Eyal, N. (2014). *Hooked: How to Build Habit-Forming Products.* New York: Penguin.

Harris, T. (2016, May 18). How technology is hijacking your mind – from a magician and Google design ethicist. *Medium.* Retrieved from https://medium.com/thrive-global/how-technology-hijacks-peoples-minds-from-a-magician-and-google-s-design-ethicist-56d62ef5edf3.

Hobson, K. (2017, March 6). Feeling lonely? Too much time on social media may be why. *NPR*. Retrieved from http://www.npr.org/ sections/health-shots/ 2017/ 03/ 06/ 518362255/ feeling-lonely-too-much-time-on-social-media-may-be-why.

Jacquet, J. (2015). *Is Shame Necessary?* New York, NY: Pantheon Books.

Karadag, E., Tosuntas, S., Erzen, E., Duru, P., Bostan, N., Sahin, B. Culha, I. & Babadag, B. (2015, May 27). Determinants of phubbing, which is the sum of many virtual addictions: a structural equation model. *Journal of Behavioral Addictions.*, *4*(2), 60-74.

Kelly, H. & Regan, J. (2017, June 27). Inside Apple: how the iPhone almost never happened. *CNN*. Retrieved from http://money.cnn.com/ 2017/06/27/technology/gadgets/creation-iphone-history/index.html

Kuss, D. & Griffiths, M. (2011, September). Online social networking and addiction – A review of the psychological literature. *International Journal of Environmental Research and Public Health*, *8*(9), 3528-3552.

La Monica, P. (2018, April 25). Snapchat redesigns its app again. Stock plunges. *CNN*. Retrieved from http://money.cnn.com/2018/04/25/ technology/snapchat-redesign-app-stock/index.html.

Levy, N, Cortesi, S., Gasser, U., Crowley, E., Beaton, M., Casey, J. & Nolan, C. Bullying in a networked era: a literature review. *Kinder & Braver World Project: Research Series*. 2012-17, 1-61. Retrieved from http://ssrn.com/abstract=2146877.

Licht, C. (Producer). (2016, March 26). *CBS this morning: Saturday*. [Television broadcast]. New York, NY: Central Broadcasting Service. Retrieved from http://www.cbsnews.com/videos/the-phenomenon-ofinternet-shaming/.

Lorenz, T. (2018, February 11). Snapchat's new update triggers revolt by millions of teens. *The Daily Beast*. Retrieved from https://www.the dailybeast.com/ snapchats- new- update- triggers- revolt- by- millions-of-teens.

Lynd, R. & Lynd, H. (1929). *Middletown: A Study in Modern American Culture*. New York: Harcourt Brace & Company.

Marantz, A. (2018, March 19). Reddit and the struggle to detoxify the Internet. *The New Yorker.* Retrieved from https://www.newyorker.com/ magazine/2018/03/19/reddit-and-the-struggle-to-detoxify-the-internet.

Mariani, M. (2016, September/October). The antisocial network. *Psychology Today.*

Marwick, A. & boyd, d. (2011). The drama! Teen conflict, gossip, and bullying in networked publics. *A Decade in Internet Time: Symposium on the Dynamics of the Internet and Society,* September 2011. Retrieved from http://papers.ssrn.com/sol3/ papers.cfm?abstract_id=1926349.

Mercado, M., Holland, K., Leemis, R., Stone, D. & Wang, J. (2017, November 21). Trends in emergency department visits for nonfatal self-inflicted injuries among youth aged 10 to 24 years in the United States, 2001-2015. *Journal of the American Medical Association,* 318(19), 1931-1933.

Merchant, B. (2017). *The One Device: The Secret History of the iPhone.* New York: Little, Brown and Company.

Morgans, J. (2017, May 19). Your addiction to social media is no accident. *Vice.* Retrieved from https://www.vice.com/en_us/article/vv5jkb/the-secret-ways-social-media-is-built-for-addiction.

Morris, B. (2017, January 11). The next big thing in smartphones? The software. *Wall Street Journal.* Retrieved from http://www.wsj.com/ articles/the-next-big-thing-in-smartphones-the-software-1484139602.

Michael, D. (2017). Is the Internet engineered to be addictive? *The Doctor Weighs In.* Located at https://thedoctorweighsin.com/is-the-internet-engineered-to-be-addictive/.

Mojtabai, R., Olfson, M. & Han, B. (2016). National trends in the prevalence and treatment of depression in adolescents and young adults. *Pediatrics, 138*(6).

Oberst, U., Wegmann, E., Stodt, B., Brand, M. & Chamarro. (2016, December 19). Negative consequences from heavy social networking in adolescents: the mediation role of fear of mission out. *Journal of Adolescence, 55,* 51-60.

Olweus, D. (1994). Bullying at school: basic facts and effects of a school-based intervention program. *Journal of Child Psychology and Psychiatry, 35*(7), 1171-1190.

Pellegrini, A. (2002). Bullying and victimization in middle school: a dominance relations perspective. *Educational Psychologist, 37*(3), 151-163.

Pendergrass, W. (2017). Phubbing: communication in the attention economy. *2017 Proceedings of the Conference on Information System Applied Research.* Retrieved from http://proc.conisar.org/2017/pdf/ 4526.pdf.

Phillips, Whitney. (2015). *This Is Why We Can't Have Nice Things: Mapping the Relationship between Online Trolling and Mainstream Culture.* Cambridge, MA: The MIT Press.

Primack, B., Shensa, A., Sidani, J., Whaite, E., Lin, L., Rosen, D., Colditz, J., Radovic, A. & Miller, E. (2017). Social media use and perceived social isolation among young adults in the U.S. *American Journal of Preventive Medicine, 53*(1), 1-8.

Przybylski, A., Murayama, K., DeHaan, C. & Gladwell, V. (2013). Motivational, emotional, and behavioral correlates of fear of missing out. *Computers in Human Behavior, 29*, 1841-1848.

Roberts, J. (2016). *Too Much of a Good Thing: Are You Addicted to Your Smartphone?* Austin: Sentia Publishing.

Roberts, J. (2016b, December 14). Is 'phubbing' ruining your relationship? *CNN.* Retrieved from http://www.cnn.com/2016/12/14/health/ phubbing-phones-relationships/index.html.

Roberts, J. & David, M. (2016, January). My life has become a major distraction from my cell phone: Partner phubbing and relationship satisfaction among romantic partners. *Computers in Human Behavior, 54*, 134-141. Retrieved from http://www.sciencedirect.com/science/ article/pii/S0747563215300704#articles.

Sonawane, V. (2014, March 11). Cyber bullying increases suicidal thoughts and attempts: study. *HNGN.* Retrieved from http://www.hngn.com/ articles/ 26245/ 20140311/ cyber- bullying- increases- suicidal-thoughtsattempts-study.htm.

Stern, J. (2013, May 29). Cellphone users check phones 150x/day and other Internet fun facts. *ABC News*. Retrieved from http://abcnews.go.com/ blogs/ technology/ 2013/ 05/ cellphone- users- check- phones- 150xday-and-other-internet-fun-facts/.

Sweney, M. (2018, February 12). Is Facebook for old people? Over-55s flock in as the young leave. *The Guardian*. Retrieved from https://www. theguardian.com/ technology/ 2018/ feb/ 12/ is- facebook- for- old-people-over-55s-flock-in-as-the-young-leave.

Tokunaga, R. (2010). Following you home from school: a critical review and synthesis of literature on cyberbullying victimization. *Computers in Human Behavior*, *26*(3), 277-287.

Turkle, S. (2011). *Alone Together: Why We Expect More from Technology and Less from Each Other*. New York: Basic Books.

Twenge, J. (2017a, July 1). Steve Jobs, Apple and social anxiety: the iPhone's birthday is nothing to celebrate. *Newsweek*. Retrieved from http:// www.newsweek.com/ steve- jobs- apple- and- social- anxiety-iphones-birthday-nothing-celebrate-630416.

Twenge, J. (2017b, September). Have smartphones destroyed a generation? *The Atlantic*. Retrieved from https://www.theatlantic.com/ magazine/ archive/2017/09/has-the-smartphone-destroyed-a-generation/534198/.

Twenge, J., Joiner, T., Rogers, M. & Martin, G. (2018). Increases in depressive symptoms, suicide-related outcomes, and suicide rates among U.S. adolescents after 2010 and links to increased new media screen time. *Clinical Psychological Science*, *6*(1), 3-17.

Ugar, N. & Koc, T. (2015). Time for digital detox: misuse of mobile technology and phubbing. *Procedia – Social and Behavioral Sciences*, *195*, 1022-1031.

Valkenburg, P. & Peter, J. (2007). Online communication and adolescent well-being: testing the stimulation verses the displacement hypothesis. *Journal of Computer-Mediated Communication.*, *12*, 1169-1182.

Warner, R. (2013, August 17). Are public shaming and cyberbullying the same? *The Huffington Post*. Retrieved from http://www.huffington post.com/russ-warner/are-public-shaming-and-cy_b_3443957.html.

Yin, R. (2009). *Case Study Research: Design and Methods. Fourth Edition.* Thousand Oaks, CA: Sage.

Zimmer, B. (2016, December 22). A new word, 'phubbing,' catches on, thanks to a plot. *Wall Street Journal.* Retrieved from http://www.wsj.com/articles/a-new-word-phubbing-catches-on-thanks-to-a-plot-14824378.

In: Digital Technology
Editor: Michelle F. Wright
ISBN: 978-1-53616-438-1
© 2019 Nova Science Publishers, Inc.

Chapter 8

PROBLEMATIC INTERNET USE

Michelle F. Wright
Penn State University, Pennsylvania, US
Masaryk University, Brno, Czechia

ABSTRACT

The general public and academic researchers have been concerned with problematic internet use (PIU) over the last decades. Various causes and consequences of PIU among adolescents have been discussed in the literature. The purpose of this chapter is to examine the risk factors and consequences associated with PIU. The chapter begins by discussing the benefits and risk of digital technology use, explains behavioral addictions, and describes the classification and measurement of PIU. The prevalence of PIU among adolescents is discussed next, along with the demographic, biological and genetic, behavioral, psychological, and social predictors of PIU. The physical, behavioral, psychological, social, and academic outcomes of PIU are explained next. Recommendations for research and practice conclude the chapter. The research reviewed in this chapter is multi-disciplinary and includes cross-sectional and longitudinal studies.

PROBLEMATIC INTERNET

Digital technologies are enmeshed in adolescents' lives, with many of them utilizing such technologies every day and admitting that they are sometimes constantly connected (Lenhart, 2015). There are many opportunities associated with adolescents' digital technologies use, such as rapid communication at all times of the day, information/knowledge for leisure and school assignments, and entertainment (e.g., YouTube). Adolescents also experience negative online situations due to their use of digital technologies. Some of these negative online situations include accidental exposure to gory and sexually explicit content through videos, images, and text, identity theft, sexual predation, and cyberbullying. Problematic internet use (PIU) is another risk associated with digital technology use among adolescents.

Defined as the desire/compulsion for and use of the internet and/or other digital technologies, PIU is characterized by tolerance and symptoms of withdrawal (Young, 1998). The aim of this chapter is to describe multi-disciplinary literature on PIU among adolescents. The studies reviewed include cross-sectional, longitudinal, qualitative, quantitative, and mixed-methods research designs. There are eight major sections of this chapter, including:

1) Digital Technology Use – provides details about the benefits and risks associated with adolescents' digital technology use,
2) Behavioral Addictions – discusses the current literature on the criteria of behavioral addictions,
3) Problematic Internet Use – explains the definitions, prevalence rates, characteristics, symptoms, and measurement of PIU,
4) Predictors of PIU – describes the predictors of PIU, such as demographic, biological and genetic, behavioral, psychological, and social predictors,
5) Outcomes of PIU – discusses the physical and behavioral, psychological and social, and academic outcomes of PIU,

6) Models of PIU – explains different models which provide explanations as to why adolescents develop PIU,

7) Recommendations for Future Research and Practice – describes recommendations for future research and practice, specifically what schools and parents should do about PIU,

8) Conclusion – provides concluding remarks about the state of the literature on PIU.

Digital Technology Use

Digital technologies have influenced the lives of people of all ages and from all over the world. Such technologies have redefined social relationships, social interactions and communication, leisure time, and work and career. Being able to access the internet using a high-speed internet connection has drastically changed people's lives and has triggered sudden cultural change (Odlyzko, 2003). The diminishing cost of cellular technology and hardware, as well as computer software and hardware, has increased the number of people connected to the internet (Diamandis & Kotler, 2012). High-speed internet access is available almost anywhere, including libraries, primary and secondary schools, and colleges and university. Developed nations, such as the United States, continue to experience high amounts of digital technologies saturation. Approximately 76.2% of the United States population has access to the internet, regardless of gender, making the United States one of the largest online market (The Statistical Portal, 2018). There are still some disparities in online access, with higher socio-economic status having more access. The United States also ranks 4th in the Freedom House Index of 2017, indicating that the population has ample freedom in terms of their access to online content. Roughly 98% of United States adolescents access the internet, suggesting that they spend an incredibly amount of time engaged in online activities. Given such high online saturation among United States adolescents, it is important to examine their online experiences. Their online experiences affect their psychological, behavioral, and academic outcomes. Adolescence also represents a unique developmental context in which autonomy and independence are desired.

Digital technology saturation has permeated many cultures across the world, with people spending a lot of time interacting with such technologies (Newell, Pilotta, & Thomas, 2008). Adolescents have access to various online databases of information for leisure and academic purposes, social and entertainment media, and the capability of interacting and communicating with just about anyone, anywhere, and at any time. There is also an increased desire to implement digital technologies to help students develop 21st century skills (Voogt, Erstad, Dede, & Mishra, 2013). Studies have also found positive correlations between internet use for academic purposes (e.g., research, reading, learning) and academic achievement (Kumar & Manjunath, 2013; Zhu, Chen, Chen, & Chern, 2011).

Regardless of the many benefits associated with adolescents' digital technology use, researchers, educators, parents, and clinicians are concerned with the psychological risks and addictive properties of such technologies (Young, 1998). Research has revealed that excessive internet use is related to depression, anxiety, attention disorders, and obsessive behaviors (Huang, Wang, Qian, Zhong, & Tao, 2007; Kuss, Griffiths, & Binder, 2013; Weinstein & Lejoyeux, 2010). Although prohibiting the use of digital technologies is not feasible, there is a need to investigate the risks and outcomes associated with PIU.

Behavioral Addictions

First described in the 1970s, and gaining attention in the 1980s and 1990s, behavioral addiction is non-chemical and does not involve the consumption of substances (Griffiths, 1996; Marks, 1990). Behavioral addiction gained attention due to increased attention given to addictive behaviors, such as gambling and videogame playing, eating, exercise, and sex. Behavioral addiction has many of the same psychological, social, and cultural characteristics as substance addiction (Griffiths, 1996, 1998). Behavioral and substance addictions are reinforced by use and people acquire tolerance and experience dependency, withdrawal symptoms, and affective mood changes. Furthermore, both types of addiction involve comparable perceptions of what behaviors are deemed meaningful or due to pursuit of similar lifestyles. There are also similar contextual factors among certain groups of users. Culturally, perceptions of behavioral and substance addictions are similar such that excessive use of "something" is not desirable, should be forbidden, and relate to negative long-term consequences.

Debate continues regarding the classification of behavioral addictions and whether such addiction is a "true" form of addiction (Erickson, 2008). Addiction typically involves a clinical diagnosis involving the ingestion of chemicals or substances, such as alcohol or drugs (Griffiths, 1998). The Diagnostic and Statistical Manual or Mental Disorders (DSM-IV) implemented the terminology of "dependence" to replace "addiction" in an effort to limit the conceptualization to the involvement of substances only. Based on the revised clinical perspective of addiction, "internet addiction" might be inappropriate terminology because such an addiction does not involve ingestion of chemicals or substances (Erickson, 2007). Therefore, Young (1996) proposed that "internet addiction" is any online-related, compulsive behavior which interrupts normal living and contributes to stress in individuals' relationships and employment.

When someone has internet addiction, the compulsive behavior dominates their life, leading them to neglect family, friends, work, and hygiene. Some researchers argue that there is a need to relax the strict clinical conceptualization of addiction in order to consider "certain behaviors" as sources of addiction (Griffith, 1996; Holden, 2001). To support the clinical legitimacy of behavior addictions, descriptions of Internet Gaming Disorder and Internet Use Disorder are provided in the appendix of the DSM-V (Griffiths, 1998; Petry & O'Brien, 2013). The inclusion of behavioral addiction in the appendix of the DSM highlights the international recognition of addictions. There is also evidence from the field of neuroscience that justifies the consideration of behavioral addictions. Functional Magnetic Resonance Imaging of gamblers' brains showed similar brain activity and biochemistry as the brains of individuals with substance addiction and dependencies (Holden, 2001; Ko et al., 2009). Such a finding suggests that gambling can be addictive without having to ingest any chemicals and that such behaviors can trigger neural activities/circuitry just like chemicals do. Results from neuroimaging studies suggest similarities in brains of individuals with behavioral and substance addiction, particularly concerning molecular (e.g., decreased dopaminergic activity), neuroadaptive (e.g., structural changes in the brain), and cognitive (e.g., behaviors constricted to similar areas in the brain) correlates (Kuss & Griffiths, 2012). Because of the debate regarding the strict clinical perspective on addiction and the expanded concept of addiction, there have been many different terms for internet addiction, including excessive internet use, maladaptive internet use, and internet over-use (Beard, 2005; Caplan, 2010; Davis, Flett, & Besser, 2002; Whang, Lee, & Chang, 2003). There is no consensus on a specific terminology.

Problematic Internet Use

PIU is the terminology used in this chapter because it is less controversial (Griffiths, 1996; Young, 1998). It is also a broader term encompassing excessive attachment to the internet and to specific uses of the internet, including chatting, gaming, online pornography, shopping, gambling, and social media, which increases psychological and emotional distress and interferes with individuals' daily life (Griffiths, 1996; Young, 1998). Caplan (2010) found that individuals with PIU preferred online social interactions over face-to-face interactions, spent more time online for mood regulation, experienced cognitive preoccupations with using digital technologies, and had an inability to regulate their technology use. Emerging as a new disorder in 1996, PIU is conceptualized as an addiction that does not involve the use of intoxicants (Griffiths, 1996; Young, 1996). The behaviors of PIU might include short-term rewards for users and can result in persistent effects, although users acknowledge and are aware of adverse effects (Grant, Potenza, Weinstein, & Gorelikc, 2010; Griffiths, 1996). Excessive internet and digital technologies use might be a symptom of boredom, desire to reduce feelings of loneliness and sadness, boost morale, increase positive mood, and/or to avoid face-to-face interactions (Kuss et al., 2014). Individuals with PIU display resentment, anger, and rage when confronted with the excessive amount of time they spend online or using digital technologies.

PIU includes five subtypes: (1) cyber sexual addiction (i.e., excessive use of adult websites to view cyber porn and/or engage in cybersex), (2) cyber-relationship addiction (i.e., excessive amount of online relationships and/or obsesses about making online relationships), (3) net compulsions (e.g., online gambling, shopping or day-trading done at an obsessive rate), (4) information overload (i.e., compulsion to surf the internet or search databases), and (5) computer addiction (i.e., playing computer games at obsessive rates; Young, 2004). PIU is a behavioral addiction disorder and it can also be classified as an impulse control disorder. Like impulse control disorder, PIU develops during adolescence or young adulthood, impacts individuals from different cultures and geographical locations, and can persistent across the lifespan (Young & de Abreu, 2012). Research suggests that PIU is associated with functional impairment uniquely and independently from other psychopathological conditions in both cross-sectional and longitudinal research studies (Tokunaga, 2015). Therefore, PIU is conceptualized as a genuine condition and distinctive from the consequences of another underlying and/or psychopathological condition, suggesting the need for diagnostic criteria of PIU.

Prevalence rates of PIU have been examined in the literature. Among adolescents in India, Goel, Subramanyam, and Kamath (2013) found that 74.5% of their sample ($n = 987$) were moderate users, 24.8% were classified as possible addicts, and 0.7% were deemed to be addicted. In another study among 475 Finnish adolescents, 61.5% were classified as mild over-users, 22.9% as moderately addicted, and 1.3% as seriously addicted (Sinkkonen et al., 2014). Differences in these prevalence rates reflect variations in samples, sampling techniques, measurement of PIU, and the country of origin.

Measurement of PIU

There are various proposals for diagnostic criteria and screening tools for PIU, with most focused on PIU in adolescents and young adults (Beard, 2005). Issues with diagnosing PIU include no standard definitions, little clinical evidence supporting diagnostic criteria for PIU, and a lack of clinically validated scales with comparable cut-off points. Such issues make it difficult for researchers and clinicals to estimate the prevalence rates of PIU among adolescents. *Internet Addiction Diagnostic Questionnaire* (IADQ; Young, 1998) was one of the first screening tools developed for diagnosing PIU. This questionnaire includes eight criteria and considers both non-essential use of internet and computers. The screening tool has been validated in multiple samples from different geographical regions. Another tool, the *Internet Addiction Test* (IAT), was developed for use with adolescents and adults, and it is widely used (Young, 1998). The IAT is validated and includes 20-items concerning the frequency of recreational use of the internet during a period of one year, each rated on a 5-point Likert scale. Scores are summed and higher scores indicate greater severity of internet compulsivity and addiction. Complaints associated with PIU include salience, excessive use, neglect of work, anticipation, lack of control, and neglect of relationships, interactions, or social life. Such symptoms correspond to the diagnostic criteria for pathological gambling in the DSM-IV. The adaptation of the IAT includes 12-items, with four categories of PIU severity, such as normal, mild, moderate, and severe (Pawlikowski, Altstotter-Gleich, & Brand, 2013; Widyanto & McMurran, 2004). Other validated PIU scales include *Pathological Internet Use Scale* (Morahan-Martin, & Schumacher, 2000), the *Internet Related Problem Scale* (Armstrong, Phillips, & Saling, 2000), the *Internet Addiction Scale* (Nichols & Nicki, 2004), and the *Internet Over-Use Scale* (Jenaro, Flores, Gomez-Vela, Gonzalez-Gil, & Caballo, 2007). Many screening tools for PIU include symptoms of preoccupation, regulation problems, functional and social impairment, and tolerance or withdrawal, and some include secretive use and the role of internet use in distraction from daily life (Armstrong et al., 2000; Caplan, 2000; Davis et al., 2002; Young, 1998). The screening tools described thus far have been validated exclusively with adolescents and adults and in one culture, except for the IADQ, and do not consider the use of various data collection methods, such as online administration.

Koronczai et al., (2011) described the six basic requirements for assessing PIU, including i) comprehensive by examining all aspects of PIU, ii) concise as possible such that the survey is time-limited, iii) reliable and valid for different methods of data collection (e.g., online, face-to-face), iv) appropriate for different age groups, such as for both adolescents and adults, v) appropriate in different cultural settings, and vi) incorporate cut-off scores. The *Problematic Internet Use Questionnaire* (PIUQ) addresses several of the six criteria described by Koronczai and colleagues (2011). The PIUQ considers obsession (i.e., obsessive thoughts regarding the internet and withdrawal symptoms when not using the internet), neglect (i.e., failing to attend to basic needs and everyday activities), and control disorder (i.e., difficulties with regulating or controlling internet use). The PIUQ has reliable factor structures and is validated with different data collection methods on adults and adolescents (Demetrovics et al., 2008; Koronczai et al., 2011).

Predictors of PIU

Attention has been given to understanding the predictors of PIU. A number of predictors have been identified in the literature. This section is organized according to demographics, biological, behavioral, psychological, and social correlates.

Demographic Predictors

Compulsive use of the internet is typically reported by older, male adolescents and adults than younger, female adolescents and adults (Bakken et al., 2009; Durak & Senol-Durak, 2014). Furthermore, Goel et al. (2013) found that adolescents in their study had highest levels of PIU than adults, with social networking websites as the technology they utilized excessively. Similarly, Kwon (2012) found that adolescents were twice as likely to meet the criteria for PIU when compared to younger children and adolescents between the ages of nine and fifteen.

Biological and Genetic Predictors

Research on the genetic predictors of PIU is still in its infancy. Lee and colleagues (2009) found that adolescents diagnosed with PIU had the genetic polymorphisms of the serotonin transporter gene when compared to healthy control adolescents. PIU was associated with higher frequencies of the long-arm allele. Ultimately, this study concluded that adolescents with PIU had similar genetic and personality traits as depressed adolescents. Brains areas of adults with PIU are activated most in the areas of general reward sensitivity (Dong, Huan, & Du, 2011). Few studies have been conducted on the biological predictors of PIU, with most of these studies linking sleep patterns with PIU. Sleep difficulties (i.e., insomnia, snoring, sleep apnea, nightmares, difficulty staying aware during the daytime) were associated positively with PIU among adolescents (Choi et al., 2009).

Behavioral Predictors

Adolescents with PIU were more likely to have attention deficit/hyperactivity disorder, as well as problematic alcohol use (Ko et al., 2009). Furthermore, adolescents with PIU were more likely to report self-harm tendencies than adolescents without PIU (Bakken et al., 2009; Lam, Peng, Mai, & Jing, 2009; Montag et al., 2010). Research has also focused on the association between PIU and other internet-related behaviors. In one study, Eijnden et al., (2008) examined 663 adolescents (12-15 years old) from the Netherlands to examine the association between the use of digital technologies and PIU. The findings revealed a positive relationship between the use of internet applications in which real-time conversations (e.g., instant messenger, chat rooms) and PIU six months later. Furthermore, German adolescents with high levels of PIU were more likely to use the internet in private and hide their use (Guertler et al., 2014). Other research has revealed positive associations between PIU and spending more time on leisurely internet activities among adolescents (Bakken et al., 2009; Montag et al., 2010).

Psychological Predictors

Findings from various studies suggest that PIU is associated with various psychological predictors. High levels of anxiety and depression, feeling sad, low self-esteem, poor social skills, social phobias, and higher levels of shyness are related to higher levels of PIU among adolescents (Armstrong et al., 2000; Caplan, 2002; Shapira, Goldsmith, Keck, Khosla, & McElroy, 2000). PIU, conceptualized as an impulse control issue, involves the inability to resist the impulse, desire, and temptation to avoid excessively using the internet, even if it causes harm to oneself (Young, 1998). Therefore, self-control could be an important predictor of PIU among adolescents. Low self-control was related positively with PIU and self-control was more strongly associated with PIU than other variables, while higher self-control is negatively related to PIU (Kim, Namkoong, Ku, & Kim, 2008; Li et al., 2013). Resiliency was negatively associated with PIU among adolescents (Li et al., 2013; Nam et al., 2018; Park, Kang, & Kim, 2014). Research has also revealed that hostility and impulsivity were positive predictors of PIU (Bakken et al., 2009; Montag et al., 2010). Lower meaning of life and self-efficacy were also associated with higher levels of PIU.

Social Predictors

Insecure attachment attitudes, parental use of psychological control, strict parental rules, poor quality parent-teen communications about internet use, weakened family unit, and higher levels of parent-adolescent conflict and family conflict were associated positively with PIU among adolescents (Li et al., 2013; Kuss et al., 2014; Park et al., 2014). Research has also focused on the role of parent-children relationship quality and its relationship to PIU. Taiwanese adolescents ($n = 555$) with lower-quality relationships with their parents were more likely to engage in PIU (Liu & Kuo, 2007).

Outcomes of PIU

There are various outcomes associated with PIU. This section includes physical and behavioral, psychological and social, and academic outcomes of PIU.

Physical and Behavioral Outcomes

Few cross-sectional and longitudinal studies have been conducted on the negative physical outcomes associated with PIU. Adolescents with PIU are less likely to exercise when compared to adolescents without PIU (Li et al., 2010). Carpal tunnel syndrome, weight gain or weight loss, headaches, neckaches, back problems, and dry and red eyes are associated positively with PIU. Adolescents with PIU have unhealthy patterns in their daily routines, including bedtimes and diet (Lam et al., 2009; Li et al., 2010). Research has also indicated that PIU is related to poor sleep quality, as well as insomnia, snoring, sleep apnea, teeth grinding, and nightmares (Choi et al., 2009). In longitudinal studies on the physical outcomes of PIU, PIU was positive associated with sleep disturbances (i.e., insomnia, fragmented sleep, premature awakening) one year later (Thomee, Eklof, Gustafsson, Nilsson, & Hagberg, 2007; Thomee, Harenstam, & Hagberg, 2011). Furthermore, PIU was related positively to lifetime smoking, lifetime marijuana use, aggression, getting into serious fights, and carrying a weapon among adolescents (Liu, Desai, Krishnan-Sarin, Cavallo, & Potenza, 2011).

Psychological and Social Outcomes

PIU is associated with poor self-esteem and psychological well-being, problems in family relationships, and low quality family and social relationships (Kuss et al., 2013). Other research has revealed that PIU is associated with higher levels of depression and anxiety among Indian adolescents (Goel et al., 2013). Furthermore, greater pathological issues and loneliness were related to high levels of PIU for Chinese adolescents. PIU increased Finnish adolescents' reliance on online life and reduced their self-esteem and desire to pursue real-life social relationships (Sinkkonen et al., 2014). In addition, Mexican adolescents with higher rates of PIU reported that they had difficulties regulating their mood and issues with self-regulation of online activities, as well as problems managing their daily lives (Gamez-Guadiz, Villa-George, & Calvete, 2012). Peer victimization is also related to higher levels of PIU among adolescents (Kuss et al., 2013; Lin et al., 2015).

Harsh parenting style was indirectly related to PIU among adolescents through their emotional dysregulation (Wang & Qi, 2017). Forgiveness also moderated these indirect relationships, with lower levels of forgiveness having the strongest influence. Effortful control buffered against the risk of maladaptive cognitions for PIU (Li et al., 2010). Furthermore, self-esteem was a mediator and self-control was a moderator in the association between adolescents' social relationships and PIU (Park et al., 2014).

Many of the studies reviewed in this subsection are cross-sectional. Much of the longitudinal studies reveal similar patterns as those found in cross-sectional studies. PIU and depression and anxiety are positively associated in longitudinal studies using adolescent samples (Dong, Lu, Zhou, & Zhao, 2011; Gentile et al., 2011; Lam et al., 2009). PIU was also linked to hostility one year later, after controlling for previous levels of hostility (Dong et al., 2011).

Academic Outcomes

PIU is linked positively to academic performance problems among adolescents (Stieger & Burger, 2010). Adolescents with PIU are more likely to neglect their schoolwork than adolescents without PIU (Sinkkonen et al., 2014). Furthermore, adolescents with PIU have greater absenteeism in school and declines in official and self-reported grades. Furthermore, Vila et al. (2018) found that adolescents with PIU had lower test scores and failed more classes than adolescents without PIU. Li et al. (2015) examined deviant peer affiliation, school connectedness, self-control, and PIU. They found that deviant peer affiliation partially mediated the association between school connectedness and PIU, and that this relationship was stronger for adolescents with lower self-control.

Models of Problematic Internet Use

This section describes different models used to explain the development of PIU among adolescents.

Impulse Control Disorder Model

Young (1996) developed the impulse control model to explain how individuals with PIU have similar symptoms as those individuals who suffered from pathological gaming and the dependency on alcohol and drugs. Considering PIU as an impulse control problem suggests that PIU involve pathological problematic internet use. Shapira et al. (2000) explained that PIU is uncontrollable, markedly distressing, time-consuming, and results in social, occupational, or financial difficulties, and is not the result of hypomania or manic symptoms. Applying DSM-IV criteria, Shapira et al. classified 17 of the 20 adults included in their study as having Impulse Control Disorder Not Otherwise Specified, with the other three meeting the criteria for Obsessive Compulsive Disorder. Based on these findings, PIU is characterized by unspecified impulse control disorder than obsessive compulsive disorder. Treuer and colleagues (2001) conducted a similar study as Shapira et al. (2000). In their study, Treuer et al. (2001) considered an individual as having PIU if the individual had the urge to be online even when the internet was unavailable, had thoughts that a world without the internet was dull and empty, had daytime fantasies about internet use, were nervous when the internet connection was slow, depression and guilt occurred after using the internet for prolong periods, and were aggressive when internet use was interrupted. Given these criteria, Treuer et al. argued that PIU should be considered a new subtype of impulse control disorder. PIU as a type of impulse control disorder indicates that individuals take risky actions because they seek risky reward and do not foresee risks (Shapira, 2003).

Cognitive-Behavioral Model

According to the Cognitive-Behavioral Model, PIU occurs from problematic cognitions as well as behaviors that intensify or maintain maladaptive responses (Davis, 2001). Davis applied the cognitive-behavioral model by categorizing individuals with PIU into two groups. The first group are specified problematic internet users, who use the internet for specific services or content. The second group is called the generalized problematic internet users, who are attracted to the internet itself. The generalized problematic internet users are most vulnerable to internet-related issues, like PIU, as they are unable to stop using the internet regardless of the services or content available. These users are also likely to engage in behaviors that occur online only. On the other hand, specified problematic internet users can stop using the internet because they are able to find alternative sources of content. Davis distinguished between these two groups because specific pathological internet use involves individuals engaging in activities that are commonly conducted offline as well as online, suggesting that they are "addicted on the internet" versus "addicted to the internet" (Davis, 2001).

Davis (2001) argued that psychopathology is present or has previously occurred for symptoms of PIU to occur. The psychopathology is not an underlying symptom of PIU, but it is important for understanding how PIU develops. Therefore, Davis suggests that the symptoms associated with PIU should be considered separately from the psychopathology experienced. Furthermore, the internet does not mitigate or reduce the symptoms underlying psychopathology, but instead is a contributory factor to triggering PIU. Reinforcement from stimuli (e.g., tactile sensation from typing on a keyboard) also has a role in the development of PIU, contributing to the maintenance of the associated symptoms. Another feature of PIU is rumination, and this can involve constantly trying to determine why overusing the internet, and reading about and researching PIU, as well as talking to friends about one's overuse of the internet. Another aspect of rumination is recalling reinforcing memories regarding the internet, which can further the cycle of PIU.

Expanding on Davis's research, Caplan (2002, 2010) integrated research on face-to-face interpersonal communication with interpersonal communication through digital technologies. Caplan (2002) also integrated his own research on online social interactions and the socio-cognitive model of unregulated internet use to develop the revised Cognitive-Behavioral Model of PIU. This model includes four core components, such as preference for online social interactions, mood regulation, deficient self-regulations, and negative outcomes (Caplan, 2010). Preference for online social interactions involves the individual believing that they are safer, more efficacious, and more confident when engaging in online interpersonal interactions than face-to-face interactions. The preference for online social interactions is an explanatory factor in why some individuals exhibit cognitive and/or behavioral indicators of PIU, such as using the internet for mood regulation and failing to regulate their own use of the internet. Support for this proposal is found in Caplan's (2002) research. He found that adults with higher social anxiety and low social support preferred online interpersonal interactions because the online environment was considered safer and more comfortable than face-to-face interactions. Another component of this model is the motivation to utilize the internet to diminish distressing feelings for mood regulation (Kim et al., 2009; LaRose et al., 2003). Using the internet for mood regulation is associated with failure to monitor internet use, which increases behavioral symptoms and negative outcomes (Caplan, 2010).

Research provides support for the basic tenets of the Cognitive-Behavioral Model. Compulsive use of the internet and preference for online social interactions is linked to higher incidences of PIU (e.g., Caplan, 2010; Fioravanti, Dettore, & Casale, 2012; Kim et al., 2009; van den Eijnden et al., 2008). Mood regulation is also a predictor of negative outcomes associated with PIU (Caplan, 2002; Caplan & High, 2007; Gamez-Guadix et al., 2012).

RECOMMENDATIONS FOR RESEARCH AND PRACTICE

Based on the literature reviewed in this chapter, there are few longitudinal studies on the predictors and outcomes of PIU. Future research should incorporate longitudinal designs to better disentangle the temporal ordering of PIU, its predictors, and outcomes. Children are using digital technologies at younger ages, and the aim of follow-up research should be to incorporate longitudinal designs following children around the time they first use these technologies until they are adolescents or young adults. Such a design will allow for a better understanding of the predictors or risk that might relate to PIU development during adolescence and adulthood. Little attention in the literature has been given in the contextual predictors of PIU. More research should be given to the role of parents/family, peers, and schools in understanding how these contexts might relate to PIU.

Educational curriculum should include modules on digital skills. Such modules should not only focus on negative online interactions, such as cyberbullying, cyberstalking, and cyberhate. These modules should incorporate information about PIU, particularly the symptoms and outcomes of PIU, along with discussing appropriate use of digital technologies. Programs should also teach moderation of digital technologies use, instead of focusing on abstaining from such use. Encouraging moderation of digital technologies use should also take into account homework or other assignments. Excessive amounts of assignments that utilize digital technologies or that require large amounts of time online should be minimized. If not realistic or possible, segments of the assignments should be completed at school in which teachers and school staff can better monitor adolescents' use of digital technologies. When schools are informed about the symptoms associated with PIU, they are better able to identify "red flags" and administer or recommend treatment for any adolescents affected.

Parents should receive training and/or awareness of the symptoms of PIU. Such knowledge has the potential to help parents recognize digital technology overuse and to mitigate the negative impacts of PIU. Understanding PIU can help parents know when to seek treatment for their child. Parents could also plan "no digital technology" days in their households in which parents also disengage from technology. Modeling such behaviors might help adolescents to diminish their use as well.

CONCLUSION

The aim of the chapter was to describe the literature on PIU among adolescents through a discussion of behavioral addiction, and the predictors and outcomes associated with PIU. Recommendations for future research and practice are also described. It is through follow-up research and the application of research to practice that we can learn how to mitigate the negative effects of PIU or reduce the risk of developing this addiction. Gaps in the literature of PIU are clear, and more longitudinal studies are needed to better understand the temporal ordering of predictors and outcomes of PIU. Future research should consider various contextual predictors of PIU, including parents, schools, peers, and communities.

REFERENCES

Armstrong, L., Phillips, J. G., & Saling, L. L. (2000). Potential determinants of heavier internet use. *International Journal of Human-Computer Studies*, 53(4), 537-550.

Bakken, I. J., Wenzel, H. G., Gotestam, K. G., Johansson, A., & Oren, A. (2009). Internet addiction among Norwegian adults: A stratified probability sample study. *Scandinavian Journal of Psychology, 50*(2), 121-127. doi: 10.1111/j.1467-9450.2008.00685.x.

Beard, K. W. (2005). Internet addiction: A review of current assessment techniques and potential assessment questions. *Cyber Psychology & Behavior, 8*, 7-14. doi: 10.1089/cpb.2005.8.7.

Caplan, S. E. (2002). Problematic internet use and psychosocial well-being: Development of theory-based cognitive-behavioral measurement instrument. *Computers in Human Behavior, 18*(5), 553-575. doi: 10.1016/S0747-5632(02)00004-3.

Caplan, S. E. (2010). Internet use: A two-step approach. *Computers in Human Behavior, 26*(5), 1089-1097. doi: 10.1016/j.chb.2010.03.012.

Caplan, S. E., & High, A. C. (2007). Beyond excessive use: The interaction between cognitive and behavioral symptoms of problematic internet use. *Communication Research Reports, 23*, 265-271.

Choi, K., Son, H., Park, M., Han, J., Kim, K., Lee, B., & Gwak, H. (2009). Internet overuse and excessive daytime sleepiness in adolescents. *Psychiatry in Clinical Neuroscience*, 63(4), 455-462. doi: 10.1111/j.1440-1819.2009.01925.x.

Davis, R. A. (2001). A cognitive-behavioral model of pathological internet use. *Computers in Human Behavior, 17*(2), 187-195. Doi: 10.1016/S07 47-5632(00)00041-8.

Davis, R. A., Flett, G. L., & Besser, A. (2002). Validation of a new scale for measuring problematic internet use: Implications for pre-employment screening. *CyberPsychology & Behavior, 5*(4), 331-345.

Demetrovics, Z., Szeredi, B., & Rozsa, S. (2008). The three-factor model of internet addiction: The development of the problematic internet use questionnaire. *Behavioral Research Methods, 40*(2), 563-574.

Demetrovics, Z., Orsolya, K., Koronczai, B., Griffiths, M. D., Nagygyorgy, K., Elekes, Z., … Urban, R. (2016). Psychometric properties of the Problematic Internet Use Questionnaire Short-Form (PIUQ-SF-6) in a nationally representative sample of adolescents. *PLoS One, 11*(8). doi: 10.1371/journal.prone, 0159409.

Diamandis, P. H., & Kotler, S. (2012). *Abundance: The future is better than you think*. New York, NY: Free Press.

Dong, G., Lu, Q., & Zhao, X. (2011). Precursor or sequala: Pathological disorders in people with internet addiction disorder. *PlosONE.* oi: 10.1731/journal.pone.0014703.

Durak, M., & Senol-Durak, E. (2014). Which personality traits are associated with cognitions related to problematic internet use. *Asian Journal of Social Psychology, 17*(3), 206-218. doi: 10.1111/ajsp. 12056.

Erickson, C. K. (2007). *The science of addiction: From neurobiology to treatment*. New York: W. W. Norton & Co.

Fioravanti, G., Dettore, D., & Casale, S. (2012). Adolescent internet addiction: Testing the association between self-esteem, the perception of internet attributes, and preference for online social interactions.

CyberPsychology, Behavior, & Social Networking, 15(6), 318-323. doi: 10.1089/cyber.2011.0358.

Gamez-Guadix, M., Villa-George, F., & Calvete, E. (2012). Measurement and analysis of the cognitive-behavioral model of generalized problematic internet use among Mexican adolescents. *Journal of Adolescence, 35*(6), 1581-1591. doi: 10.1016.j.adolescence. 2012. 06.005.

Goel, D., Subramanyam, A., & Kamath, R. (2013). A study on the prevalence of internet addiction and its association with psychopathology in Indian adolescents. *Indian Journal of Psychiatry, 55*(2), 140-143. doi. 10.4103/0019-5545.111451.

Grant, J. E., Potenza, M. N., Weinstein, A., & Gorelick, D. A. (2010). Introduction to behavioral addictions. *American Journal of Drug & Alcohol Abuse,* 36(5), 233-241. doi: 10.3109/00952990.2010.491884.

Griffiths, M. (1996). Behavioural addiction: An issue for everybody. *Employee Councelling Today,* 8(3), 19-25. doi: 10.1108/ 1366562910116872.

Griffiths, M. (1998). Internet addiction: Does it really exist? In J. Gackenbach (Ed.), *Psychology and the Internet* (pp. 61-73). San Diego: Academic Press.

Guertler, D., Rumpf, H., Bischof, A., Kastirke, N., et al., (2014). Assessment of problematic internet use by the compulsive internet use scale and the internet addiction test: A sample of problematic and pathological gamblers. *European Addiction Research,* 20(2), 75-81. Doi: 10.1159/ 000355076.

Holden, C. (2001). 'Behavioral' addictions: Do they exist? *Science,* 294(5544), 980-982. doi: 10.1126/science.294.5544.980.

Huang, Z., Wang, M., Qian, M., Zhong, J., & Tao, R. (2007). Chinese internet addiction inventory: Developing a measure of problematic internet use for Chinese college students. *CyberPsychology & Behavior, 10*(6), 805-811.

Jenaro, C., Flores, N., Gomez-Vela, M., Gonzalez-Gil, F., & Caballo, C. (2007). Problematic internet and cell-phone use: Psychological behavioral, and health correlates. *Addiction Research & Theory*, 15(3), 309-320. doi: 10.1080/16066350701350247.

Kim, E. J., Namkoong, K., Ku, T., & Kim, S. J. (2008). The relationship between online game addiction and aggression, self-control and narcissistic personality traits. *European Psychiatry, 23*(3), 212-218. doi: 10.1016/j.europsy.2007.10.010.

Kim, J., LaRose, R., & Peng, W. (2009). Loneliness as the cause and the effect of problematic internet use: The relationship between internet use and psychological well-being. *CyberPsychology & Behavior, 12*(4), 451-455. doi: 10.1089/cpb.2008.0327.

Ko, C. H., Liu, G. C., Hsiao, S., Yen, J. Y., Yang, M. J., Lin, W. C., ... Chen, C. S. (2009). Brain activities associated with gaming urge of online gaming addiction. *Journal of Psychiatry Research*, 43(7), 739-747. doi: 10.1016/j.psychires.2008.09.012.

Koronczai, B., Urban, R., Kokonyei, G., Paksi, B., Papp, K., Kun, B., ... Demetrovics, Z. (2011). Confirmation of the three-factor model of problematic internet use on off-line adolescent and adult samples. *CyberPsychology, Behavior, & Social Networking, 14*, 657-664. doi: 10.1089/cyber.2010.0345.

Kumar, B. T. S., & Manjunath, G. (2013). Internet use and its impact on the academic performance of university teachers and researchers: A comparative study. *Higher Education, Skills and Work-Based Learning*, 3(3), 219-238. doi: 10.1108/HESWBL-09-2011-0042.

Kuss, D. J., & Griffiths, M. D. (2012). Online gaming addiction in children and adolescents: A review of empirical research. *Journal of Behavioral Addiction, 1*(1), 3-22. doi: 10.1556/JBA.1.2012.1.1.

Kuss, D. J., Griffiths, M. D., Karila, L., & Billieux, J. (2014). Internet addiction: A systematic review of epidemiological research for the last decade. *Current Pharmaceutical Design, 20*(25), 4026-4052.

Kwon, J. (2012). Toward the prevention of adolescent internet addiction. In K. S. Young & C. N. de Abreu (Eds.), *Internet addiction: A handbook and guide to evaluation and treatment*. Hoboken: John Wiley & Sons.

Lam, L. T., Peng, Z. W., Mai, J. C., & Jing, J. (2009). Factors associated with internet addiction among adolescents. *CyberPsychology & Behavior*, 12(5), 551-555. doi: 10.1089/cpb.2009.0036.

LaRose, R., Lin, C. A., & Eastin, M. S. (2003). Unregulated internet usage: Addiction, habit, or deficit self-regulation. *Journal of Media Psychology, 3*, 225-253. doi: 10.1207/S1532785XMEP0503_01.

Lenhart, A. (2015). *Teens, social media & technology overview 2015.* Retrieved from: http://www.pewinternet.org/2015/04/09/teens-social-media-technology-2015/.

Li, D., Li, X., Wang, Y., Zhao, L., Bao, Z., & Wen, F. (2013). School connectedness and problematic internet use in adolescents: A moderated mediation model of deviant peer affiliation and self-control. *Journal of Abnormal Child Psychology, 41*(8), 1231-1242. doi: 10.1007/s10802-013.9761-9.

Li, D., Zhang, W., Li, X., Zhen, S., & Wang, Y. (2010). Stressful life events and problematic internet use by adolescent females and males: A mediated moderation model. *Computers in Human Behavior, 26*, 1199-1207.

Lim, J., Gwak, A. R., Park, S. M., Kwon, J. et al., (2015). Are adolescents with internet addiction prone to aggressive behavior: The mediating effect of clinical comorbidities on the predictability of aggression in adolescents with internet addiction. *CyberPsychology, Behavior, & Social Networking, 18*(5), 260-267. doi: 10.1089/cyber.2014.0568.

Liu, C. Y., & Kuo, F. Y. (2007). A study of internet addiction through the lens of the interpersonal theory. *CyberPsychology & Behavior, 10*(6), 799-804.

Liu, T. C., Desai, R. A., Krishnan-Sarin, S., Cavallo, D. A., & Potenza, M. N. (2011). Problematic internet use and health in adolescents: Data from a high school survey in Connecticut. *Journal of Clinical Psychiatry*, 72(6), 836-845. doi: 10.4088/JCP.10m06057.

Marks, I. (1990). Behavioural (non-chemical) addictions. *Addiction, 85*(11), 1389-1394. doi: 10.1111/j.1360-0443.1990.tb01618.x.

Montag, C., Jurkiewicz, M., & Reuter, M. (2010). Low self-directedness is a better predictor for problematic internet use than high neuroticism.

Computers in Human Behavior, 26(6), 1531-1535. doi: 10.1016/j.chb. 2010.05.021.

Morahan-Martin, J., & Schumacher, P. (2000). Incidence and correlates of pathological internet use among college students. *Computers in Human Behavior, 16*, 13-29. doi: 10.11016/S0747-5632(99)00049-7.

Nam, C. R., Lee, D. H., Lee, J. Y., Choi, A. R., *et al.,* (2018). The role of resilience in internet addiction among adolescents between sexes: A moderated mediation model. *Journal of Clinical Medicine, 7*(8). doi: 10.3390/jcm7080222.

Newell, J., Pilotta, J. J., & Thomas, J. C. (2008). Mass media displacement and saturation. *The International Journal of Media Management, 10*(4), 131-138. Doi: 10.1080/14241270802426600.

Nichols, L. A., & Nicki, R. (2004). Development of a psychometrically sound internet addiction scale: A preliminary step. *Psychology of Addictive Behaviors, 18*(4), 381-384. Doi: 10.1037/0893-164X.18. 4.381.

Odlyzko, A. (2003). Internet traffic growth: Sources and implications. *Proceedings of SPIE – The International Society for Optical Engineering, 5247,* 1-15. doi: 10.1117/12.512942.

Park, S., Kang, M., & Kim, E. (2014). Social relationship on problematic internet use (PIU) among adolescents in South Korea: A moderated mediation model of self-esteem and self-control. *Computers in Human Behavior, 38,* 349-357. doi: 10.10116/j.chb.2014.06.005.

Pawlikowski, M., Altstoetter-Gleich, C., Brand, M. (2013). Validation and psychometric properties of a short version of Young's Internet Addiction Test. *Computer in Human Behavior, 29*(3), 1212-1223.

Petry, N. M., & O'Brien, C. P. (2013). Internet gaming disorder and the DSM-5. *Addiction, 108*(7), 1186-1187. doi: 10.1111/add.12162.

Shapira, N. A., Lessig, M. C., Goldsmith, T. D., Szabo, S. T., *et al.,* (2003). Problematic internet use: Proposed classification and diagnostic criteria. *Depression & Anxiety, 17*(4), 207-216.

Sinkkonen, H. M., Puhakka, H., & Merilainen, M. (2014). Internet use and addiction among Finnish adolescents (15-19 years). *Journal of Adolescence, 37*(2), 123-131.

Stieger, S., & Burger, C. (2010). Implicit and explicit self-esteem in the context of internet addiction. *CyberPsychology, Behavior, & Social Netowkring*, 13(6), 681-688.

The Statistical Portal. (2018). *Share of adults in the United States who use the internet in 2018, by age group.* Retrieved from: https://www. statista.com/ statistics/ 266587/ percentage- of- internet- users- by- age-groups-in-the-us/.

Thomee, S., Eklor, M. Gustafsson, E., Nilsson, R., & Hagberg, M. (2007). Prevalence of perceived stress, symptoms of depression and sleep disturbances in relation to information and communication technology (ICT) use among young adults – an explorative prospective study. *Computers in Human Behavior, 23*(3), 1300-1321. doi: 10.1016/j. chb.2004.12.007.

Thomee, S., Harenstam, A., & Hagberg, M. (2011). Mobile phone use and stress, sleep disturbances, and symptoms of depression among young adults – a prospective cohort study. *BMC Public Health, 11*(66), 1-11. doi: 10.1186/1471-2458-11-66.

Tokunaga, R. S. (2015). Perspectives on internet addiction, problematic internet use, and deficient self-regulation: Contributions of communication research. *Annals of the International Communication Association, 39*(1), 131-161. doi: 10.1080/23808985.2015.11679174.

Treuer, T., Fabian, Z., & Furedi, J. (2001). Internet addiction associated with features of impulse control disorder: Is it a real psychiatric disorder? *Journal of Affective Disorder, 66*(2-3), 283.

van den Eijnden, R. J., Meerkerk, G. J., Vermulst, A. A., Spijkerman, R., & Engels, R. C. (2008). Online communication, compulsive internet use, and psychosocial well-being among adolescents: A longitudinal study. *Developmental Psychology, 44*(3), 655-665. Doi: 10.1037/0012-1649.44.3.655.

Voogt, J., Erstad, O., Dede, C., Mishra, P. (2013). Challenges to learning and school in the digital networked world of the 21st century. *Journal of Computer Assisted Learning, 29,* 403-411. doi: 10.1111/jcal.12029.

Wang, M., & Qi, W. (2017). Harsh parenting and problematic internet use in Chinese adolescents. *Computers in Human Behavior*, 77, 211-219.

Weinstein, A., & Lejoyeux, M. (2010). Internet addiction or excessive internet use. *American Journal of Drug & Alcohol Abuse, 36*(5), 277-283. doi: 10.3109/00952990.2010.491880.

Whang, L. S., Lee, S., & Chang, G. (2003). Internet over-users' psychological profiles: A behavior sampling analysis on internet addiction. *CyberPsychology & Behavior, 6*(2), 143-150.

Widyanto, L., & McMurra, M. (2004). The psychometric properties of the Internet addiction test. *CyberPsychology & Behavior,* 7, 443-450.

Young, K. S. (1998). Internet addiction: The emergence of a new clinical disorder. *Cyber Psychology & Behavior, 1*(3), 237-244.

Young, K. S. (2004). Internet addiction: A new clinical phenomenon and its consequences. *American Behavioral Scientist, 48*(4), 402-415. doi: 10.1177/000276404270278.

Young, K. S., & de Abreu, C. N. (2012). *Internet addiction: A handbook and guide to evaluation and treatment.* Hoboken: John Wiley & Sons.

Zhu, Y., Chen, L., Chen, H., & Chern, C. (2011). How does internet information seeking help academic performance? – The moderating and mediating roles of academic self-efficacy. *Computers & Education, 57*(4), 2476-2484. doi :10.1016/j.compedu.2011.07.006.

In: Digital Technology
Editor: Michelle F. Wright

Chapter 9

SCREEN USE AND SUICIDE IN US YOUTH: WHAT IS THE EVIDENCE?

*Daniel Romer**
Annenberg Public Policy Center, University of Pennsylvania,
Philadelphia, PA, US

ABSTRACT

Recent increases in suicide in U. S. adolescents have raised concerns about the effects of heavy screen-media use by young people. We review the evidence regarding changes in adolescent health and well-being over the past several decades and evaluate the hypothesis that increasing screen use by adolescents and young adults (ages 15-24) is the source of increases in suicide in the past decade. We compare this screen-dysphoria hypothesis with one that focuses on economic challenges that confront both parents and young people and that have intensified since the 2008 financial crisis.

* Corresponding Author's E-mail: dan.romer@appc.upenn.edu.

TODAY'S ADOLESCENTS ARE RELATIVELY HEALTHY

Despite recent concerns about rising suicide rates in U. S. adolescents and young adults (National Center for Health Statistics, 2018; Orben & Przybylski, 2019a; Twenge, Cooper, Joiner, Duffy, & Binau, 2019; Twenge, Joiner, Rogers, & Martin, 2018), adolescents have experienced steady declines in unhealthy outcomes. As seen in Figures 1 to 3, there has been steady improvement in adolescent pregnancy, drug use, and driver fatalities over the past several decades. In contrast, although suicide rates among both males and females have declined since the 1980's, they have increased again since 2008 (Figure 4). According to the Youth Risk Behavior Survey (YRBS; Centers for Disease Control and Prevention, 2018), the rise in suicide has been paralleled by an increase in reports of suicidal ideation, which are now on the rise after falling throughout the 1990's (Figure 5). Due to an increase in gun violence, there has also been a more recent increase in homicide among young people (Yablon & Ness, 2018). However, homicide differs from suicide in that it tends to be clustered in low-income urban areas, whereas suicide is more common in suburban and rural areas (Branas, Nance, Elliott, Richmond, & Schwab, 2004). In either case, however, it is noteworthy that the rise in suicide and homicide has departed from the more general and favorable decline in other indicators of ill-health among young people.

Twenge and colleagues (2018) have suggested that the increase in suicide and related outcomes in recent years reflects increasing social isolation and other adverse effects of online social networking. They found that depressive symptoms as reported in the Monitoring the Future Study and the YRBS were positively related to screen use, especially social media use. At the same time, engaging in sports and attending religious services were negatively related to those symptoms.

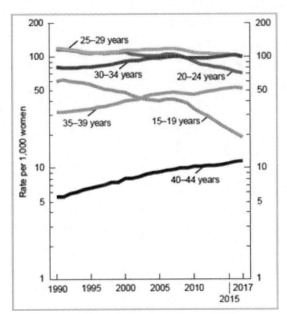

Source: Martin, Hamilton, Osterman, Driscoll, & Drake, 2018.
Note: Rates are plottes on a logarithmic scale.

Figure 1. Decline in birth rates in U. S. for 15-to-24 year olds since 1990.

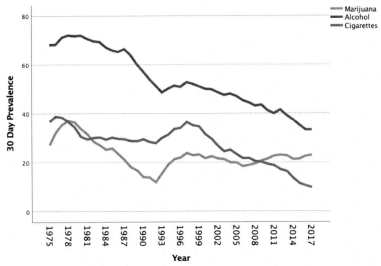

Source: (Johnston et al., 2018).

Figure 2. Declines in use of drugs since 1970's among high school seniors.

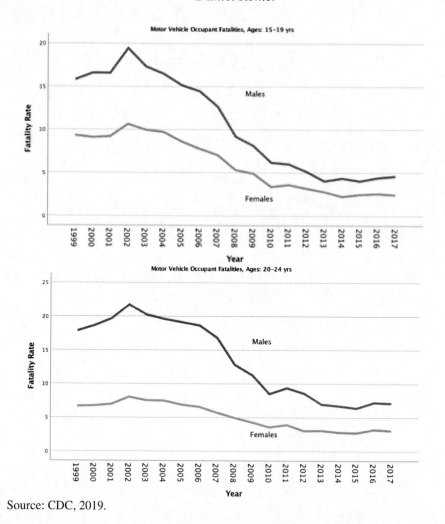

Source: CDC, 2019.

Figure 3. Declines in motor vehicle fatalities since 1999 for 15-19 and 20-24 year olds.

In this chapter, we evaluate this screen-dysphoria hypothesis in contrast to increasing stress placed on youth to succeed academically in combination with recent economic constraints brought on by the financial crisis of 2008. This interpretation is consistent with economic trends during the 1990's when the US economy was doing well. Consumer confidence was high and the economy grew at a strong pace. In keeping with an economic analysis, we see that suicide rates declined dramatically in young people ages 15 to 24 during the 1990's (Centers for Disease Control and Prevention, 2019).

This trend reversed abruptly with the financial crisis of 2008, when the rates went up again (see Figure 4).

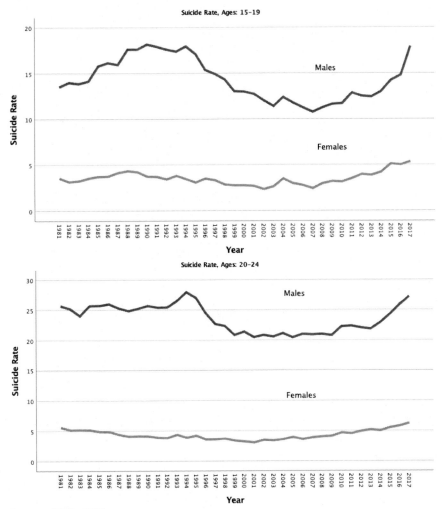

Source: CDC, 2019.

Figure 4. Suicide rates among 15-19 and 20-24 year olds since 1981.

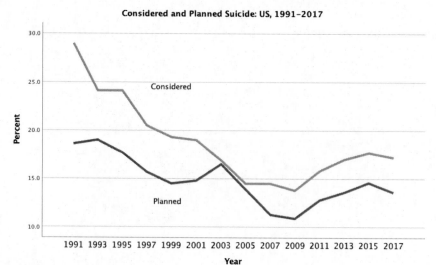

Source: CDC, Youth Risk Behavior Survey, 2018.

Figure 5. Trends in percentage of high school students reporting suicidal ideation since 1991.

SUICIDE AND THE ECONOMY

Evidence regarding economic trends and suicide is strong. A study of 63 countries from 2000 to 2011 found an aggregate relationship between unemployment trends and suicide across age groups (Nordt, Warnke, Selfritz, & Kawohl, 2015). The rise in suicide was pronounced following the 2008 financial crisis. Suicide differs from other types of death during recessions which appear to decline in aggregate with greater unemployment (Ariizumi & Schirle, 2012; Bilal et al., 2017), suggesting that the relationship between unemployment and mortality is complex. Nevertheless, a study in Sweden found that length of unemployment was associated with a rise in suicide at the individual level (Garcy & Vagero, 2012). Suicide rates are also tempered by the policy response to financial hardships, with less of an effect in countries that have stronger economic safety nets for their workers (Stuckler & Basu, 2013).

We examined U. S. suicide trends from 1990 to 2017 in two young age groups (15-19 and 20-24) in relation to various economic indicators, including rates of household poverty and income as well as unemployment. In support of an economic analysis, the trends in suicide were highly related to poverty and income in males, and less so in females (see Figure 6). However, in the last two years of available data (2016-2017), the suicide rates of young people diverged from the economic trend. Although the economy did well in those years, suicide rates increased, bucking the trend seen prior to 2016. As seen in Table 1, the economic trends in income and poverty aligned more closely for both males and females prior to 2016 but less so when including the last two years. Unemployment rates were less strongly related to suicide in these age groups.

SUICIDE AND INTERNET USE

Data on social media use in adults began to be collected starting in 2005 by the Pew Internet and Technology program. According to their surveys, young people ages 18-29 have been the strongest users of social media. Indeed, by 2008, about two-thirds of this age group was already using these media. By 2010, this grew to about 80% and has since plateaued at about 88% (https://www.pewinternet.org/fact-sheet/social-media/). It is likely that adolescents were even more heavily engaged in social media.

Given the powerful relation between suicide rates and household income/poverty rates from 1999 to 2015, the rise in social media use by young people is unlikely to have triggered the rise in suicide that started in 2009 and that has produced the gains that have persisted since that time. Furthermore, the rise in 2016-2017 that diverged from economic trends was no more likely to have coincided with social media use, which did not change dramatically at this time. The economic trends provide a strong alternative explanation for the rise in suicide since 2008, although the most recent rises in 2016-2017 defy easy explanation.

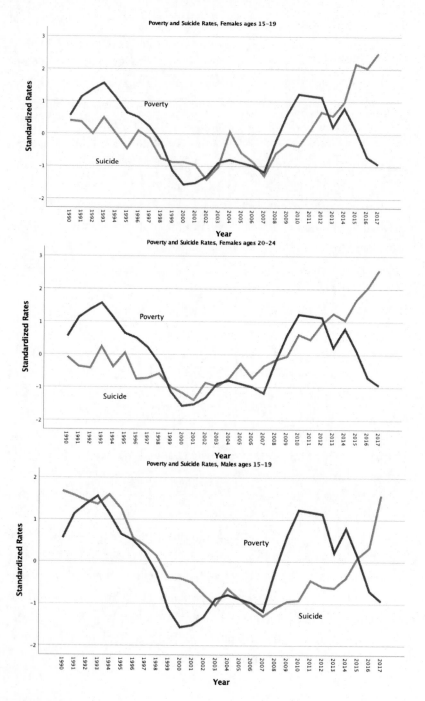

Figure 6. (Continued).

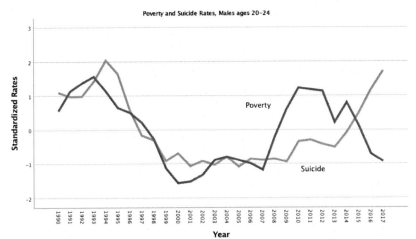

Source: Suicide rates are from CDC, 2019; Poverty rates are from US Census, 2019.

Figure 6. Suicide rates and household poverty rates from 1990 to 2017 for four gender by age groups. Note the divergence in years 2016-2017.

Table 1. Correlations between economic indicators and suicide rates, U. S., 1990-2017

Gender/Age	Correlation from 1990-2017 (n = 28)			Correlation from 1990-2015 (n = 26)		
	Unemployment	Income	Poverty	Unemployment	Income	Poverty
Female						
15-19	.08	-.07	.32	.31	-.47	**.63**
20-24	.22	.04	.28	**.53**	-.34	**.59**
Male						
15-19	-.08	**-.51**	.47	.00	**-.73**	**.58**
20-24	.01	**-.49**	**.53**	.13	**-.79**	**.70**

Note: Bolded entries are $p < .01$. Economic data are from the US Census.

WHAT ACCOUNTS FOR THE DECLINE IN MOST INDICATORS OF ADOLESCENT ILL-HEALTH BUT AN INCREASE IN SUICIDE?

A recent analysis by Doepke and Zilibotti (2019) helps to understand both the favorable and less favorable trends in adolescent health. They examined parenting practices across the world in relation to economic and psychological forces. Building on Baumrind's (1978) model of parenting styles, they defined two dimensions of parenting: intensity and responsiveness. Authoritative and authoritarian parenting are high in intensity but differ in responsiveness, with authoritative parents more responsive to the needs of their children than authoritarian parents. An interesting feature of the model is the distinction between permissiveness and neglect. Permissiveness is responsive but less controlling than authoritative parenting, and neglect is low in both intensity and responsiveness. They find evidence that the US and other countries with high levels of competitiveness for education and job success have a surplus of intensive parenting, and especially authoritative parenting in middle-income households. Countries that have less competition for education and job success (e.g., the Scandinavian countries) tend to have parents with a more permissive style and happier adolescents. Greater concern about obtaining a college degree in the US has been a trend since at least the late 1990's, but it has escalated since the great recession of 2008. It is also related to a country's level of inequality, with high levels exacerbating stress on adolescents. Notably, Twenge et al. (2017) also reported a relationship between depression and economic inequality.

In line with Doepke and Zilibotti, changes in parenting have had large scale effects on children over the past 50 years. First, family sizes have declined since the 60's and 70's. In an analysis done by the Pew Research Center (2015), 40% of women ages 40 to 44 in 1976 had given birth to four or more children; while in 2014, the corresponding percentage was only 14. With fewer children per household, parents have been able to devote more time to each of their children, and this is likely to have reduced many indicators of ill-health in adolescents. An analysis of time spent caring for children indicates that rates of this behavior increased dramatically starting in the early 1990's (see Figure 7; Ramey & Ramey, 2010). This pattern was evident even for non-college educated parents, but it was stronger for those who had a college degree.

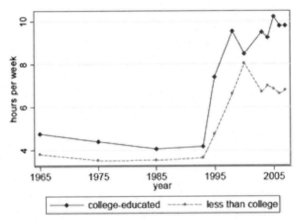

Source: Ramey & Ramey, 2010.

Figure 7. Time devoted to childcare since 1965 for mothers and fathers by college education.

But not all of the increased attention from parents may have been healthy. In particular, the increasing need for academic success, which also increased in the 1990's, may have had adverse effects on adolescents. More intensive parenting may have put additional stress on children to succeed academically, which could have led to increases in risk for suicide (see also, Mueller & Abrutyn, 2016).

In a recent study of young people ages 18-29, we found that students in this age group were particularly at risk for suicide compared to non-students (Arendt, Scherr, Pasek, Jamieson, & Romer, 2019). This is consistent with the hypothesis that economic pressures to obtain post-secondary education have placed increased stress on young people, especially those striving for such degrees.

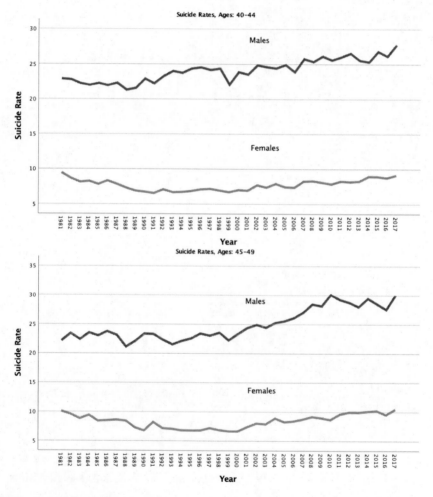

Figure 8. (Continued).

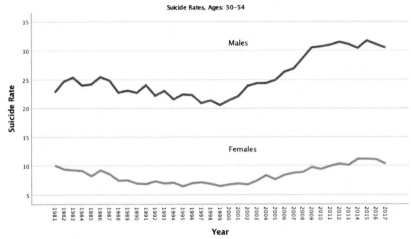

Source: CDC, 2019.

Figure 8. Trends in suicide for adults ages 40-54.

Parents have also experienced greater stress since at least 2000 when the economic expansion of the 1990's ended. As seen in Figure 8, suicide rates in persons ages 40 to 54 have been on the upswing since about 1999, especially in those ages 45 to 54. These are the likely ages of parents of the young people now experiencing the suicide uptick. The recent scandal involving celebrities paying exorbitant fees to enroll their adolescents in college illustrates the extreme measures parents are willing to take in order to manage the academic success of their children.

What we are suggesting is that more intensive parenting has likely helped to reduce otherwise unhealthy behavior in adolescents, but at the same time has passed on the stress that results in increased suicidal ideation. As noted above, reports of suicidal ideation in adolescents declined during the prosperous 1990's but began to reverse since 2008. This reversal is more likely associated with the financial crisis than with anything to do with social networking.

DOES ONLINE SOCIAL NETWORKING LEAD
TO DEPRESSION?

Evidence regarding the effects of social networking has been mixed. While it has reduced the need for face-to-face interaction, it has also likely kept youth off the road thereby helping to reduce driving fatalities (see Figure 3). But the 2008 economic crisis has likely added to the decline as well given the sharp drop in driver fatalities at this time. Nevertheless, for those adolescents who drive, the distraction produced by phones has likely halted the trend of declining driving injuries. It is noteworthy however that recent changes in motor vehicle fatalities have been far greater for middle-aged pedestrians than for youth (not shown in the figure).

Heavy use of online media may also be a result rather than a cause of depression. In our longitudinal study of media use by young people ages 14 to 22 (Romer, Bagdasarov, & More, 2013), we found that over a year's time, those who experienced an increase in depression tended to withdraw from social activity, such as sports and clubs, while also spending more time on the internet. A more recent study of early adolescents and college students in Canada (Heffer, Good, Daly, MacDonell, & Willoughby, 2019) also found that symptoms of depression predicted later use of social media in adolescent females and that greater participation in clubs or sports predicted less depression later in the study among the college students. These findings suggest that the correlation that Twenge et al. (2018) found between depression symptoms and time spent online was at least partly due to a response to depression rather than a cause.

We have also studied youth with symptoms of internet addiction and found that there is a tendency for such youth to report unhappy relations with parents, which may also lead to withdrawal (Bleakley, Ellithorpe, & Romer, 2016). Thus, associations between heavy online media use and depression may be the result of poor relationships with parents in some youth.

There is also evidence that the type of content that young people access online is important in determining its effects. For example, online engagement with educational and informational sources is beneficial for youth (Romer et al., 2013). Youth who do not use these resources for whatever reason are also less likely to do well in school, which may also lead to unhappiness. We have also found that the type of content that young people find online can affect their mental health. Those who frequent online chat sites in search of information and support regarding suicide were found to be at greater risk of subsequent suicidal ideation (Dunlop, More, & Romer, 2011). This was in contradiction to finding that exposure to suicide on social networks such as Facebook did not enhance subsequent suicidal ideation, perhaps because it also tended to be accompanied by supportive messages from friends.

A large study of online media use in the UK suggests that the association between heavy use and depression is small in magnitude (Orben & Przybylski, 2019b). In addition, three large scale studies by the same team found very small relations between screen use and depression (Orben & Przybylski, 2019a). This conforms to evidence that it is the purpose of media use that determines its effects by potentially displacing otherwise healthy and productive use of time rather than by being directly depressogenic.

In sum, the greater use of online media by today's youth has complex effects that must be considered in the context of the economic pressures that have increased competition among youth in the U. S. for post-secondary training. These pressures appear to have increased the intensity of parenting which has had both helpful and, in some cases, stressful effects on youth.

The recent increases in suicide in young people which depart from trends in both screen use and economic hardship will require further study to determine their likely sources. Whether these are just short-term departures from economic trends or evidence of other major influences will be answered in part by suicide rates in subsequent years.

References

Arendt, F., Scherr, S., Pasek, J., Jamieson, P. E., & Romer, D. (2019). Investigating harmful and helpful effects of watching season 2 of 13 Reasons Why: Results of a two-wave U. S. panel survey. *Social Science & Medicine.* https://doi.org/10.1016/j.socscimed.2019.04. 007.

Ariizumi, H., & Schirle, T. (2012). Are recessions really good for your health? Evidence from Canada. *Social Science & Medicine,* 74, 1224-1231. https://doi.org/10.1016/j.socscimed.2011.12.038.

Baumrind, D. (1978). Parental disciplinary patterns and social competence in children. *Youth and Society,* 9(3), 239-276.

Bilal, U., Cooper, R., Abreu, F., Nau, C., Franco, M., & Glass, T. A. (2017). Economic growth and mortality: Do social protection policies matter? *International Journal of Epidemiology.* https://doi.org/10.1093/ije/dyx016.

Bleakley, A., Ellithorpe, M. E., & Romer, D. (2016). The role of parents in problematic internet use among US adolescents. *Media and Communication,* 4(3), 24-34. https://doi.org/10.17645/mac.v4i3.523.

Branas, C. C., Nance, M. L., Elliott, M. R., Richmond, T. S., & Schwab, C. W. (2004). Urban-rural shifts in intentional firearm death: Different causes, same results. *American Journal of Public Health,* 94(10), 1750-1755.

Centers for Disease Control and Prevention. (2018). *Trends in the prevalence of suicide-related behaviors, National YRBS: 1991-2017.* Retrieved from https://www.cdc.gov/healthyyouth/data/yrbs/pdf/trends /2017_suicide_trend_yrbs.pdf.

Centers for Disease Control and Prevention. (2019). *Fatal injury reports, national, regional and state, 1981-2017.* Retrieved from National Center for Injury Prevention and Control website: https://webappa.cdc. gov/sasweb/ncipc/mortrate.html.

Doepke, M., & Zilibotti, F. (2019). *Love, money & parenting: How economics explains the way we raise our kids.* Princeton, NJ: Princeton University Press.

Dunlop, S., More, E., & Romer, D. (2011). Where do youth learn about suicides on the Internet, and what influence does this have on suicidal ideation? *The Journal of Child Psychology and Psychiatry*, 52(10), 1073-1080. https://doi.org/10.1111/j.1469-7610.2011.02416.x.

Garcy, A. M., & Vagero, D. (2012). The length of unemployment predicts mortality, differently in men and women, and by cause of death: A six year mortality follow-up of the Swedish 1992-1996 recession. *Social Science & Medicine*, 74, 1911-1920. https://doi.org/10.1016/j. socscimed.2012.01.034.

Heffer, T., Good, M., Daly, O., MacDonell, E., & Willoughby, T. (2019). The longitudinal association between social-media use and depressive symptoms among adolescents and young adults: An empirical reply to twenge et al., (2018). *Psychological Science*. https://doi.org/10.1177/ 2167702618812727.

Johnston, L. D., Miech, R. A., O'Malley, P. M., Bachman, J. G., Schulenberg, J. E., & Patrick, M. E. (2018). *Monitoring the future: National survey results on drug use: 1975-2017*. Ann Arbor, MI: Institute for Social Research, University of Michigan.

Martin, J. A., Hamilton, B. E., Osterman, M. J. K., Driscoll, A. K., & Drake, P. (2018). *Births: Final data for 2017* (No. Vol. 67, No. 8). Hyattsville, MD: National Center for Health Statistics.

Mueller, A. S., & Abrutyn, S. (2016). Adolescents under pressure: A new Durkheimian framework for understanding adolescent suicide in a cohesive community. *American Sociological Review*, 81(5), 877-899. https://doi. org/10.1177/0003122416663464.

National Center for Health Statistics. (2018). *Suicide mortality in the United States, 1999-2017* (No. NCHS Data Brief, no 330). Retrieved from https://www.cdc.gov/nchs/data/databriefs/db330-h.pdf.

Nordt, C., Warnke, I., Selfritz, E., & Kawohl, W. (2015). Modelling suicide and unemployment: A longitudinal analysis covering 63 countries, 2000-11. *Lancet Psychiatry*, 2, 239-245. https://doi.org/10.1016/ S2215-0366(14)00118-7.

Orben, A., & Przybylski, A. K. (2019a). Screens, teens, and psychological well-being: Evidence from three time-use-diary studies. *Psychological Science.* https://doi.org/10.1177/0956797619830329.

Orben, A., & Przybylski, A. K. (2019b). The association between adolescent well-being and digital technology use. *Nature Human Behavior*, 3, 173-182. https://doi.org/10.1038/s41562-018-0506-1.

Pew Research Center. (2015). *Parenting in America: Outlook, worries, aspirations are strongly linked to financial situation.* Retrieved from https:// www.pewresearch.org/ wp-content/ uploads/ sites/ 3/ 2015/ 12/ 2015-12-17_parenting-in-america_FINAL.pdf.

Ramey, G., & Ramey, V. A. (2010). *The rug rat race. Brookings Papers on Economic Activity, pp. 129-176.* Washington, DC: The Brookings Institution. doi: 10.1353/eca.2010.0003.

Romer, D., Bagdasarov, Z., & More, E. (2013). Older versus newer media and the well-being of United States youth: Results from a national longitudinal panel. *Journal of Adolescent Health*, 52, 613-619. https:// doi.org/10.1016/j.adohealth.2012.11.012.

Stuckler, D., & Basu, S. (2013). *The body economic: Why austerity kills.* New York: Basic Books.

Twenge, J. M., Cooper, A. B., Joiner, T. E., Duffy, M. E., & Binau, S. G. (2019). Age, period, and cohort trends in mood disorder indicators and suicide-related outcomes in a nationally representative dataset, 2005-2017. *Journal of Abnormal Psychology*, 128(3), 185-190. https://doi. org/10.1037/abn0000410.

Twenge, J. M., Joiner, T. E., Rogers, M. L., & Martin, G. N. (2018). Increases in depressive symptoms, suicide-related outcomes, and suicide rates among U. S. adolescents after 2010 and links to increased new media screen time. *Clinical Psychological Science*, 6(1), 3-17. https://doi.org/10.1177/2167702617723376.

Yablon, A., & Ness, D. (2018). *U. S. gun death rate hit 20-year high in 2017, CDC data shows.* Retrieved from The Trace website: https:// www.thetrace.org/rounds/gun-death-rate-2017-increase-cdc-suicide/.

In: Digital Technology   ISBN: 978-1-53616-438-1
Editor: Michelle F. Wright   © 2019 Nova Science Publishers, Inc.

Chapter 10

NEGATIVE CYBER EFFECTS: WHY DIGITAL TECHNOLOGIES CONTRIBUTE TO AGGRESSION AND DECREASE THE ABILITY TO JUDGE THE CREDIBILITY OF DIGITAL LIES (FAKE NEWS)

*Catarina Katzer**

Institute of Cyberpsychology and Media Ethics Cologne,
Cologne, Germany

ABSTRACT

Digital technology plays an important role in peoples´ daily lives. Most smartphone users are always "On", with 30% of adults and nearly 2/3 of the 12-18 years old using their smartphones at night in their bedroom (Cisco Connected Word Technology Report 2012; Pronova BKK 2017; https:// www.t-online.de/ digital/ handy/ id_ 83971634/ das- handy- in- meinem- bett- weniger- schlaf- durchs- smartphone. html). Moreover,

---

* Corresponding Author's E-mail: dr-katzer@netcologne.de.

approximately every 7-minutes, German students interrupt their actions to look at their smartphones (Markowetz 2016). Furthermore, 70% of German toddlers and preschoolers (2-5 years old) use their parent's smartphone for about ½ hour per day (BLIKK Study 2017). Undoubtedly, the digital revolution effects human behavior, emotions, perception, and cognition for better and worse. Especially effects of the problematic use of internet technology seem to increase: 1. The rise of Online Aggression (as Hate speech, Shitstorms, Cyberbullying) and 2. the impact of digital lies (manipulation by Fake News). The first psychological glance at those phenomenon reveals, that behavior we show online as the way of information processing and the formation of opinion are highly affected by the usage of digital technologies. New strategies to stop those dilemmas are needed, which will be also discussed in this chapter.

INTRODUCTION

Whatever we interact with online, whether fake news in election campaigns in Europe or in the US or aggression as hate speech, shitstorms, or cyberbullying, the use of digital technologies seems to stimulate deviant behavior and decrease our ability to distinguish between fake news and real news online. The purpose of this chapter is to focus on the problematic use of digital technologies. There are two visible negative consequences of digital technology use that will be discussed: 1) the impact of Digital Lies (i.e., manipulation by Fake News), and 2) the rise of Online Aggression (i.e., Hate speech, Shitstorms, Cyberbullying). As will be highlighted by this chapter, the virtual environment has changed the world. In addition, consequences of digital technology in relation to our physical environment will be discussed (e.g., Can virtual aggression lead to real aggression on the streets? Do we lose digital moral and ethical standard?) in this chapter, as well as new strategies to prevent online aggression and manipulation through fake news.

THE IMPACT OF DIGITAL LIES: CYBERPSYCHOLOGICAL EFFECTS OF FAKE NEWS MANIPULATION

Fake News or false truth is not an invention of the digital age. Documents show that the Soviets were spending billions on external propaganda and influence campaigns during the Cold War and targeted American audiences with fake news (Hindman 2018). Therefore, influencing people´s attitudes and behaviors by manipulating facts is not new. However, digital technologies have changed the dissemination of fake information and the effects on human perception in beliefs. Through digital technologies, it can take a few seconds for a message to reach millions of recipients. False news stories about Hillary Clinton ordering the murder of a FBI agent or participating in a satanic child abuse ring were shared thousands of times on social media during the 2016 election (Silverman 2016). Furthermore, the quality of information is decreasing. Traditional journalism receives tremendous competition from influencing, blogging, and youtubing. Every internet user can release information or news feeds and become a news ticker. The problem is that the proof of quality is difficult to determine because every internet user has become a gatekeeper. But what does this mean for the recipients? How does this digital change in news influence the way internet users perceive material and the method of information processes?

Studies show alarming results. The majority of American students are "clueless about evaluating the accuracy and trustworthiness of what they find online" (Shellenbarger 2016). In addition, 82% of middle-schoolers in the United States could not distinguish between advertising content and a real news story on a website. Moreover, they had trouble sorting facts from fiction and their ability to judge the credibility of digital lies is lacking. Findings are similar in Europe; in particular, 86% of swiss students have problems distinguishing between fake or real news, whether information is superficial, and they have no cognitive strategies for determining real versus fake news (https:// www.jugendundmedien.ch/ themen/ fake- news-manipulation.html). How can we explain what is happening with our cognitive procedures? What lays behind those developments? And how can we get out of this dilemma?

The Rhythm of the Internet and the Lack of Digital Consciousness Influence Perception, Information Processing, and Credibility of Information Sources

Concerning the impact of digital lies (fake news), it seems that we must distinguish between different effects which are working together like a vicious circle. Undoubtedly the internet rhythm has a tremendous influence on perception and information processing. Most of us get more and more trained to interrupt current activities, similar to Pavlov dogs. Germans between 18 - 21 years interrupt their actions more than 135 times per day to look at their smartphones (Markowetz 2016). This behavior has different emotional and cognitive effects (Lachmann et al. 2018). On the emotional level, we get habituated to stay in constant interaction with our digital devices and develop a "habit to check" (i.e., to look onto smartphone screen), although nothing really happened (Katzer 2018b; Renzulli 2019) or nomophobia (i.e., fear to be offline, separation anxiety; Seunghee et al. 2017). The need to look at our smartphone screens increases. This is similar to an "Cyberautomatism" which happens unconsciously. Therefore, when someone forgets their phone at home, misplaces it, or if it is on low battery, they might panic. Moreover, studies on smartphone addiction (e.g., Machado Khoury et al. 2019) show that abruptly stopping the use of smartphones can increase stress levels and cause withdrawal symptoms. We also begin to develop a new relationship towards our smartphone and digital devices. Research has suggested that smartphones have become a part of our bodies, like an extension of hands and arms (Liepelt et al. 2015). On the cognitive level, we must face the huge diversity of cyberspace, which confronts us through a plurality of apps, and simultaneously we have to act in our physical environment. Today we act constantly connected on different levels of perception or consciousness (Katzer 2016b).

The consequences of smartphone saturation include negative effects on concentration and memory, including the quality (e.g., we make more mistakes) and speed of our activities (e.g., slowing down; Sana et al. 2013). Therefore, our perception of information gets affected and becomes superficial. Of the documents searched for online, only 10-15% are read (see also Nicholas 2014) while the rest of the information is scanned and forgotten. Furthermore, we are unable to find cognitive structures (Minear et al. 2013; Uncapher et al. 2017). We can easily become victims of a "Context collapse". We are prone to forgetting tasks, such as getting out of the train or buying the wrong product in the supermarket, because we are too engaged with digital technologies. The consequence is an overstraining effect and digital cognitive congestion. We lose digital consciousness.

Manipulation by Fake News: How the of Lack of Digital Consciousness Leads to a "Digital Mind Trap"

To prevent losing digital consciousness and ease the process of overstraining, we adapt to new cognitive strategies. However, these strategies have negative effects on information processing, opinion making, and perceived credibility of information sources. Therefore, those cognitive strategies follow the rule - short means fast, easy, and convenient. The success of Twitter is not surprising. The limitation of information means a relief for our brain. It shortens the perception process, but the reception of data and information becomes superficial. We begin to accept statements and news without questioning and avoid material which is not coherent. We prevent cognitive dissonance (Katzer 2017b). Augmentative thinking and scrutinizing are strained and because of the need for convenience we try to evade. These strategies of perception facilitate manipulation of thinking and opinion making. On one side, digital perception online is managed by data or information which are familiar or corresponding with one's own experiences and attitudes. "One of the tricks our mind plays, is to highlight evidence which confirms what we already believe" (Stafford 2017). Because of cognitive congestion, this effect, we call "confirmation bias", works especially well online. When known information is paired with false news, we might not notice it at all. Furthermore, our own beliefs lead to digital perception. Moreover, what we see online influences what we believe. Our trust in information gets generated only by prior exposure. This illusory truth effect shows that a single exposure online increases subsequent perception of accuracy, despite a low level of overall believability (Pennycook et al. 2018). Only a small plausibility of information is sufficient for repetition to influence the belief towards facts or news (Pennycook et al. 2018). Therefore, the scope of repetition on beliefs is larger than has been assumed.

Not only are one's beliefs or the exposure itself leading to digital perceptions, the content plays an important role as well. Emotional information, including feelings of anger, fear, sorrow, or happiness, influence perception and blurs cognitive reflection. More emotion means stronger perception of information, including fake information (Katzer 2018a). Besides the information itself, the source and its authenticity and credibility determine what we think is true or false. Sources involving traditional gatekeepers, like journalists from newspapers, we trust the most. Nearly the same happens with people we meet/encounter online. We may know a lot about someone online, because they post a lot, share many photos, or includes work-related details on social networks. These features conceptualize this person as an expert and enhances trustworthiness (Katzer 2017b). Furthermore, we frequently encounter this information about a person online which improves the feeling of sympathy, closeness, trust, and credibility (see mere exposure effect; Zajonc 2001). This process happens online automatically; we are continuously confronted with posts and information by people we follow on Twitter or Facebook (i.e., Influencer). Therefore, we are online in a recurring loop of self-confirmed thinking and live in a filter-bubble (Katzer 2017a). Being a member of a group strengthens the believability of information and sources. It is akin to us being prisoners in a vicious circle of self enhancement. Moreover, the group size is essential. A huge group of followers initiates a special way of thinking. In particular, when lots of people follow and "like" someone, then they must know something about this person's likeability, and subsequently their credibility.

But How Can We Stop the Digital Fake News Dilemma? What Solutions Can Prevent Manipulation through Fake News?

It is important to acknowledge whether it is enough to discuss fake news in public to enhance attention or whether it is necessary to improve the ability to distinguish between fake or real news. Unfortunately, studies testify that frequent discussions about fake news in general can lead to worse outcomes (see Van Duyn & Collier 2018). Priming effects concerning believability and identification of fake news have a negative influence on perceptions of fake news and public´s evaluation of news media. Exposure to elite discourse about fake news leads to lower levels of trust in media and less accurate identification of real news. Therefore, frequent discussion of fake news may affect whether individuals trust news media and the standards with which they evaluate it. Those discussions may also increase the dissemination of false information, especially when discourse of fake news by elites happens without context and thoughtfulness (Van Duyn & Collier 2018). To get out of this dilemma, what we really need, is to develop new digital strategies to adjust the way of changing perception and thinking online. Every Internet User needs to know about the shortcomings of information processes online. Moreover, we need to develop a new digital consciousness. All users should confront their cognitive dissonance, begin purposeful discussions, and always consider the opposite perspective, even if it is straining. People must become more skeptical and critical towards the things they get in contact with, especially when we look onto to the effectiveness of deep fakes (Lifhits 2018; Stauffacher 2019), as the need for strong skepticism is obvious. Therefore, we should focus the blindspot in our imagination on the ways information and sources could be different from how we first assume they were (Stafford 2017). Thus, people should question their own feelings and own digital behavior, and whom they follow online and why. To scrutinize our own beliefs and the confirmation of those beliefs, we should ask the right questions about news information and our own attitudes or prejudices. Deeply analyzing means to inquire where information or data came from, what is known about the source, and whether we can find different information, similar photos, or material on other websites. Therefore, we should take the stance that information online should not be trusted easily and that we should think slowly about the information we encounter. Thus, we should not always obey the rhythm of the internet.

THE RISE OF ONLINE AGGRESSION: PSYCHOLOGICAL BACKGROUND, EFFECTS ON MORAL STANDARDS, REAL LIFE BEHAVIOR AND SOLUTIONS

Many examples from politics, economics (Strohm 2013), or showbiz (Friese 2015) indicate that aggressive behavior online is not unusual. In Germany, research has found that hate speech increased in 2018 (Forsa Hate Speech Report 2018). Nearly every other internet user has observed hate or aggressive behavior, with roughly 20% responding to the incident and 80% doing nothing (Bitkom 2018). It might seem that many people accept these incidents online as "common" (Katzer 2018a). In 2014, the former Google chairman Eric Schmidt described the need to do something against negative experiences online. He suggested that we should think about using technical tools as filter systems against hate and harassment (Hern 2015). Before describing a strategy of action, more detail is needed about online aggression. The next section will address the following questions: In which way does the virtual environment change the conditions for Hate speech, Shitstorms, Cyberbullying, and what are the effects for perpetrators? Does virtual aggression lead to real-world aggression? Do we lose digital moral and ethical standards?

Negative Consequence of Computer Mediated Communication (CMC): Increasing Infrahumanization and Aggressive Behavior as Hate Speech, Shitstorms, and Cyberbullying

The virtual environment and CMC have changed not only the conditions for human behavior, but our perceptions of oneself and others (Katzer

2018a). Experiments demonstrate that CMC leads to a greater infrahumanization as face to face interactions and that human emotions are stronger in face to face situation than in CMC (Hoffman et al. 2010; Leyens et al. 2000). Of vital importance is the utmost difference between face to face communication and CMC. In particular, there is the separation of our physicalness from our concrete actions online. With our body we stay in real life situations in front of the screen, but with our minds we immerse ourselves in the virtual environment using technical tools, such as laptop or smartphone. Online actions happen disembodied, which changes our perception of own behavior. The separation of the real-world and online activity, of body and mind, originates psychologically as a huge emotional distance to oneself as actor and to others, the recipients (Katzer 2016b, 2019). On one hand, this process leads to decreasing awareness of our own deviant actions. What we do not see, we will not feel. Online self-categorization and social standards or norms influence behavior in the real-world. Perpetrators of negative online behavior might lose the ability to understand how they harm others. The emotions of victims of hate speech, cyberbullying, or shitstorms are not physical visible. Therefore "digital empathy" (Katzer 2016a) is fading, and emotional bunting (Katzer 2016a) and disinhibition (Lapidot-Lefler & Barak 2012) are increasing. Moreover, the immersion into a huge group of Internet Users on social media enhances these processes, as our "self" gets invisible, we become deindividualized, and we only feel as a part of the group. Therefore, the online community itself supports the decrease of self-awareness and self-control. This reduces the inhibition threshold (Dodd 2001) and responsibility for own behavior - it is getting transformed onto the group, our own guilty conscience turned off.

However, membership of a homogeneous online group on Facebook, Twitter, Instagram, or WhatsApp intensifies those effects. Being a real member (i.e., follower) in an anonymous environment, i.e., of an aggressive group or right-wing community, fortifies conformity and social influence to follow an aggressive social norm (see Katzer 2016a; Rösner and Krämer 2016). Therefore, online processes of group dynamics are extremely effective (e.g., social influence by norms and standards). The more salient group identity and being among many individuals, we don´t feel ourselves and social influence becomes the stronger (Reicher et al. 1995), which is in line with the theory of De-Individuation (SIDE Model; Reicher et al. 1995; Postmes et al. 2001; Kugihara 2001; Reicher et al. 1995; Diener 1980). Those psychological processes show a strong interaction between situate conditions (e.g., being part of an Online group), internal factors (e.g., fading self-awareness), and actual behavior (e.g., lack of self-control leads to actions we normally don´t show; De-Individuation SIDE Model; Reicher et al. 1995; Postmes et al. 2001; Kugihara 2001; Reicher et al. 1995; Diener 1980).

Immersion into a group and cohesiveness increase conformity. Similarly, those processes stimulate the development of new rules/norms and moral opinion within the group (i.e., emergent norm). Thus, aggression becomes standard behavior against other people, specifically those considered the outgroup. Group effects increase by size, such that the bigger the ingroup, the stronger conformity and standardizing of rules and norms become. Moreover, we can testify that aggression or hate speech happen in a virulent way. Like a spiral of negative emotional contagion, aggression becomes worse over time.

Analysis of shitstorms show that the more people engaged, the more harmful, aggressive, or fecal speech becomes (Katzer 2018c; Rauschnabel et al. 2016). Moreover, the need for affiliation strengthens those effects and the influence on future behavior.

Consequences of Virtual Aggression on Physical Environment: Do We Lose Moral and Ethical Standard?

One important issue future research should bring into focus is the effects of virtual aggressive behavior on real-world behavior.

The internet is not a one-way street. In the last few years, we observed an increasing transfer from social network groups (i.e., of right-wing radicalism (Künast 2019) or citizens against journalists (Feindbild Journalist Studie 2019) to real acts of deviant behavior. Undoubtedly, Cyberspace is an environment where users learn opinion making and get role models for own behavior, even behavior in the real-world (Katzer 2017a).

Moral standards and ethics are potentially highly affected by the content people see and do online, which has the potential to carry-over from the digital world to the offline world. Therefore, there is a risk to lose social standards in moral and ethics and create a new mind set full of antisocial behavior and attitudes. Virtual communities and CMC can increase inhuman or deviant uninhibited behavior, and aggressive actions or crime, but it is not an automatism. Deindividuation processes may also support prosocial behavior, help, or solidarity (see candy storms; Herbold 2015).

One positive example is the German Facebook group #ichbinhier, which acts forceful against hate and has gotten different awards for their social action (www.ichbinhier.eu/ich-bin-hier). The internet can strengthen both- the bad and the good in our behavior. Therefore, in anonymous and physical invisible environments, the way of social influence (e.g., norms, standards, opinions of a group we want to be part of; need of affiliation) is of great importance.

SOLUTIONS: WHAT WE NEED TO DO AGAINST ONLINE HATE

The discourse above has shown that the virtual environment has changed conditions and affects aggressive behavior. Therefore, we have to discuss new strategies for prevention which need to be comprehensive on different levels. The first level is education of abilities and knowledge. Individuals, especially youth, should develop abilities, such as socioemotional skills (e.g., digital empathy, self-control) and learn the potential psychological changes in their perceptions concerning themselves and others. Schools have a very important role regarding this issue. They need new structures (e.g., peer to peer teams to help and educate), cyberguidelines (e.g., restrictions, rules how and when to use digital technology in school), and new educational topics (e.g., a combination of cyberpsychology knowledge and computer science to learn the ability to estimate different effects of new technical tools on society as beneficial or harmful). Another level is to make the online environment safer. On the behavioral level, a new way to trigger more self-control by users could be to activate psychological knowledge about one's behavior, i.e., incorporate a "rethink button" into social networks. It works like pop ups before posting comments and raises awareness of the actual behavior (see also www.rethinkwords.com/ whatisrethink). Moreover, governmental guidelines and framework- or laws should remind providers, social networks, and internet industry of their responsibilities, which require more than mere self-regulation. One example is the German "Netzwerkdurchsetzungsgesetz," (https://www.bundestag. de/ dokumente/ textarchiv/ 2017/ kw26-de-netzwerkdurchsetzungsgesetz-513398) which is estimated by many European countries as a right way to fight online hate, aggression, and violence. Accordingly, in May 2019, France President Macron explained a new law against hate similar to Germany (Pany 2019). Moreover, a stronger victim protection and a new and effective reporting and investigation system is needed, such as an obligatory national First Aid button on websites of all social networks/providers. Those buttons increase awareness anytime users are online and should enable victims or observers of aggression to get access to psychological assistance immediately. Furthermore, prevention on a technological level, should use automatic detection/filter systems, which automatically delete threats, photos or violent video clips. However, technological prevention strategies might be monitored by administration. Therefore, we should also think about reforming penal law, i.e., including cyberbullying into the penal code (which has already happened in some countries) or enacting a new cyberbullying law, as has been done in parts of the United States, New Zealand, Singapore, Austria, or Italy. We should not forget that people are cyberspace - they create the Internet. Thus, the users should develop more digital bravery and moral courage as to not lose human standards and ethical behavior.

CONCLUSION

The virtual environment is changing conditions and effects aggression and the ability to judge credibility of digital lies. The rhythm of the internet (i.e., continuous interruptions influence perception and information processing) and the lack of digital consciousness (as a result of simultaneously behavior on different levels of consciousness and environment: Online on social networks like Twitter, WhatsApp, Facebook or Youtube, Instagram, Searching machines, Gaming etc. and physically in family, school, work setting etc.) leads into "Cyberautomatism" (i.e., superficial information reception, accepting statements without questioning, avoidance of cognitive dissonance, and online living in homogenous groups which work as filter bubble). Those mistakes of perception make it easy to manipulate thinking and opinion making (Katzer 2017a, 2018a). The anonymous environment and the separation of physicalness from the actions online (we act disembodied) changes perception of oneself (as perpetrator) and others (as victims). Emotional distance towards oneself as actor and the others as recipients, decreasing awareness of own deviant actions and empathy, the huge group of Internet users enhances processes of digital De-Individuation (SIDE Model), and the behavior of others in homogeneous online groups (see social modeling, role models, affiliation) reduces the inhibition threshold, influences future behavior, and the development of aggressive rules/ norms within the group (i.e., emergent norm). Moreover, those effects of manipulation and aggressive behavior are increasing with group size.

The detailed review of the psychological background mentioned above addressed the effects on moral standard and behavior in the real-world. Therefore, we have to assume a reciprocal effect. This involves acknowledging that Online behavior does not stay online because it may relocate onto the streets and may influence ethics in the offline world. Furthermore, the change in online perception and information processing modifies our information processing as evidence by superficial procedures, not reading and only scanning papers and information, decision finding and opinion making without deep scrutinizing, and convenient mind patterns (as follow a huge group size.). Such processes can lead us into a digital mind trap and influence thinking and behavior in real life situations. To address this issue, a new digital consciousness must be developed which raises awareness of how the rhythm of the internet and the lack of digital consciousness influence perception, information processing, and credibility of information sources. We should use a mix of new strategies to learn about manipulation procedures (e.g., how the of lack of digital consciousness leads into a "digital mind trap") and change our perceptions of oneself and others. Governmental institutions have to administrate their huge responsibility towards society and facilitate urgent changes concerning digital education (i.e., Schools) and creating a safer online environment. Therefore, stricter governmental ruling and regulation of online supply/digital industry (e.g., social networks or providers as Facebook, Twitter, Reddit etc.) which enhance protection (i.e., rethink button or filter systems) and support (i.e., obligatory First Aid Button, revision of statute) are needed.

Over time human being and digital technologies will be connected more and more. Therefore, to prevent drowning in cyberpsychological effects and to become competent cybernauts, we must be aware of changes in ourselves and train a critical mind to gain skills for estimating digital benefit or damage.

REFERENCES

Bitkom 2018, *Press Information: Hate Speach-Every 9th Internet User has become a victim.* https://www.bitkom.org/Presse/Presseinformation/ Hasskommentare- Jeder- neunte- Internetnutzer- war- selbst- schon-Opfer.html.

BLIKK Study 2017. *Federal government's commissioner for drug related issues et al.* (2017), press release 29.5.2017. www.drogenbeauftragte. de/ fileadmin/ dateien-dba/ Drogenbeauftragte/ 4_ Presse/ 1_ Pressemitteilungen/ 2017/ 2017_ II_ Quartal/ 2017- 05-29_ PM_ Blikk. pdf (1.9.2018).

Cisco Connected Word Technology Report 2012: Generation Y-Whole Communication is linked with the internet. www.bisculm.com/studie-die- kommunikation- der- generation- y- ist- mit- dem- netz- verknupft- -8890/.

Diener, E. (1980.) Deindividuation: The absence of self-awareness and self-regulation in group members. In P. B. Paulus (Ed.), *Psychology of group influence*, (pp. 209 - 242). Hillsdale, NJ: Eribaum.

Dodd, David K. (2001): Robbers in the classroom: a deindividuation exercise. In: Griggs, Richard A. (Hrsg.): *Handbook for teaching introductory psychology,* Volume 3, S. 251 - 253. Mahwah, New Jersey/London.

Feindbild Journalist Report 2018. European Centre for Press and Media Freedom. https://www.ecpmf.eu/files/feindbild_3_-_rueckblick_2018. pdf.

Forsa Hate Speech Report 2018, https://www.medienanstalt-nrw.de/ fileadmin/ user_upload/ lfm-nrw/ Foerderung/ Forschung/ Dateien_ Forschung/forsaHate_Speech_2018_Ergebnisbericht_LFM_NRW.PDF (search 20.03.2019); https://www.thueringer-allgemeine.de/web/ zgt/ leben/ detail/ -/ specific/ Mehr- Hass- Mobbing- und- Extremismus- im-Internet-563307770.

Hern, Alex (2015): Google`s Eric Schmidt calls for «spell-checkers for hate and harassment". In: *The Guardian*, https://www.theguardian.com/ technology/ 2015/ dec/ 08/ googles-eric-schmidt-spell-checkers-hate-harassment-terrorism (seen 6. 02. 2018).

Hindman, Matthew (2018). *Disinformation, 'Fake News' and Influence Campaigns on Twitter.* Knight Foundation.

Hoffman, B. T, Chellaney, I., Sutherland, M., Hancock, J., Manacher, M., Tan, D. (2010). *Infrahumanization in computer-mediated communication,* https://theingroup.wordpress.com/.

http://www.handelszeitung.ch/unternehmen/schwule-und-lesben-empoert-shitstorm-gegen-barilla-503061 (search 10.01.2019).

http://www.welt.de/vermischtes/article145080345/Wer-fuer-Fluechtlinge-kaempft-erntet-einen-Shitstorm.html (search 25.02.2019).

https://www.dw.com/de/hass-im-internet-gewalt-auf-der-straße/a-
19036572 (search 25.03.2019).

https://www.jugendundmedien.ch/themen/fake-news-manipulation.html
(search 10.03.2019).

https://www.tagesspiegel.de/themen/digitalisierung-ki/dem-hass-im-netz-
begegnen-shitstorm-candystorm/12279860.html (4.09.2015).

https://www.t-online.de/digital/handy/id_83971634/das-handy-in-meinem-
bett-weniger-schlaf-durchs-smartphone.html (search 20.03.2019).

Katzer, C. (2016a). *ARAG Digital Risks Survey - International expert study.*
https:// www.arag.com/ medien/ pdf/ presse/ arag_ digital_ risks_
survey.pdf.

Katzer, C. (2016b). Cyberpsychology- Life in the Net: How the Internet
changes our live. Dtv, Munich (german edition).

Katzer, C. (2017a). Funky to Fake? How serious journalism has to be? How
serious journalism can be? Crisis of credibility? Hessischer
Jungjournalistentag, Frankfurt, 10.06.2017.

Katzer, C. (2017b). *Why fake news work.* https:// faktenfinder. tagesschau.
de/ hintergrund/ interview- falschmeldungen- 101. html (search 20.03.
2019).

Katzer, C. (2018a). Psychology of digital lies and Opinion making 4.0: Why
hate speach and fake news online work so well. In: Limbourg, P. und
Grätz, R. (Hrsg.). *Medienkulturen 4: Meinungsmache im Netz: Fake
News, Bots und Hate Speech.* Steidl.

Katzer, C. (2018b). Who does not post anything, does not exist- How the
internet changes our daily lives. *PC-Welt.* https://www.pcwelt.de/a/wer-
nichts- postet- ist- nicht- existent- wie- das- internet- unser- leben-
veraendert,3463235 (03.03.2019).

Katzer, C. (2018c). *Women in shitstorms. How to deal with digital hate?*
https:// www.emotion.de/ leben-arbeit/ gesellschaft/ shitstorm-hilfe-
strategien-frauen (search 20.03.2019).

Katzer, C. (2019). *Sajber Psihologija [Cyber Psychology].*

Kugihara, Naoki (2001): Effects of aggressive behaviour and group size on
collective escape in an emergency: A test between a social identity

model and deindividuation theory. In: *British Journal of Social Psychology,* 40 (4), S. 575 - 598.

Künast, R. (2019). *Protect Children against radicalism.* https:// www. belltower. news/ interview- zu- hate- speech- renate- kuenast- 83755/ (search 09.04.2019).

Lachmann, B., Sindermann, C., Sariyska, R., Luo, R., Melchers, M., Becker, B. and Montag, C. (2018). The Role of Empathy and Life Satisfaction in Smartphone Use Disorder. *Frontiers in Psychology,* 9, 398.

Lapidot-Lefler, N. and Barak., A. (2012). Effects of anonymity, invisibility, and lack of eye-contact on toxic online disinhibition. *Computers in Human Behavior,* Volume 28, Issue 2, March 2012, Pages 434 - 443.

Leyens, J. Ph., Paladino, M. P., Rodriguez, R. T., Vaes, J., Demoulin, S., Rodriguez, A. P. and Gaunt, R. (2000). "The emotional side of prejudice: The attribution of secondary emotions to ingroups and outgroups". *Personality and Social Psychology Review,* 4 (2): 186 - 197.

Liepelt, R., Dolk, T. and Hommel, B. (2015, März). When objects become part of the body. Vortrag auf der 57. Tagung experimentell arbeitender Psychologen (TeaP). Hildesheim, Deutschland.

Lifhits, J. (2018). Deepfakes Are Coming. And They're Dangerous. *Washingtonn Examiner,* 20. July, 2018. https://www.weeklystandard. com/ jenna-lifhits/ deepfake- videos- are- a- national- security- threat (search 20.07.2018).

Machado Khoury, J., Silva Codorino Couto, S., de Almeida Santos, D., de Oliveira e Silva, V., Sousa Drumond, S. P., Lopes de Carvalho e Silva, L., Malloy-Diniz, L., Albuquerque, M. R., de Castro Lourenço das Neves, M. and Frederico Duarte Garcia (2019). Bad Choices Make Good Stories: The Impaired Decision-Making Process and Skin Conductance Response in Subjects With Smartphone Addiction. *Front. Psychiatry,* 22 February 2019.

Markowetz, A. (2016). *Digitaler Burnout.*

Minear, M., Brasher, F., McCurdy, M., Lewis, J., Younggren, A.(2013). Working memory, fluid intelligence, and impulsiveness in heavy media multitaskers. *Psychol. Bull. Rev.,* 2013 Dec.; 20(6):1274 - 81.

Nicholas, D. (2014). The Google generation, the mobile phone and the 'library' of the future: Implications for society, governments and libraries in A. Noorhidawati et al. (Eds.) ICOLIS-2014, Kuala-Lumpur DLIS, FCSIT, 2014: pp 1 - 8.

Pany, T. (2019). *Macron will fight Online Hate*. https:// www.heise.de/tp/ features/ Macron- will- den- Hass- im- Netz- schaerfer- bekaempfen-4316584.html (22.02.2019).

Pennycook, G., Cannon, T. D. and Rand, D. G. (2018). Prior exposure increases perceived accuracy of fake news. *Journal of Experimental Psychology: General,* 147(12), 1865 - 1880.

Postmes, T., Spears, R., Sakhel, K. and de Groot, D. (2001). Social Influence in Computer-Mediated Communication: The Effects of Anonymity on Group Behavior. *Personality and Social Psychology Bulletin,* 27, 1242 - 1254.

Pronova BKK (2017): *Addictions of the Germans.* www.pronovabkk.de/ suechte_2017.

Rauschnabel, Philipp A. Kammerlander, Nadine and Ivens, Björn S.(2016). Collaborative Brand Attacks in Social Media: Exploring the Antecedents, Characteristics, and Consequences of a New Form of Brand Crises, *Journal of Marketing Theory and Practice,* vol. 24, no. 4 (Fall 2016), pp. 381 - 410.

Reicher, Stephen D., Spears, Russell and Postmes, Tom. (1995): A Social Model of Deindividuation Phenomena. *Journal European Review of Social Psychology,* Volume 6, 1995 - Issue 1, S. 161 - 198.

Renzulli, K. A. (2019). *Americans touch their smartphones 2,617 times a day—a 'digital declutter' could help you regain hours.* https:// www.cnbc.com/ 2019/ 04/ 09/ cal-newport-a-digital-declutter-can-help-you-reduce-smartphone-time.html, (20.04.2019).

Rösner, L. and Krämer, N. (2016). Verbal Venting in the Social Web: Effects of Anonymity and Group Norms on Aggressive Language Use in Online Comments. *Social Media + Society* July-September 2016: 1 - 13.

Sana, Faria, Weston, Tina, Cepeda, Nicholas J. (2013): Laptop multitasking hinders classroom learning for both users and nearby peers. In: *Computers and Education*, 62 (1), S. 24 - 31.

Seunghee Han, Ki Joon Kim and Jang Hyun Kim. (2017). Understanding Nomophobia: Structural Equation Modeling and Semantic Network Analysis of Smartphone Separation *Anxiety, Cyberpsychology, Behavior, and Social Networking,* (2017). DOI: 10.1089/cyber.2017. 0113.

Silverman, Craig (2016). "This Analysis Shows How Viral Fake Election News Stories Outperformed Real News on Facebook," *BuzzFeed*, November 16, 2016, https://www.buzzfeed.com/craigsilverman/viral-fake-election-news-outperformed-real-news-on-facebook.

Shellenbarger, S. (2016). Most Students Don't Know When News Is Fake, Stanford Study Finds. *Wall Street Journal*, Nov 21, 2016. https://www. wsj.com/ articles/ most- students- dont- know- when- news- is- fake-stanford-study-finds-1479752576 (search 09.10.2018).

Stafford, T. (2017). *How do you persuade somebody of the facts? Asking them to be fair, impartial and unbiased is not enough.* http:// www.bbc.com/ future/ story/ 20170131-why-wont-some-people-listen-to-reason (Search 24.04.2019).

Stauffacher, R. (2019). Deepfakes: Can I still believe what I see? *Neue Zürcher Zeitung*, 11.03.2019, https://www.nzz.ch/digital/deepfakes-kann- ich- ueberhaupt- noch- glauben- was- ich- sehe- ld. 1457416 (search 11.03.2019).

Uncapher, Melina. R., Lin, Lin, Rosen, Larry D., Kirkorian, Heather L., Baron, Naomi S., Bailey, Kira, Cantor, Joanne, Strayer, David L., Parsons, Thomas D., Wagner, Anthony D. (2017): Media Multitasking and Cognitive, Psychological, Neural, and Learning Differences. In: *Pediatrics,* 140 (S2), S. 62 - 66.

Van Duyn, Emily and Collier, Jessica. (2018). Priming and Fake News: The Effects of Elite Discourse on Evaluations of News Media. *Mass Communication and Society,* 10.1080/15205436.2018.1511807.

Catarina Katzer

Zajonc, R. B. (2001). Mere Exposure: *A Gateway to the Subliminal*, Volume: 10 issue: 6, page (s): 224 - 228. Issue published: December 1, 2001.

In: Digital Technology　　　　ISBN: 978-1-53616-438-1
Editor: Michelle F. Wright　　© 2019 Nova Science Publishers, Inc.

Chapter 11

(UN)DOING DEVIANCE: SOCIAL CATEGORIZATION IN USER REACTIONS TO PROANOREXIA VIDEOS ON YOUTUBE

Anu Sirola[*], *Markus Kaakinen, Tuuli Turja*
and Atte Oksanen
Tampere University, Tampere, Finland

ABSTRACT

Proanorexia ("promoting anorexia") is an online-based phenomenon that is popular among young women. It is publicly seen as a deviant activity that is attached with the stigma of eating disorders. This chapter explores how the proana identity is categorized in comments on proanorexia videos on YouTube. Using the search word "pro-ana," twenty-five popular YouTube user channels were selected. The comments (n = 2122) of these channels' videos were analyzed using membership categorization analysis. Proanas are categorized as a deviant out-group because of activities such

---

[*] Corresponding Author's E-mail: anu.sirola@tuni.fi.

as spreading harmful ideals, and for attributes such as grotesque appearance. Commenters position themselves in relation to proanorexia with various self-categories, which is used as a rhetorical device to justify one's stance. While proanas defend their in-group identity and distinguish themselves from hateful outsiders, extreme categorizations reinforce deviant attributes and stigma towards those identifying as proanas and may strengthen the attractiveness of the risky in-group.

Keywords: eating disorders, anorexia, social identity, social media, membership categorization analysis

INTRODUCTION

Proanorexia (i.e., *proana*) is an Internet-based phenomenon that typically glamorizes the anorexic body and promotes eating-disordered behavior. Generally, it challenges the medical view of anorexia as a disorder (Conrad & Rondini, 2010) and promotes an "anti-recovery" stance on anorexia (Fox et al., 2005; Oksanen, Garcia & Räsänen, 2016). Proanorexia content includes inspirational videos and images (i.e., "thinspiration") that aim to motivate weight loss (Borzekowski et al., 2010; Norris et al., 2006). Exposure to proanorexia content is associated with increased eating pathology and negative body image (Rodgers et al., 2016). The majority of people using proanorexia websites are young women (Csipke & Horne, 2007), who are also in the high-risk group for anorexia (Fairburn & Harrison, 2003). The mortality rate in anorexia is one of the highest among psychiatric disorders (Smink et al., 2012), which makes promoting anorexia a dangerous activity. Because of its extreme ideals and risky health behavior, proanorexia is publicly considered to be a deviant and dangerous phenomenon, and, as such, it provokes strong criticism among outsiders (Giles, 2006; Knapton, 2013; Marcus, 2016).

This chapter focuses on public reactions to proanorexia videos on the popular video sharing site, YouTube. We will also provide new perspective on YouTube commenting that is popular among young people. While there is a growing body of research on proanorexia, studies on YouTube remain scarce. A study by Syed-Abdul et al. (2013) found that there are thousands of videos promoting anorexia on YouTube, and that they are also more popular compared to informative anorexia videos. As the users on YouTube mainly communicate by commenting on videos, the sense of community is looser as any registered user can leave comments on public videos (Oksanen et al., 2015). Due to controversial and counter-normative nature of proanorexia, and due to YouTube's high popularity and easy accessibility, YouTube is a fruitful context to study public reactions and criticism concerning proanorexia phenomenon. Drawing from the literature on stigma, deviance, and social categorization, we examine what kinds of resources are used to (de)construct proanorexia as a deviant phenomenon in user comments for the most popular proanorexia videos.

STIGMA AND THE DEVIANCE OF PROANOREXIA

As with other psychological disorders, negative attitudes and stigma towards individuals with eating disorders are common (Easter, 2012; Mond et al., 2006; Rich, 2006). In a stigma theory proposed by Erving Goffman (1963), a perceived negative attribute serves to distinguish a person from others as "less human." Individuals with anorexia are often perceived as seeking attention (Mond et al., 2006; Rich, 2006) and responsible for their illness (Stewart et al., 2006), while an anorexic body is perceived as unhealthy and grotesque (Marcus, 2016). In proanorexia phenomenon, an anorexic ideal is celebrated, which further provokes negative attitudes and hostility in outsiders (Giles, 2006; Knapton, 2013; Marcus, 2016).

Communities based on risky health behavior are often considered deviant, as they are seen to deviate from the cultural norms (Adler & Adler, 2008). According to Howard Becker (1963), social groups construct deviance by reference to a set of rules, which then enables them to label or categorize other people; "The deviant is one to whom that label has successfully been applied; deviant behavior is behavior that people so label" (p. 9). Scott and Lyman (1970), in turn, defined a deviant as an individual whose actions are perceived as a possible threat to the common good and who is held responsible for deviant action. Thus, we are interested in what kinds of social and cultural resources are used in online interaction to construct, maintain, and resist the stigma and deviance of the proanorexia phenomenon and proana identity.

PROANOREXIA AND THE INTERNET: THE SOCIAL IDENTITY APPROACH

Various studies show that those identifying as proanas are motivated to search for online support because they do not receive understanding and non-judgmental support for disordered eating habits offline (Casilli et al., 2012; Rich, 2006; Tong et al., 2014; Yeshua-Katz and Martins, 2013). Proanorexia is widely spread to different kinds of social media platforms, such as Tumblr (Park et al., 2017), Instagram (Marcus, 2016), Flickr (Yom-Tov, Fernandez-Luque, Weber, & Crain 2012), blogs (Tong et al. 2014), YouTube (Syed-Abdul et al., 2013), and discussion forums (Giles, 2006). Platforms have their unique characteristics that differ, for example, in terms of the sense of community and support they offer for users (e.g., Brotsky & Giles, 2007), which influence social identity practices and group behavior.

Social identity refers to identification within certain social groups, in which social categorization serves as a resource. In social identity theory (SIT), social categorization refers to the need to achieve or maintain positive social identity by evaluating one's in-group as positively differentiated from relevant out-groups (Tajfel & Turner, 1979; Turner & Reynolds 2010). For example, in proanorexia communities, those identifying as the in-group of proanas wish to maintain their authenticity and distinguish from outsiders, such as "wannabes", "fakers" and "haters", that are seen to threaten their positive in-group identity (Giles, 2006). According to the minimal group paradigm, favoring one's own in-group over a perceived out-group is activated, even in the most minimal group conditions (Tajfel et al., 1971), which may be especially relevant in a visually anonymous online context.

In a social identity approach, the starting point for social identity formation is self-categorization. Self-categorization theory emphasises how individuals within a particular context cognitively define themselves in terms of social category memberships rather than a unique personal identity (Turner, 1985; Turner et al., 1987; Turner et al., 1994). This shift from personal identity to collective group identity is called depersonalization (Turner et al., 1987). In the proanorexia phenomenon, self-categorizations vary in terms of embodied and metaphorical descriptions (Bates, 2015), and anorexia itself is categorized, for example, as a disorder or a lifestyle (Brotsky and Giles, 2007; Csipke and Horne, 2007; Giles, 2006) or even a skill or religion (Knapton, 2013). These differing self-categorizations provoke debates in terms of the "authentic" identity of proana (Boero and Pascoe, 2012; Giles, 2006). Proanorexia sites also contain subgroups advocating healthy eating habits and ways of recuperating from anorexia (Borzekowski et al., 2010; Conrad & Rondini, 2010; Yom-Tov et al., 2012). These kinds of recovery-oriented communities represent an opposite approach to proanorexia, and these two camps mostly coexist separately without high levels of inter-group interaction (Oksanen et al., 2015; Yom-Tov et al., 2012).

Although social categorization and depersonalization are fundamental parts of group processes and structuring the social world (Billig, 2002; Tajfel, 1978; Tajfel, 1981), group comparison and negative out-group categorization may sometimes culminate in extreme hate towards and even dehumanization of the perceived out-group (Haslam & Loughnan, 2014; Tajfel, 1978). Dehumanization occurs when the "humanness" of others is dismissed or denied, which thereby constitutes others as animal-like or mechanical objects (Haslam, 2006). Dehumanization varies from subtle and relatively mild to more blatant and severe forms, in which absolute judgments about a particular target are made and its humanity is outright denied (Haslam & Loughnan, 2014). However, as Billig (2002) noted, even though dehumanization illustrates an extreme form of depersonalization, SIT fails to elaborate on the continuum between depersonalization and dehumanization or between "ordinary" and "abnormal" forms of social categorization (p. 181).

Some characteristics of computer-mediated communication (CMC) make group processes even more salient in online interaction than in face-to-face interaction. According to the social identity model of deindividuation effects (SIDE), the visual anonymity aspect present in social media interaction reduces the amount of personal information available to other users and thus enhances contextually relevant social identities, which may lead to categorization of other people based on their group memberships rather than on their personal attributes (Lea et al., 2001; Postmes et al., 2001; Reicher et al., 1995; Spears et al., 2002). This enhanced depersonalization may further activate stereotypes and hostility towards a perceived out-group (Billig, 2002). Anonymity may also lead to stronger group polarization (Sia et al., 2002). On YouTube, interaction is based on relatively high anonymity which may be useful for people wishing to spread hateful messages (Oksanen et al., 2014). YouTube is based on pseudonymity-based interaction where usernames and profiles are visible, but visual anonymity of online interaction is still present. While interaction is not fully anonymous, hostile and offensive speech (i.e., "flaming") is very common on YouTube (Moor et al., 2010). This makes it interesting to examine intergroup categorizations concerning proanorexia phenomenon from a social psychological perspective.

OVERVIEW OF THE STUDY

In this chapter, we combine theoretical frameworks of social identity and discursive identity practices to study proanorexia discussions on YouTube. We use the social identity approach as a starting point to understand in-group and out-group differentiation as a need to maintain positive identity and self-enhancement within those identifying as proanas and outsiders. However, as we are analyzing naturally occurring online data, we do not have access to commenters' cognitive states. Instead, we conceive social categories and deviance as constructions that are produced in discursive action (Billig, 2002; Goode, 2015; Lamerichs & Te Molder, 2003; Potter & Reicher 1987). We approach intergroup behavior as a social construction process in which the social context influences one's perception of the self and others as representatives of certain social categories, distinguishing "us" from "them" (Turner et al., 1994). It is important to gain knowledge on online behavior around proanorexia that is mainly an Internet-based phenomenon and attracts particularly young women. This kind of knowledge may help to understand how online group distinctions and social categorizations on popular social media platforms may affect the attractivity of risky in-groups among young people.

Our research questions are:

1. How are proanas categorized as a deviant out-group?
2. How do proanas defend their in-group from outsiders' criticism?

DATA AND METHODS

Data Collection

Our data consist of user comments on proanorexia-related videos on YouTube's most popular proanorexia channels. During October 15 - 29, 2014, 25 of the most popular proanorexia user channels on YouTube were selected using the search word "pro-ana." The popularity of the channels was based on the video views and channel subscriptions. All the chosen channels included videos that promoted anorexia and had been commented on during the previous 24 months. The selected 25 YouTube channels included a total of 214 videos. User comments on those videos were then gathered systematically with a web crawler using the YouTube Data Application Programming Interface (YouTube, 2016). Two independent coders checked all the videos available on these channels and excluded the videos that did not concern proanorexia. The interrater agreement was 94.76% (Cohen's $\kappa = .88$) (Oksanen et al., 2015). The final data consisted of 2,122 comments on 133 proanorexia-related videos containing only comments to videos that the coders had mutually marked as relating to proanorexia.

All of the channel proprietors were identified as having a positive stance on anorexia. Twenty-four of the 25 channel proprietors were identified as women, and only one channel did not reveal any gender identity. Videos included thinspiration videos of extremely thin women and users' own video blogs in which they talked about their dieting progress, shared extreme weight-loss tips, and presented their bodies to the camera. As we focus on public reactions to proanorexia more generally, we have not distinguished between comments on different genres such as thinspiration videos or video blogs in our analysis.

We have carefully considered ethical guidelines of the Internet research (see Markhan & Buchanan, 2012) before conducting this research. All the videos and comments were publicly accessible on YouTube. We do not see that our research would inflict any harm to the proana individuals or commenters. Also, we have focused on public reactions in general, not on the particular individuals. To respect privacy matters, we do not identify video proprietors or commenters, and all user names have been excluded from the data. The comment extracts are identified only by reference to their data file numbers (presented in square brackets). All the extracts are identical to the data, including spelling and grammar errors. Extracts that are parts of longer comments are signalled with ellipses.

Membership Categorization Analysis

To examine intergroup behavior and categorization, we analyzed the comment data with tools of membership categorization analysis (MCA). MCA, which was originally developed by Harvey Sacks, draws from the ethnomethodological tradition in order to examine interactional and textual practices (Stokoe, 2012). MCA is a method to examine categories and descriptions (that also serve as identities) that refer to a certain person or group (Sacks, 1992; Schegloff, 2007; Silverman, 1993). In MCA, categorization is seen as an interactional activity in which the focus is the category (or identity) that is invoked in a particular occasion and the kinds of implications these category selections have (Jayyusi 1991). An individual can be categorized, for example, by gender, age, occupation, or appearance, and all these categories are loaded with different kinds of category-bound activities and attributes that we expect to be fulfilled in different situations (Stokoe, 2012). Categories that are closely related to each other, such as "baby," "mother," and "father", are organised into category collections, in this case "family" (Schegloff, 2007).

Categories and their collections include shared cultural common-sense knowledge that enables people to orient themselves in relation to those categories and their attributes in a relatively similar manner; that is, to "know" what category members are like, what kinds of attributes they have, and how they are related to each other (Sacks, 1992; Shegloff, 2007). This knowledge contains category-bound attributes and activities that serve as a resource to identify the existence of a particular category, even when that category is not explicitly mentioned (Sacks, 1992; Schegloff, 2007). From the description "The X cried. The Y picked it up," we are likely to recognize "X" as the baby and "Y" as the baby's mother (or parent), although these identities are not explicitly mentioned (Silverman, 1993). This is possible because, in our cultural knowledge, crying is a category-bound activity of the baby and the attribute of the mother is to take care of the baby. Although interpretations of categories are not always correct, this example reveals the cultural power of category knowledge in making sense of the world.

Categorizations are not just neutral descriptions; instead, there is always a moral dimension in categorizing people, both self and others, with different labels (Jayyusi, 1984, 1991). In terms of self-categorization, categories and their perceived attributes can be used as entitlements for various kinds of acts and to undermine others (Potter, 1996). Categorization also serves as a political and rhetorical strategy to justify one's stance (Goodman & Speer, 2007). Moreover, failing to fulfil expectations of a certain category is often perceived as morally punishable (Jayyusi, 1991). Accounts are needed, especially in situations where a person is perceived as behaving in a way that deviates from normative, that is, culturally acknowledged moral behavior.

In earlier studies concerning risky health behavior, MCA has been successfully applied to studying interaction and social categorization in online settings (Giles, 2006; Smithson et al., 2011; Stommel & Koole,

2010). Although MCA is often used as a co-method with Sack's tradition of conversation analysis (CA; e.g., Goodman & Speer, 2007; Stommel & Koole, 2010), the analytical focus in MCA is not as strictly based on sequential matters, and it is thus possible to apply to more diverse textual and interactional settings (see Giles, 2006; Stokoe, 2012).

As the focus of our analysis is on social categorization between groups, the results do not represent all comments from our data. For example, the comments that did not concern proanorexia directly (e.g., "I love this song!") were excluded from the analysis. Instead, in order to examine intergroup categorization between "proanas" and "outsiders," we focused on the comments with a reference to one's membership category (i.e., self-category) in relation to proanorexia (i.e., those who glamorize anorexia, "proanas," and those who do not glamorize anorexia, "outsiders") and a stance on proanorexia. While self-categories were not always explicitly mentioned, they could be identified with category-bound attributes (see Sacks, 1992; Schegloff, 2007). For example, if a commenter strongly criticized the anorexic body and message of the video, we took it as an "outsider," whereas, if a commenter described the anorexic body as beautiful and worth achieving, we took it as "proana." With MCA, we examine what kinds of attributes are given to proanas and what kinds of category distinctions are made in order to dismiss them and perceive them to be deviant as well as how those identifying as proanas defend their in-group identity from this criticism.

RESULTS

Doing Deviance: Dismissing the Proana Identity

In the first section of analysis, we examine how those identifying as outsiders distinguish themselves from proanas. We focus on what kinds of attributes are given to proanas and how categorizations of self and others work as entitlements to undermine proanas as a perceived out-group.

Distinguishing "Anorexic" from "Proana"

A large portion of the critical comments in our data are from those who claim to have experience with eating disorders. Thus, they act as entitled authorities to describe why promoting anorexia is wrong. The dual distinction between conflicting categories of "proana" and those who express suffering from eating disorders is illustrated in the following extract where the commenter explicitly wishes to distinguish oneself from the former category:

> . . . But I'M NOT PRO ANA! I've just had (and still now) problem with anorexia and bulimia. [78]

Distinguishing oneself from the negatively perceived category "proana" serves as normalizing the category membership of having "problem with anorexia and bulimia." The following extracts also show how the self-category (individual with eating disorder) is used as a justification for categorizing proanas as a deviant out-group that differs from "us," or people suffering from eating disorders. Commenters distinguish themselves from the negative attributes of proanas, such as "encouraging people to kill themselves":

> these things are sick. i suffer ana, but i would NEVER make one of these videos. you are encouraging people to kill theirselves. [1164]

> i cant believe this i almost died having a eating disorder and this is put up F#@$! This. [249]

However, the analysis of the data also shows that proanas can be categorized without such a strict group distinction. Even though the following extracts also categorize proanorexia as problematic and dangerous, it is made with the mention of two sides of eating disorders, and there is an implicit option of moving between these two groups (compare Stommel & Koole, 2010). Proanas are seen more as moving towards a wrong direction, and self-categories such as "recoverer" are used as a rhetorical device to justify one's stance:

> this is dangerous, what you're doing here. It's not a game. As a recoverer, take it from me. I've seen both sides. [63]

> I am very curious and not trying to be rude but why are you posting "pro ana/mia" videos? In doing this you are actively helping others get sicker. It is helping others hurt themselves. I personally don't think that is okay to do. I am just wondering why you take part in it. I have an eating disorder myself and just don't seem to understand this side of things. [1790]

> You are sick and you need help! i know this from personal experience. this disease WILL KILL YOU! don't think it won't, don't think you are in control. i know it sucks but you will end up killing yourself. [638]

As anorexia is categorized as a "disease" and something that "can kill," proanas are categorized as "sick" and in need of help. The following extracts show that even without an explicit self-category, anorexia is categorized as belonging to a category collection of deadly disorders, which makes proanas' category-bound activity of promoting it questionable:

> pro ana? Are you stupid . . . Thats not a diet, thats a disorder. [225]

> you sick fucks are adoring a serious medical condition??? . . . to praise ones own sickness and weakness is terribly sad . . . [944]

> why would you be "pro ana" . . . you want to be for something that kills people?? That's like saying . . . can i be "pro aids??" weird. [1076]

In sum, anorexia is categorized as an unwanted disorder that has negative and dangerous implications for health. Proanas become categorized as a problematic group that has false thoughts about anorexia, and they are seen to threaten the culturally shared knowledge that disorders are something negative that individuals suffer from. Those self-categorizing as former anorexics use their experience to entitle their criticism as a warning as they claim to understand the reality of anorexia better nowadays, whereas those without an explicit self-category construct anorexia as belonging to a category collection of disorders as factual knowledge.

Proanas as Failed Women

As proanorexia is a predominantly female phenomenon, the category "woman" and its normative attributes, especially beauty, are essential in debates on proanorexia. Although proanorexic individuals admire extremely skinny bodies, outsiders tend to see them as unattractive and unhealthy (see also Marcus, 2016). In some criticizing comments from outsiders, commenters identify themselves as men. Because categories "woman" and "man" are mutually related, the self-category "man" is used as a rhetorical device to justify what is expected from the category "woman." An anorexic woman is constructed as undesirable because extreme thinness challenges the ideal female body in the eyes of men and is seen as a deviant attribute of womanhood:

> anorexia looks DISGUSTING! it is in no way attractive (coming from a guy, and every guy I've asked agrees with me) . . . [591]

> . . . in my opinion along with other men who will agree with me that anorexia is just wrong women who smell like vomit is wrong, women with hair loss is wrong, women with no teeth is wrong . . . [269]

Even without an explicit self-category, anorexic attributes are defined in relation to the categories "girl" and "woman" and to their normative attributes, such as naturality and healthiness. These can be interpreted to come from those who position themselves into the self-category "real women" or at least "we who know what is needed to be a real woman." Categories such as "kid" and "freak" are juxtaposed with proanas, constructing proanas as deviating from what is expected as being an adequate woman:

> ew that's not hot, thats ugly!! You need to put on weight, you look like a little kid. [216]

> ew, nasty unhealthy anorexic freaks. girls thats not the type of body any one should want. [5]

Even though proanas are criticised for their extreme thinness, the following extracts reveal that thinness is also recognized as a normative attribute of beauty. However, there are two contrasting categories that are both based on an attribute of thinness: proanas with grotesque and skeletal appearance, and thin people who are normal, healthy, and attractive. This distinction constructs proanas as a deviant out-group:

> Im all for being toned and thin. But i do NOT believe in doing it with anorexia or bulimia . . . [441]

> yes its nice to be thin but damn you people just cross the line for real . . . [2001]

> ehh sorry. i like thinspo and it inspires me but i dont want to be thin enough to look like a skeleton. just to look hot. [1978]

In sum, proanas become categorized as failed women, as they are perceived as not fulfilling the adequate attributes of womanhood. While criticism is aimed at proanas as individuals, the cultural ideal of a thin body is celebrated and proanas are seen as crossing the line between acceptable and unacceptable thinness. Thus, anorexic thinness is seen as challenging the pressure to conform to Western beauty standards, which constructs proanas as a deviant out-group of women with questionable beauty ideals.

Proanas as Guilty Malefactors

As proanorexia is advocated in YouTube via videos, the video uploaders become constructed as guilty and even inhuman malefactors who spread harmful material to others. In the following comments, self-categorizations are not explicitly mentioned but can be interpreted as a wider self-category of "moral online users" who criticize spreading harmful content online:

> Making these videos is a CRIME against humanity. It should be a punishable offense with PRISON time. They encourage vulnerable young girls to commit slow suicide... it ruins lives and hurts many people . . . [1986]

> . . . you know as well as anyone, that someone who promotes this evil shit is just as guilty as any criminal who kills someone with their own hands! Supporting and promoting a wicked problem like EDs is pure rotten behavior and should be punished! [1021]

> People that post this kind of stuff are as bad as murderers. You should be thrown into jail and starved. [1084]

Proanas are categorized as belonging to the same category collection of guilty and dangerous people such as "criminals" and "murderers" who deserve punishment for their deviant and antisocial actions. They are seen to share dangerous influences, especially towards young girls, who are constructed as victims. Categorizing eating disorders as a "wicked problem" and promoting them as a "crime" construct the category of proanas as a deviant out-group.

At its most extreme, group comparison culminates in dehumanizing comments, which dismiss and deny the human value of proanas. Although self-category is not explicitly mentioned, the extracts illustrate an extreme group distinction to "us" as human and moral individuals and "them" as a deviant out-group:

. . . you are a horrible person for condoning anorexia and deserve to be stoned to death and then chucked into a volcano . . . [1893]

HOW DARE YOU PUBLISH THIS! the net hates you I hope you die from your obsession. Cause truning normal KIDS into pro ana kids it diservs painful death. [1015]

Pro anorexics who try to influence others to join in their delusional ideal of beauty are faggots. If you've got this problem, by all means talk about it to people but if you try to get them to do the same like this video is encouraging, then you deserve to die . . . [2024]

The activity of spreading proanorexia material is seen as a threat against the common good that justifies dehumanization. Proanas become categorized as a fundamentally distinct out-group with unhuman attributes such as "horrible" and "evil." In extract 2024, however, the commenter makes a distinction between two out-groups of proanas: those who only have the "problem" and those who encourage others. The commenter suggests that the normative activity of proanas (or individuals with anorexia) is to seek help for their "problem," while counter-normative and deviant activity is to encourage others. These differing categorizations suggest that two groups of proanas should also be treated differently, as only those who spread their ideals to others are seen as a problematic out-group that deserve punishment.

In addition to spreading dangerous material to other people, deviant thoughts are construed as differing from what is seen as culturally acceptable human activity, which serves as distinguishing proanas from other people and justifying dehumanization:

I feel sorry for you and your small brain. Don't ever have kids, they will probably end up like a low life peice of shit like you . . . [2011]

when some girls and even some guys are dumb enough to think that the better way to lose body fat (and they are never satisfied with the result) is to just stop eating, or fake a eat to then vomit it, than it's better that this loosers die feeling a lot of pain and very slowy. [1460]

In sum, proanas become categorized as guilty malefactors who are harmful to others and responsible for their actions, which underlines their perceived deviance (see Scott & Lyman 1970). The antisocial action of spreading proanorexic material is constructed as worthy punishment, and proanas become categorized as a fundamentally distinct out-group that differs from the whole human race. Wishing extreme punishment and even death for perceived out-group members can be considered a blatant and absolute form of dehumanization, in which the out-group is seen as lacking humanity outright (Haslam & Loughnan, 2014), even going so far as to see death as a justified punishment for perceived deviant behavior and thoughts.

Undoing Deviance: Defending the Proana Identity

In the second section of the analysis, we examine how those identifying as "proana" defend and normalize their identity category from outsiders' criticism. We are interested in what kinds of accounts they offer for their perceived deviant actions and how they wish to maintain positive social identity with group differentiation.

Accounts for Deviant Behavior and Identity

Because of the public stigma of eating disorders, those identifying as proanas have an accountability to justify their behavior that is often perceived as deviant by outsiders. This includes defending the proana identity and its attributes such as extreme thinness. The following extracts reveal what kinds of positive attributes are attached to proana identity:

Because, Its Not A Disorder. Its Perfection . . . [1006]

. . . I started as a way of control, of making my body mine after someone tried to take it from me. I wanted to be pure, clean, empty, delicate, floating. Complete control of what went into my body. The way

for me to monitor how in control I was was to weigh myself . . . So I want
to be thin, because thin is control, delicacy, beauty and perfection. [2059]

being too skinny is closer to what nature intended us to be. nature
never intended us to be fat and eat refined carbs and sit all day on the
computer. so yay to thin! [1641]

Proanorexia is defined with attributes such as "perfection," "willpower,"
"beauty," and "control," which is also a rhetorical device to distinguish
proanorexia from the negative category collection of disorders. In extract
1641, thinness is also categorized as something natural, healthy, and worth
achieving compared to its counterpart, fatness. These categorizations serve
as normalizing deviance and challenging the public negativity of
proanorexia and proana identity.

In some comments from those self-categorizing as proana, it is
considered a deviant but also misunderstood identity. The following extract
reveals how deviance is resisted by categorizing an eating disorder as an
active agent that possesses its victim, which serves as a rhetorical device and
an account for proana identity:

what people don't realize is that eds take control of you. Don't get me
wrong; i am 100% pro ana and think bones are beautiful but i know that
that is a distorted truth and ''m pretty sure that what i see in the mirror isn't
the truth but i keep losing weight:' (it's a sick vicious cycle that we have
no control over. it does take over your life. It's something that i want to get
away from so badly but it's already embedded into me that i can't find
beauty in anything that isn't bone. [1472]

The commenter explicitly uses the self-category "proana" but also
recognizes the perceived deviant and distorted attributes that are often
culturally category-bound to eating-disordered individuals. People with
eating disorders are implicitly categorized as victims, whereas an eating
disorder is an active agent and a guilty malefactor. Thus, "proana" is defined
as an identity-based category in which category-bound attributes include
both valuing extreme thinness and being a victim of a disorder. This kind of

victim speech also challenges the generally used definition of proanorexia as a lifestyle choice.

Distinguishing "Us" from "Outsiders"

In order to maintain a positive social identity when their in-group identity is threatened by outsiders, those identifying as proanas defend their in-group with strict group distinction. In the following extract, "thin people" are contrasted with "fat people," constructing the former category as superior compared to the latter that is perceived as harmful and blameworthy:

> Blame every thing and everyone but yourselves? Fat people are the cause. Little girls look at these hulking beef bags and they get traumatized by what they see. . . . Thin women really are far superior to fatties. This anti ANA stuff needs to stop. 200 people die from it each year compared to 400,000 who die from obesity. Fat people suck! [2056]

Group distinction is also explicit in the following extracts, where the out-group of hateful outsiders, "haters," is categorized as a deviant and antisocial group that differs from "us":

> . . . if you guys who areextremely opposed to what we do, why are you watching videos like this? . . . if you dont like what you see, stop watching. [1307]

> if your not pro ana. then stop watching this and LEAVING RETARTED COMMENTS. becuase you guys ovbiously dont understand . . . [1785]

> why are you haters watching this if you dont support/like it . . . leave us alone! [1049]

Those self-categorizing as proana defend their identity by differentiating their in-group positively from the perceived out-group. The out-group of "haters" is constructed as ignorant and hostile people whose actions are questionable. Perceived hostility from outsiders may even strengthen the group boundaries and desire to attach to one's own in-group, as in extract 1049, where the commenter asks "haters" to leave "us" alone.

DISCUSSION

This chapter examined social categorization and group distinction in the comments on proanorexia videos on YouTube. The commenters positioned themselves in various categories in relation to proanorexia and proanas, such as (recovering) anorexics, healthy people, "real" women, men, or moral online users in general. These self-categorizations can be approached as flexible definitions of the individual and a rhetorical device that reflect a particular context (Turner et al., 1994). Proanas were depicted as false anorexics, failed women, criminals, and even inhuman agents who advocate harm and victimize other users. In order to defend their identity from outsiders' criticism, those identifying as proanas gave accounts of their perceived deviant actions by normalizing their behavior and attaching positive attributes to their in-group in relation to perceived out-groups, such as "fat people" and "haters" (compare Giles, 2006; Marcus, 2016). Dealing with haters was executed with strict group distinction, such as categorizing them as a hostile and antisocial out-group. These discursive actions and group comparisons can be interpreted as attempts to maintain positive social identity and to boost self-enhancement (Tajfel & Turner, 1979).

Hostility in our data illustrates the normative nature of offensive communication on the Internet and especially YouTube (Moor et al., 2010), as anonymity is connected to stronger group polarization (Sia et al., 2002) and, according to SIDE, identifying more strongly to contextually relevant social identities (Postmes et al., 2001; Reicher et al., 1995; Spears et al., 2002). This, in turn, tends to intensify reactions to other groups (Billig, 2002). This may be particularly true in the case of reactions to counter-normative online groups such as proanas, especially in the context of YouTube, where interaction is based on a relatively high anonymity (see Oksanen et al., 2014). Hostile categorization of proanas on public social media platforms, like YouTube, construct and normalize deviant attributes towards eating disorder-affected individuals, and strict group distinctions may further unite the harm-advocating proanorexia communities (see also Knapton, 2013).

Our results also demonstrated supportive understanding and warnings from those self-categorizing themselves as having experience with eating disorders. The beneficial role of peer support in terms of a shared recovery-oriented social identity is acknowledged in a study concerning eating disorder support groups online (McNamara & Parsons, 2016), but, according to our results, YouTube is not necessarily a fruitful platform for forming a shared identity. Thus, it is important to understand the group dynamics in a particular social media platform, as using online communities and sites related to eating disorders can reinforce but also undermine the effects of clinical interventions (see also Yom-Tov et al., 2012). As young people are active online users and prefer Internet as a help source for various health-related problems (Ali et al., 2015), it is crucial to gain understanding of ways to utilize recovery-oriented online support and interventions.

From the theoretical and methodological points of view, our analysis revealed that intergroup behavior in the context of YouTube contains rich identity work. Analyzing CMC on social media platforms benefits from combining theoretical approaches of intergroup behavior with discursive tools on identity practices. Social media platforms like YouTube form a special kind of interactional context, which challenges the original theories of intergroup behavior (Moor et al., 2010). As such, in the context of social media, intergroup behavior must be approached from a wider perspective than theories were originally developed to achieve. The SIDE model drawing from the tradition of SIT is one example of trying to examine the role of anonymity in group processes in CMC (Lea et al., 2001; Reicher et al., 1995; Spears et al., 2002), but both SIT and SIDE would benefit from applying a more discursive approach to identity practices, especially in the context of social media (see also Lamerichs & Te Molder, 2003).

Future studies should aim to scrutinize the different levels of anonymity and its influence on intergroup communication on various social media platforms (see also Keipi, 2017). In addition, the concept of dehumanization must be elaborated upon and extended on public social media platforms. This kind of approach would be vital in examining what Billig (2002) noted as lacking in SIT: elaborating the continuum between "ordinary" and "abnormal" forms of social categorization in terms of dehumanization towards the out-group (p. 181). In the context of the Internet, anonymity, pseudonymity and hostility constitute an even greater challenge to this elaboration, as degrading and threatening out-group categorization has become quite an "ordinary" form of communication on different social media platforms (Foxman and Wolf, 2013).

As we examined categorizations only in textual practices in naturally occurring online data, we cannot test the full social identity process. However, the social identity approach as a starting point formulated a fruitful ground for examining social identities in discursive action online (see also Lamerichs and Te Molder, 2003). Our analysis was also only focused on video comments on YouTube, and the results are not representative of all proanorexia discussions online. However, we feel that this chapter has shed light on public reactions to the proanorexia phenomenon and has contributed to CMC studies in terms of intergroup behavior and group dynamics on social media, particularly on YouTube.

The category "proana" is constructed on YouTube as a negative identity with deviant attributes such as grotesque appearance, harmful activity, and delusional thoughts. People seeking and promoting ways to achieve an anorexic state are perceived as a deviant group who are distinguished from the category of individuals suffering from an eating disorder. Therefore, the proana identity is not only carrying the stigma of anorexia and eating disorders in general but also, and maybe even more importantly, the deviance of *promoting* a stigmatized illness (see also Easter, 2012). Whereas those identifying as proanas wish to defend their identity from outsiders' criticism, public hostility can be seen as constructing and maintaining deviance towards the phenomenon and the individuals advocating it, which may serve as strengthening the group boundaries and uniting the in-group of proanas. These findings give an important insight to health professionals working with young people with eating disorders.

ACKNOWLEDGMENTS

We would like to thank Dr. David Garcia (Complexity Science Hub Vienna and Medical University of Vienna) for collaboration on data collection.

REFERENCES

Adler, P. A. & Adler, P. (2008). The cyber worlds of self-injurers: Deviant communities, relationships, and selves. *Symbolic Interaction, 31*(1), 33–56. doi: 10.1525/si.2008.31.1.33.

Ali, K., Farrer, L., Gulliver, A. & Griffiths, K. M. (2015). Online peer-to-peer support for young people with mental health problems: a systematic review. *JMIR mental health, 2*(2). doi: 10.2196/ mental.4418.

Bates, C. F. (2015). 'I am a waste of breath, of space, of time': Metaphors of self in a pro-anorexia group. *Qualitative Health Research, 25,* 189–204. doi: 10.1177/1049732314550004.

Becker, H. (1963). *Outsiders: Studies in the sociology of deviance.* New York, NY: Free Press.

Billig, M. (2002). Henri Tajfel's 'cognitive aspects of prejudice' and the psychology of bigotry. *British Journal of Social Psychology, 41*(2), 71–188. doi: 10.1348/014466602760060165.

Boero, N. & Pascoe, C. J. (2012). Pro-anorexia communities and online interaction: Bringing the pro-ana body online. *Body & Society, 18*(2), 27–57. doi: 10.1177/1357034X12440827.

Borzekowski, D. L., Schenk, S., Wilson, J. L. & Peebles, R. (2010). e-Ana and e-Mia: A content analysis of pro-eating disorder web sites.

American Journal of Public Health, 100(8), 1526. doi: 10.2105/AJPH.2009.172700.

Brotsky, S. R. & Giles, D. (2007). Inside the "pro-ana" community: A covert online participant observation. *Eating Disorders, 15*(2), 93–109. doi: 10.1080/10640260701190600.

Casilli, A. A., Tubaro, P. & Araya, P. (2012). Ten years of Ana: Lessons from a transdisciplinary body of literature on online pro-eating disorder websites. *Social Science Information, 51*(1), 120–139. doi: 10.1177/0539018411425880.

Conrad, P. & Rondini, A. (2010). The Internet and medicalization: Reshaping the global body and illness. In E. Ettorre (Ed.), *Culture, bodies and the sociology of health,* (pp. 107–120). Farnham: Ashgate.

Csipke, E. & Horne, O. (2007). Pro-eating disorder websites: Users' opinions. *European Eating Disorders Review, 15*(3), 196–206. doi: 10.1002/erv.789.

Easter, M. M. (2012). "Not all my fault": Genetics, stigma, and personal responsibility for women with eating disorders. *Social Science & Medicine, 75*(8), 1408–1416. doi: 10.1016/j.socscimed.2012.05.042.

Fairburn, C. G. & Harrison, P. J. (2003). Eating disorders. *The Lancet, 361*(9355), 407–416. doi: 10.1016/S0140-6736(03)12378-1.

Fox, N., Ward, K. & O'Rourke, A. (2005). Pro-anorexia, weight-loss drugs and the internet: an 'anti-recovery' explanatory model of anorexia. *Sociology of Health & Illness, 27*(7), 944-971. doi: 10.1111/j.1467-9566.2005.00465.x.

Foxman, A. H. & Wolf, C. (2013). *Viral hate: Containing its spread on the Internet.* New York, NY: Palgrave MacMillan.

Giles, D. (2006). Constructing identities in cyberspace: The case of eating disorders. *British Journal of Social Psychology, 45*(3), 463–477. doi: 10.1348/014466605X53596.

Goffman, E. (1963). *Stigma: Notes on the management of spoiled identity.* New Jersey: Prentice-Hall.

Goode, E. (2015). *Deviant behavior.* London: Routledge.

Goodman, S. & Speer, S. A. (2007). Category use in the construction of asylum seekers. *Critical Discourse Studies, 4*(2), 165–185. doi: 10.1080/17405900701464832.

Haslam, N. (2006). Dehumanization: An integrative review. *Personality and Social Psychology Review, 10*(3), 252–264. doi: 10.1207/s15327957 pspr1003_4.

Haslam, N. & Loughnan, S. (2014). Dehumanization and infrahumanization. *Annual Review of Psychology, 65,* 399–423. doi: 10.1146/annurev-psych-010213-115045.

Jayyusi, L. (1984). *Categorization and the moral order.* Boston, MA: Routledge & Kegan Paul.

Jayyusi, L. (1991). Values and moral judgement: Communicative praxis as a moral order. In G. Button (Ed.), *Ethnomethodology and the human sciences* (pp. 227–251). Cambridge: University Press.

Keipi, T. (2017). Relatedness Online: An Analysis of Youth Narratives Concerning the Effects of Internet Anonymity. *Young, 26*(2), 91–107. doi: 10.1177/1103308817715142.

Knapton, O. (2013). Pro-anorexia: Extensions of ingrained concepts. *Discourse and Society, 24,* 461–477. doi: 10.1177/0957926513482067.

Lamerichs, J. & Te Molder, H. F. (2003). Computer-mediated communication: From a cognitive to a discursive model. *New Media & Society, 5*(4), 451–473. doi: 10.1177/146144480354001.

Lea, M., Spears, R. & de Groot, D. (2001). Knowing me, knowing you: Anonymity effects on social identity processes within groups. *Personality and Social Psychology Bulletin, 27*(5), 526–537. doi: 10.1177/0146167201275002.

Marcus, S. R. (2016). Thinspiration vs. thicksperation: Comparing pro-anorexic and fat acceptance image posts on a photo-sharing site. *Cyberpsychology, 10*(2), article 5. doi: 10.5817/CP2016-2-5.

Markham, A. N. & Buchanan, E. (2012). *Ethical Decision-Making and Internet Research: Recommendations from the AoIR Ethics Working Committee* (Version 2.0). Retrieved from https://aoir.org/ reports/ ethics2.pdf.

McNamara, N. & Parsons, H. (2016). 'Everyone here wants everyone else to get better': The role of social identity in eating disorder recovery. *British Journal of Social Psychology, 55,* 662–680. doi: 10.1111/ bjso.12161.

Mond, J. M., Robertson-Smith, G. & Vetere, A. (2006). Stigma and eating disorders: Is there evidence of negative attitudes towards anorexia nervosa among women in the community? *Journal of Mental Health, 15*(5), 519–532. doi: 10.1080/09638230600902559.

Moor, P. J., Heuvelman, A. & Verleur, R. (2010). Flaming on YouTube. *Computers in Human Behavior, 26*(6), 1536–1546. doi: 10.1016/ j.chb.2010.05.023.

Norris, M. L., Boydell, K. M., Pinhas, L. & Katzman, D. K. (2006). Ana and the Internet: A review of pro-anorexia websites. *International Journal of Eating Disorders, 39*(6), 443–447. doi: 10.1002/eat.20305.

Oksanen, A., Hawdon, J. & Räsänen, P. (2014). Glamorizing rampage online: School shooting fan communities on YouTube. *Technology in Society, 39,* 55–67. doi: 10.1016/j.techsoc.2014.08.001.

Oksanen, A., Garcia, D., Sirola, A., Näsi, M., Kaakinen, M., Keipi, T. & Räsänen, P. (2015). Pro-anorexia and anti-pro-anorexia videos on YouTube: Sentiment analysis of user responses. *Journal of Medical Internet Research, 17*(11). doi: 10.2196/jmir.5007.

Oksanen, A., Garcia, D. & Räsänen, P. (2016). Proanorexia communities on social media. *Pediatrics, 137*(1), e20153372. doi: 10.1542/peds.2015-3372.

Park, M., Sun, Y. & McLaughlin, M. L. (2017). Social media propagation of content promoting risky health behavior. *Cyberpsychology, Behavior, and Social Networking, 20*(5), 278–285. doi: 10.1089/ cyber.2016.0698.

Postmes, T., Spears, R., Sakhel, K. & de Groot, D. (2001). Social influence in computer-mediated communication: The effects of anonymity on group behavior. *Personality and Social Psychology Bulletin, 27*(10), 1245–1254. doi: 10.1177/0146167201271001.

Potter, J. (1996). *Representing reality: Discourse, rhetoric and social construction.* London: Sage.

Potter, J. & Reicher, S. (1987). Discourses of community and conflict: The organization of social categories in accounts of a 'riot'. *British Journal of Social Psychology, 26*(1), 25–40. doi: 10.1111/j.2044-8309.1987. tb00758.x.

Reicher, S. D., Spears, R. & Postmes, T. (1995). A social identity model of deindividuation phenomena. *European Review of Social Psychology, 6*(1), 161–198. doi: 10.1080/14792779443000049.

Rich, E. (2006). Anorexic dis (connection): managing anorexia as an illness and an identity. *Sociology of Health & Illness, 28*(3), 284-305. doi: 10.1111/j.1467-9566.2006.00493.x.

Rodgers, R. F., Lowy, A. S., Halperin, D. M. & Franko, D. L. (2016). A Meta-Analysis Examining the Influence of Pro-Eating Disorder Websites on Body Image and Eating Pathology. *European Eating Disorders Review, 24*(1), 3–8. doi: 10.1002/erv.2390.

Sacks, H. (1992). *Lectures on conversation,* (Vol. *1*). Oxford: Blackwell.

Schegloff, E. A. (2007). A tutorial on membership categorization. *Journal of Pragmatics, 39*(3), 462–482. doi: 10.1016/j.pragma.2006.07.007.

Scott, M. B. & Lyman, S. M. (1970). Accounts, deviance and social order. In J. D. Douglas (Ed.), *Deviance and respectability: The social construction of moral meanings,* (pp. 89–119). New York & London: Basic Books.

Sia, C. L., Tan, B. C. & Wei, K. K. (2002). Group polarization and computer-mediated communication: Effects of communication cues, social presence, and anonymity. *Information Systems Research, 13*(1), 70–90. *doi*: 10.1287/isre.13.1.70.92.

Silverman, D. (1993). *Interpreting qualitative data: Strategies for analyzing talk, text and interaction.* London: Sage.

Smink, F. R., Van Hoeken, D. & Hoek, W. H. (2012). Epidemiology of eating disorders: Incidence, prevalence and mortality rates. *Current Psychiatry Reports, 14*(4), 406–414. doi: 10.1007/s11920-012-0282-y.

Smithson, J., Sharkey, S., Hewis, E., Jones, R. B., Emmens, T., Ford, T. & Owens, C. (2011). Membership and boundary maintenance on an online self-harm forum. *Qualitative Health Research, 21*(11), 1567–1575. doi: 10.1177/1049732311413784.

Spears, R., Postmes, T., Lea, M. & Wolbert, A. (2002). When are net effects gross products? The power of influence and the influence of power in computer-mediated communication. *Journal of Social Issues, 58*(1), 91–107. doi: 10.1111/1540-4560.00250.

Stewart, M. C., Keel, P. K. & Schiavo, R. S. (2006). Stigmatization of anorexia nervosa. *International Journal of Eating Disorders, 39*(4), 320–325. doi: 10.1002/eat.20262.

Stokoe, E. (2012). Moving forward with membership categorization analysis: Methods for systematic analysis. *Discourse Studies, 14*(3), 277–303. doi: 10.1177/1461445612441534.

Stommel, W. & Koole, T. (2010). The online support group as a community: A micro-analysis of the interaction with a new member. *Discourse Studies, 12*(3), 357–378.doi: 10.1177/1461445609358518.

Syed-Abdul, S., Fernandez-Luque, L., Jian, W. S., Li, Y. C., Crain, S., Hsu, M. H. & Liou, D. M. (2013). Misleading health-related information promoted through video-based social media: Anorexia on YouTube. *Journal of Medical Internet Research, 15*(2), 137–149. doi: 10.2196/jmir.2237.

Tajfel, H. (1978). Interindividual behavior and intergroup behavior. In H. Tajfe (Ed.), *Differentiation between groups: Studies in the social psychology of intergroup relations,* (pp. 27–60). London: Academic Press.

Tajfel, H. (1981). *Human groups and social categories: Studies in social psychology.* Cambridge: Cambridge University Press.

Tajfel, H., Billig, M. G., Bundy, R. P. & Flament, C. (1971). Social categorization and intergroup behavior. *European Journal of Social Psychology, 1*(2), 149–178. doi: 10.1002/ejsp.2420010202.

Tajfel, H. & Turner, J. C. (1979). An integrative theory of intergroup conflict. In W. G. Austin & S. Worchel (Eds.), *The social psychology of intergroup relations,* (pp. 33–47). Monterey, CA: Brooks Cole.

Tong, S. T., Heinemann-Lafave, D., Jeon, J., Kolodziej-Smith, R. & Warshay, N. (2013). The use of pro-ana blogs for online social support. *Eating Disorders, 21*(5), 408–422. doi: 10.1080/10640266.2013. 827538.

Turner, J. C. (1985). Social categorization and the self-concept: A social cognitive theory of group behavior. In E. J. Lawler (Ed.), *Advances in group processes: Theory and research,* (vol. 2), (pp. 77–122). Greenwich, CT: JAI.

Turner, J. C., Hogg, M. A., Oakes, P. J., Reicher, S. D. & Wetherell, M. S. (1987). *Rediscovering the social group: A self-categorization theory.* Oxford: Blackwell.

Turner, J. C., Oakes, P. J., Haslam, S. A. & McGarty, C. (1994). Self and collective: Cognition and social context. *Personality and Social Psychology Bulletin, 20,* 454–463. doi: 10.1177/0146167294205002.

Turner, J. C. & Reynolds, K. J. (2010). The story of social identity. In T. Postmes & N. R. Branscombe (Eds.), *Rediscovering social identity,* (pp. 13–32). New York, NY: Psychology Press.

Yeshua-Katz, D. & Martins, N. (2013). Communicating stigma: The pro-ana paradox. *Health Communication, 28*(5), 499–508. doi: 10.1080/10410236.2012.699889.

Yom-Tov, E., Fernandez-Luque, L., Weber, I. & Crain, S. P. (2012). Pro-anorexia and pro-recovery photo sharing: a tale of two warring tribes. *Journal of Medical Internet Research, 14*(6). doi: 10.2196/jmir.2239.

YouTube. (2016). *Data API.* Retrieved from https://developers.google.com/youtube/v3/docs/.

In: Digital Technology   ISBN: 978-1-53616-438-1
Editor: Michelle F. Wright   © 2019 Nova Science Publishers, Inc.

Chapter 12

TECHNOLOGY AS SKIN

Joan Ann Swanson, PhD*
Skidmore College, Saratoga Springs, NY, US

ABSTRACT

Many adolescents and emerging adults today experience technology ubiquitously, which is affecting their life choices, thoughts patterns and behaviors. This chapter explores a view of technology which is similar to that of skin; an integrated source of protection, regulation, and communication. Additionally, like skin, which is often taken for granted, adolescents and emerging adults do not recognize the significance of technology in their lives even though it impacts their identity development, thinking processes, and patterns for daily functioning. The analysis and discussion in this chapter contribute to a theoretical understanding of adolescent and emerging adult perspectives on technology in their lives.

Keywords: emerging adults, technology, developmental theory, identity development

---

* Corresponding Author's E-mail: jswanson@skidmore.edu.

INTRODUCTION

This chapter explores the relationship adolescents and emerging adults have with technology. Developmental theorists such as Erik Erikson (1968) and James Marcia (1980) emphasized the importance of identity exploration in this time period. More recent work proposes that identity exploration is a key developmental task that must be wrestled with in a period called emerging adulthood (Arnett, 2000). Significant changes have occurred in societal influences on identity development, chiefly, the ubiquitous use of technology. With each generation, the use of technology is increasing, and changing the way we think and behave (Greenfield, 2009). Youth and emerging adults are now born into a world in which technology impacts most aspects of their daily existence (Coyne, Padilla-Walker, & Howard, 2013). To that end, recent research provides insights into youth and emerging adults' dependence upon technology and technological preferences which reveals that technology could be conceptualized as if it were an extension of the human body; "technology as skin."

INFLUENCE OF TECHNOLOGY ON YOUTH AND EMERGING ADULT IDENTITY DEVELOPMENT

Self-Identity Development in Youth

The developmental period of adolescence (11-18 years of age) is widely known for being the time when individuals begin to develop their identity; in essence, their sense of self, which is greatly impacted by both internal and external factors. Erikson (1968) identified adolescence as the adolescent stage of psycho-social development when youth experience an internal crisis as a result of social interactions. Adolescents wrestle with who they are while at the same time interacting with the world around them. In Erikson's day, many of these formative social interactions emerged from face-to-face familial and community spheres. Extending Erikson's foundational work,

Marcia (1980) similarly characterized youth as a period of exploration and commitment within a developmental status continuum formed through responses to social crises in realms such as school, relationships, and establishment of values. Advancements in technology have now created an opportunity to expand the spheres of influence upon identity previously known to Erikson and Marcia.

Social-Identity Development in Youth

In addition to developing identity, including a sense of self, adolescents also develop a social identity, which may differ from their self-identity. Social identity provides individuals with a sense of belonging as a result of social interactions (Koni, 2019). Such interaction may be face-to-face or may occur in relation to digital tools. Advancements in technology have catapulted the amount of social interactions occurring among many youth. The social context for interactions began to shift in the early 1990s. Prior to this point interpersonal communication typically existed within the nearby physical radius of the individual. With the onset of technological communication advances, and especially smart mobile devices, the social arena is now amplified and extended from one's closest physical proximity to potentially global interactions. "The use of media and technology also serves as a source of relational knowledge, informing people of the configuration of relationships, expected behavior in relationships, and cultural and societal value of relationships" (Borisoff & McMahan, 2017, p. 223). Youth now create and maintain connections in many virtual ways (e.g., social media chats within Facebook messenger, Twitter, Instagram, Snapchat, and within gaming platforms). YouTube, Instagram, and Snapchat are reportedly the most popular online platforms currently used by adolescents (Anderson & Jiang, 2018). This expansion of the social sphere in which individuals interact undoubtedly is now impacting the identity formation and development of youth today. Not only is the social sphere extended, it also now has become intensified. Youth's patterns and means of bonding socially have changed. How youth relate to one another has also evolved, even to the point of redefining what is meant by the term "friend." In previous generations a close comrade who you knew well and interacted with personally was called your friend; however in more recent times, social media has morphed the concept of friend to include persons to whom one may have never actually even been formally introduced (Vatel, 2014).

Emerging Adulthood and Identity Development

During emerging adulthood, typically considered to be ages 18 through 26 years (Arnett, 2000, 2004), identity development continues to be a central developmental task. These individuals embark on a journey moving from adolescence into adulthood marked with the distinctive features of identity exploration, instability, being self-focused, feeling in-between, and having multiple options and possibilities before them (Arnett, 2000, 2004). Technology use impacts each of these distinctive developmental tasks. Self and social-identity exploration is increasing and is impacted by technological connections. The feelings of instability can be intensified and perpetuated as the world and endless possibilities are virtually at their fingertips, yet these developing individuals struggle to know where they fit in. Additionally the self-focus and self-evaluation becomes intensified as their technological devices are bombarded with images of other presenting handpicked displays of their ideal selves. Trends perpetuating self-focus are now embodied in the craze for documentation via the "selfie."

Technological advancements have impacted past generations; however, the burgeoning role of technological innovations in the lives of emerging adults today is unique to this current and future generation. According to Tapscott, (2009, p. 16), "Each generation is exposed to a unique set of events that defines their place in history and shapes their outlook." Today's emerging adults are now a generation with whom the *World Wide Web* has always been in existence (Jackson, 2013) and constant technological innovations are the norm, not the exception. Technology is so much a part of emerging adults' lives that it has become an element of their very identity. Emerging adults today have been dubbed "Digital Natives," Generation

M(edia), and the "Net Generation" (Bennett & Maton, 2010; Prensky, 2010; Rideout, Foeher, &, Roberts, 2005; Tapscott, 2009).

The mobile devices favored by many youth and emerging adults capture and store a multitude of images, recordings, and links providing social and emotional connections. Vincent (2006) remarks that the mobile phone has becomes an icon of themselves and their identity, and these devices have grown to "embody social and emotional lives, not just enable them". In other words, youth and emerging adults are intricately tied both physically and emotionally to their technological devices. In this manner, technology serves as a representation of these individual's identity. "Our experiences and the environment around us shape how we think, behave, and act" (Oblinger & Oblinger, 2005, p. 28). Nearly all youth and emerging adults in Westernized nations use the Internet; these individual's thoughts and actions commonly and naturally involve technology (Jones, 2003; Oblinger & Oblinger, 2005).

TECHNOLOGY

In most situations, technology can be defined as, "any electronically based application or piece of equipment that meets a need for access to information or communication" (Roberts, 2005, p. 3.2). Researchers should recognize that emerging adults do not view technological innovations which have existed their entire lives as technology. Levine and Dean (2013, p. 7) provide the perspective voiced by emerging adults that "it's only technology if it happens after you are born." *Educause* reports, "students have never known a world without personal access to information technologies, often take them for granted, and integrate them seamlessly into their daily lives" (Caruso, & Salaway, 2007, p. 1). The first smart phones were introduced in the early 1990s; fast-forwarding to the present, Pew Research Center reports that in 2018 95% of teens have access to a smartphone resulting in persistent and constant online activity (Anderson & Jiang, 2018).

Technology use among emerging adults is commonplace; nearly all emerging adults have access to at least one technological device such as a mobile phone (Brown & Bobkowski, 2011). One national study found 92%

of 18-24 year old participants and 100% of college student participants were Internet users (Jones, 2002). Jacobsen and Forste (2011) claim 96% of college students have cell phones. Similarly, Swanson and colleagues (2017) also noted that 94% of their collegiate participants claim to use their cell phones for academic-related purposes. With the advent of ubiquitous mobile devices, emerging adults and many youth have become available to be contacted 24 hours a day, 7 days a week. Pew Research Center notes 45% of teens reporting almost constant internet use (Anderson & Jiang, 2018). This has resulted in a rise in texting and non-verbal social networking which Coccia and Darling (2016) found correlated with increased stress and lower life satisfaction in early emerging adult years. They also noted that technology can serve as a potential protective factor against stress, but it also may lead to life dissatisfaction if the communication is not synchronous.

While technology has increased the potential for human interaction, it has also allowed for interactions between humans and machines via technological devices. Technology, especially mobile devices such as smart phones often employ automated conversation agents, commonly referred to as "chatbots." These artificial intelligence agents mimic human behavior (Candello, Pinhanez & Figueiredo, 2017). Chatbots are frequently used within business realms for customer service and education for tutoring, as well as therapeutically (Skjuve, Haugstveit, Følstad, & Brandtzaeg, 2019). However, one of the biggest uses of chatbots occurs within messaging platforms such as Facebook Messenger, WhatsApp, and WeChat (Statista, 2018). These specific messaging platforms have risen in use especially by youth and emerging adults who are now edging away from many social media realms being utilized by their parents and grandparents (e.g., Facebook).

Computerized devices and especially mobilized devices such as smart phones and wearable technology are increasingly personalized and personified through the process of anthropomorphism (Wang, 2017). These non-human devices are attributed human characteristics and abilities since they interact with the individuals using them. With repeated use, individuals begin to automatically and "mindlessly" apply human personification to technological devices (Kim & Sundar, 2012). Personal profiles are established by users on technological devices and then the onslaught of data gathering proceeds, which enables continued future human to device interactions in humanistic manners. This personification of technology is exemplified through the development of devices which facilitate social and behavioral interactions such as Apple's virtual assistant Siri, Amazon Alexa, Samsung Bixby, Google Cortana, Google Assistant, and Lyra (Hindy, 2019). Wang (2016, p. 334) describes this movement as "pervasive personification" illustrated through "anthropomorphic human-computer interactions (HCI)" which exemplifies the Computes as Social Actors (CASA) paradigm. Additionally, Childress (2018) describes technology as an extension of human capabilities.

Because of technological advancements, humans are now able to accomplish far more in all realms of their existence. In many instances, humans are even able to extend their lives because of innovations and advancements afforded though technology.

TECHNOLOGY PREFERENCES AMONG ADOLESCENTS AND EMERGING ADULTS

It is important to recognize technological preferences and patterns since Internet use, and specifically social media use is now common place and playing a significant role in shaping youth and emerging adults. Pew Research Center reports 90% of young adults use social media (Perrin, 2015). The widespread use of technology among emerging adults has influenced researchers to investigate what types of technology are used and for what purposes (Swanson & Walker, 2015).

Past researchers have focused on specific tools or apps used. For example, Rutledge, Gillmor, and Gillen (2003) cite over twenty studies which show that collegiate use of social media tools such a Facebook influence their views on body image. Social networking sites have become one of the most used modes of communication for emerging adults and are thus an important element in their development (Subrahmanyam et al. 2008).

Other researchers have focused on uses of these tools and applications in learning contexts, such as Geng (2013) who investigated the use text messages in learning; Baker, Lusk, and Neuhauser (2012) who examined electronic devices for classroom use; and Saeed, Yang, and Sinnappan (2009) who studied the incorporation of blogs, podcasts, and social bookmarks for emerging adult education.

Recent research results indicated that almost all students used both a cell phone (94%) and personal computer daily (87%), for both academic and non-academic purposes (Swanson, Renes, & Strange, 2017). Mobile technology has become significant since many adolescents and emerging adults typically have devices with them at all times, subsequently often also providing Internet access and written, visual, or spoken communication. These devices frequently are also utilized to perform computations and organizing functions. In essence, the mobile devices are mini-computers. Claims are now made that emerging adults are increasingly depending on their mobile phones for connection and access to the web as much, if not more than with actual computers, including laptops (Tapscott, 2009). These are just a few of countless studies now reporting on the impact of technology on youth and emerging adult lives.

TECHNOLOGY DEPENDENCE AND ATTACHMENT

Emerging adults both seek media to fulfill needs and are influenced by such media (Coyne, Padilla-Walker & Howard, 2013). In studies involving the assessment of emerging adult technology use, participants reported that much of their typical day involves technology for both academic and non-academic related purposes (Swanson, Renes, & Strange, 2017; Swanson & Walker, 2015). The role of technology in youth and emerging adult lives is significant considering the amount of time spent using technology. Technology has become a natural part their existence from waking to the alarm on their mobile phone, to listening to music, pod casts, news, and entertainment, and then assisting in daily activities. Technology has become a vehicle through which youth and emerging adults seek sources for information, entertainment, communication, organization, and regulation (Swanson, Renes, & Strange, 2017). And yet, technology use among many youth has risen to the level described by some as addicting and obsessive (Brody, 2006).

Personalizing user experiences with technological devices increases attachment and dependence. Research is now indicating increased dependency and addiction on technological devices, especially mobile devices such as smart phones; such attachment to digitized objects is now increasingly linked to human-like attachment issues (Bodford, Kwan, & Sobota, 2017). Smart phones are described as "primary mediators of our digital social lives in lieu of personal computers" (Wang, 2017, p. 335). Many studies remark on emotional attachment to mobile devices (Vincent, 2006). When separated from their mobile devices, Vincent (2006) reported individuals described feelings including panic, strangeness, and anxiety. After analyzing autobiographical essays of emerging adults, McMillan and Morrison (2006) found that these individuals report a growing dependency on technology in their daily lives. Additionally, researchers are finding social networking dependency is associated with mobile phone dependency, and is often an indicator of self-regulation struggles in youth and emerging adults (Burnell & Kuther, 2016). The struggle for balance rather than unhealthy dependency is a growing issue. Consequently, the dependency issue may not be recognized since many youth and emerging adults now perceive their relationship with their technological devices as if they are a part of their very being, part of their anatomy, in much the same way as skin.

TECHNOLOGY AS SKIN

From a functionalist perspective, technology use may be more fully understood by using a human body analogy (Sever, 2012). Technology serves as both an integral part of youth and emerging adults' development as well as their functioning in today's society. Comparing technology use to skin requires a foundational understanding of the role and purpose of skin. Skin is essential to the functioning of the human body. It is the largest human organ, consisting of multiple layers with the main functions of protection, regulation, and sensation (Chuon et al., 2002; McLafferty, et al., 2012; WebMD, 2009). Skin provides a" boundary between the organism and the environment" (Chuong et al., 2002, p. 160). This boundary assists in providing physical form and, in a sense, the identity of the being. Skin serves both a physiological and psychological role; not only does it function to communicate and regulate health; it also has cosmetic, aesthetic, and cultural significance (Pringle & Penzer, 2002). An individual's skin is in part representative of their personal characteristics which constitute an element of identity.

Protection

Skin serves to cover and protect human bodies by forming a barrier which holds out pathogens and holds in essential organs and fluids while also relaying sensory messages. It is a barrier protecting internal organs and preventing fluid loss, while also guarding the body from harmful pathogens and maintaining homeostasis (Chuong et al., 2002; McLafferty et al., 2012). Skin is also flexible, thus providing room to stretch and adapt to environmental changes as needed.

Technology also serves as a form of protection through social contact and communication. Individuals can interact socially via various technological modes, such as phone calls, texting, video chatting, Facebook, and Twitter exchanges, etc. Research indicates emerging adult respondents highly rank technology as a preferred means of communication, especially for non-academic purposes (Swanson & Walker, 2015). Choosing and controlling what information becomes public can serve as a protective barrier. Additionally, through technology individuals are given tools to be able to protect themselves from unwanted invasion in their personal space, similar to skin blocking pathogens.

Technology, like skin, serves to protect by being a source of information. Our skin can relay environmental conditions to our brains (e.g., too hot, cold, wet). Technology can provide access to information, or sources for information, on many subjects; provide maps and directions; and provide instructions for just about anything. In an emergency, technology serves to protect as a tool (e.g., mobile phone applications which provide a flashlight, weather or danger advisories, distress signals, and even emergency medical information and procedures).

Protection can come in the form of communicating needs or finding answers to problems. Mobile phones provide a means for contacting emergency services and are a source for safety and wellness information as needed. Emerging adults often use mapping programs (61% weekly to monthly) which can keep them from getting lost or in dangerous situations (Swanson & Walker, 2015). Additionally, online audio-visual tools such as Youtube can provide a resource for solutions to everyday problems.

Regulation

Regulation is necessary for healthy functioning. Skin serves to assist in regulating the human body's functioning. Sensory information is gathered through the skin and informative messages are then relayed through the nervous system to the brain, which we then use as a basis for our regulatory decisions. Emerging adult regulation involves technology in numerous ways including aiding with time management via calendars, alarms, and reminders. Technology additionally is useful for record keeping, organizing and planning, and researching.

The use of technology in education and business has been shown to increase motivation and achievement (Bernauer & Tomei, 2015; Grinager, 2006). Success in navigating the adolescent and emerging adult years involves increasing self-regulation. Technology can potentially aid youth and emerging adults' ability to learn and develop by providing tools to assist in gathering, organizing, and processing information, which assists them in developing foundational life schemas. As a result of consistent utilization of technology and honed regulatory skills, emerging adults have taken on a more connectivist (computer-like) manner of processing information than previous generations (Bernauer & Tomei, 2015). These individuals are now shifting to looking at information broadly for patterns and constructing new connections from which knowledge transfer is facilitated (del Moral, Cernea, & Villalustre, 2013; Siemens, 2005).

Smartphones and other wearable technologies have advanced to the point where they can detect the user's location using GPS or Wi-Fi internet connections; assess their physical environment with temperature and humidity sensors; as well as evaluate their physiological conditions including pressure and heartbeat sensors (Wang, 2017). These devices can monitor movement, and can be used to track behavioral information (diet, exercise, stress levels, even preference patterns). These advancements not only serve to aid in self-regulatory activity but also medical-related tracking. Technological devices, especially mobile ones, have assisted in regulatory activities on the go (e.g., setting up appointments and communication for pleasure and work). Vincent (2006) reported that the underlying functional purpose for technology involves attachment for both regulatory functioning and emotional attachment.

COMMUNICATION

The third primary function of skin is being a sensory agent (Chuong, et al. 2002). Often sensory information relays messages while eliciting physiological emotional responses. In this role skin enables the organism to feel the environment, while relaying necessary information for the appropriate reflexive response. Skin can be thought of as the liaison, or connection to the world in which the individual's organs are contained. This sensory role is the basis for communication which involves making connections. Communication processes involve crucial interactions which are not only essential for survival but also become building blocks of identity, as a means for social comparison and image presentation (Crocetti & Rubini, 2017).

Technology is also significant to most youth and emerging adults for the role it plays in their communication. Communication connects them both socially with friends, family, coworkers, and daily acquaintances. Using online communication mediums, and technological applications and innovations, affords emerging adults the ability to digitally create a personal representative image of their choice. By sharing personal information, preferences, relationships, involvements, and even images on social media, emerging adults practice identity formation and experimentation.

Communication serves as a key element in work, school, and emergency situations. Most emerging adult college students indicate that their preferred personal communication medium is through social media on mobile technology (74%), while 83% preferred email for academic-related communications (Swanson, Renes, & Strange, 2017). Such high percentages reveal a comfort level in using technology for communicative purposes.

CONCLUSION

Oborne (1986) alludes to the development of a symbiotic relationship between technology and humans which is the result of a revolutionary shift in the human behaviors and present-day information technology. This shift has affected people's health, education, social, leisure, and working lives. Technology provides a bridge for socialization and increasingly influences the daily practices of emerging adults. The technological practices of emerging adults naturally form a normative and cognitive framework for their development and existence.

In westernized societies today, youth and emerging adults view technology as an essential component to their existence, similar to that of skin. For many, technology has psychologically merged into part of their very essence, taking on an anatomical characteristic which carries out specific functions necessary for every day living. Technology use has impacted their identity development, thinking processes and patterns for daily functioning. To developing youth and emerging adults, technology seems to take on the functions of skin; an integrated source of protection, regulation, and communication (McLafferty et al., 2012).

Individuals do not often notice their skin, or the role it plays, unless there is some sort of disruption in skin fulfilling its role. Skin is not typically noticed unless it is damaged and/or no longer serves to protect or hold the body together (e.g., a laceration). One does not frequently consider skin unless we have a physiological reaction like "goose bumps" from a chilling breeze, or sweat drops in hot, humid weather. On a typical day, one does not stop to think about their skin. Similarly, most emerging adults do not think about their technology and its function in their lives, unless that function is disrupted.

In summary, youth and emerging adults are living with constant technology use and yet often do not realize the impact it has on their lives until they are faced with a disruption in their technological connections. Many are so connected to technology that they cannot imagine being without it (Saad, 2015). Emerging adult students have become quite facile at using technology to meet daily need for protection, regulation and communication. Additionally, with the advances in mobile devices, most emerging adults have online resources at their fingertips at all times. Technology use has shaped emerging adult identity development, thinking processes, and patterns and preferences for daily functioning. Through social media and other online ventures, these individuals are technologically forming and sending messages to the world about who they perceive themselves to be, or how they desire for the world to perceive them. As connectivist thinkers (Siemens, 2006), emerging adults are becoming increasingly networked, with daily computing. Technology is assumed to be part of emerging adults' lives. These individuals are functioning in connections, becoming natural problem solver using technology, and learning via technological routes. Their thought processes increasingly are emulating technological processes. Much like the human body, emerging adults' skin-like relationship with technology exists through connections which are increasingly networked to accomplish purposeful tasks.

This theory provides implications for a new way of viewing emerging adult technology use, in a manner similar to the concept of skin; always there and assisting in protection, regulation, and communication. Understanding the emerging adult relationship with technology from this functionalist perspective aids in understanding emerging adult developmental and functional characteristics. These implications provide a deeper understanding for educators, psychologists, sociologists, and society as a whole as they seek to understand emerging adult life patterns in today's society. Times have changed, technology has changed, and our view of the span of time between adolescence and adulthood also needs to change. Understanding the role of technology as analogous to skin in the lives of youth and emerging adults can be a foundational paradigm shift.

REFERENCES

Anderson, M. & Jiang, J. (2018). *Teens, Social Media & Technology 2018.* Pew Research Center. Retrieved from https://www.pewinternet.org/2018/05/31/teens-social-media-technology-2018/.

Arnett, J. J. (2000). Emerging adulthood: A theory of development from the late teens through the twenties. *American Psychologist, 55*(5), 469-480.

Arnett, J. J. (2004). *Emerging adulthood: The winding road from the late teens through the twenties.* New York, NY: Oxford University Press.

Baker, W. M., Lusk, E. J., & Neuhauser, K. L. (2012). On the use of cell phones and other electronic devices in the classroom: Evidence from a survey of faculty and students. *Journal of Education for Business, 87,* 275-289.

Bennett, S. & Maton, K. (2010). Beyond the 'digital natives' debate: Towards a more nuanced understanding of students' technology experiences. *Journal of Computer Assisted Learning, 26,* 321-331.

Bernauer, J. A. & Tomei, L. A. (2015). *Integrating pedagogy and technology: Improving teaching and learning in higher education.* New York, NY: Roman & Littlefield.

Bodford, J. E., Kwan, V. S. Y., & Sobota, D. S. (2017). Fatal attractions: Attachment to smartphones predicts anthropomorphic beliefs and dangerous behaviors. *Cyberpsychology, Behavior, and Social Networking, 20*(5), 320–326. doi:10.1089/cyber.2016.0500.

Borisoff, D., & McMahan, D. T. (2017). Charting the terrain of interpersonal communication and the landscape of social interaction: Traditions, challenges, and trajectories. *Atlantic Journal of Communication, 25*(4), 211-231. doi.org/10.1080/15456870.2017.1350680.

Brody, M. (2006). Understanding teens in this age of digital technology. *Brown University Child & Adolescent Behavior Letter, 22*(12), 8.

Brown, J. D., & Bobkowski, P. S. (2011). Older and new media: Patters of use and effects on adolescents' health and well-being. *Journal of Research on Adolescence, 21*, 95-113.

Burnell, K., & Kuther, T. L. (2016). Predictors of mobile phone and social networking site dependency in adulthood. *CyberPsychology, Behavior & Social Networking, 19*(10), 621–627. doi:10.1089/cyber.2016.0209.

Candello, H., Pinhanez, C., & Figueiredo F. (2017). Typefaces and the perception of humanness in natural language chatbots. In *Proceedings of the 2017 CHI Conference on Human Factors in Computing Systems* (CHI'17; pp. 3476–3487). New York, NY, USA: ACM. https://doi.com/ 10.1145/3025453.3025919.

Caruso, J. B. & Salaway, G. (2007). *The Educause Center for Applied Research Study of Undergraduate Students and Information Technology*. Boulder: CO: Educause Center for Applied Research. Retrieved January 30, 2012, from: http://net.educause.edu/ ir/library/pdf/ERS0706.pdf.

Childress, V. W. (2018). Technology - the extension of human potential. *Technology & Engineering Teacher, 77*(5), 30–35.

Chuong, C. M., Nickoloff, B. J., Elias, P. M., Goldsmith, L. A., Macher, E., Maderson, P. A., King, L. E. (2002). What is the "true" function of skin? *Experimental Dermatology, 11*(2), 159.

Coccia, C. & Darling, C. A. (2016). Having the time of their life: College student stress, dating and satisfaction with life. *Journal of the International Society for the Investigation of Stress, 32*(1). 28-35. doi: 10.1002/smi.2575.

Coyne, S. M., Padilla-Walker, L. M., & Howards, E. (2013). Emerging in a digital world; A decade review of media use, effects, and gratifications in emerging adulthood. *Emerging Adulthood, 1*(2), 125-137.

Crocetti, E. & Rubini, M. (2017). Communicating personal and social identity in adolescence. *Oxford Research Encyclopedia of Communication.* doi: 10.1093/acrefore/9780190228613.013.482.

del Moral, M. E., Cernea, A., & Villalustre, L. (2013). Connectivist learning objects and learning styles. *Interdisciplinary Journal of E-Learning & Learning Objects, 9,* 105–124.

Erikson, E. H. (1968). *Identity: Youth and crisis.* New York: Norton.

Geng, G. (2013). Investigating the use of text messages in mobile learning. *Active Learning in Higher Education, 14*(1), 77-87.

Greenfield, S. (2009). *ID: The question of meaning in the 21st Century.* London, England: Sceptre.

Grinager, H. (2006). How education technology leads to improved student achievement. *Education Issues (November 2006).* Washington, DC: National conference of State Legislatures.

Hindy, J. (2019). 10 best personal assistant apps for Android" (Updated 2019). *Android Authority.* Retrieved from https://www.android authority.com/best-personal-assistant-apps-android-667299/

Jackson, L. D. (2013). Is mobile technology in the classroom a helpful tool or a distraction?: A report of university students' attitudes, usage practices, and suggestions for policies. *The International Journal of Technology, Knowledge, and Society, 3,* 129-140.

Jacobsen, W. C., & Forste, R. (2011). The wired generation: Academic and social outcomes of electron media use among university students. *Cyberpsychology, Behavior, and Social Networking*, 14, 275-280.

Jones, S. (2002). *The Internet goes to college: How students are living in the future with today's technology.* Washington, DC: Pew Internet & American Life Project.

Jones, S. (2003). *Let the games begin: Gaming technology and college students.* Washington, DC: Pew Internet & American Life Project.

Kim, Y., & Sundar, S. S. (2012). Anthropomorphism of computers: Is it mindful or mindless? *Computers in Human Behavior, 28*(1), 241–250.

Koni E, Moradi S, Arahanga-Doyle H, Neha T, Hayhurst JG, Boyes M, et al. (2019) Promoting resilience in adolescents: A new social identity

benefits those who need it most. *PLoS ONE 14*(1): e0210521.
https://doi.org/10.1371/journal.pone.0210521.

Levine, A., & Dean, D. R. (2013). It's only technology if it happens after
you are born. *Journal of College Admission, 220*, 6-12.

Marcia, J. E. (1980). *Identity in adolescence. Handbook of adolescent
psychology, 9*(11), 159-187.

McLafferty, E., Hendry, C. & Farley, A. (2012). The integumentary system:
Anatomy, physiology and function of skin. *Nursing Standard, 27*(3), 35-
42.

McMillan, S. J., & Morrison, M. (2006). Coming of age with the Internet: A
qualitative exploration of how the internet has become an integral part
of young people's lives. New *Media & Society, 8*(1), 73–95.
doi:10.1177/1461444806059871.

Oblinger, D. G., & Oblinger, J. L. (2005). *Educating the Net generation.*
Bolder, CO: EDUCAUSE retrieved from: www.educause.edu/
educatingthenetgen/.

Oborne, D. J. (1986). Information technology and behavior: An overview of
a symbiotic relationship. *Current Psychological Research & Reviews,*
91-93.

Perrin, A. (2015). Social media usage: 2005-2015. *Pew Research Center
Internet and Technology Report.* Retrieved from http://www.
pewinternet.org/2015/10/08/social-networking-usage-2005-2015/.

Pringle, F. & Penzer, R. (2002). Normal skin; Its function and care. In Penzer
R (Ed) *Nursing Care of the Skin*, pp. 20-45. Oxford: Butterworth
Heinemann.

Prensky, M. (2010). *Teaching digital natives: Partnering for real learning.*
Thousand Oaks, CA: Corwin.

Rideout, V. J., Foeher, U. Gl, &, Roberts, D. F. (2005). *Generation M:
Media in the lives of 8-18-year-olds.* Washington, DC: A Kaiser Family
Foundation Report. Retrieved May 28, 2007 from: http://www.kff.org/
entmedia/index.cfm.

Roberts, G., (2005). "Technology and learning expectations of the Net
generation," in Oblinger, D. G., & Oblinger, J. L. (eds). *Educating the*

Net Generation, Bolder, CO: EDUCAUSE. Retrieved from: www. educause.edu/educatingthenetgen/.

Rutledge, C. M., Gillmor, K. L., & Gillen, M. M. (2013). Does this profile picture make me look fat? Facebook and body image in college students. *Psychology of Popular Media Culture, 2*(4), 251-258.

Saad, L. (2015). Nearly half of smartphone users can't imagine life without it. *Gallup.* Retrieved from: https://news.gallup.com/poll/184085/ nearly-half-smartphone-users-imagine-life-without.aspx?utm_source= Economy&utm_medium=newsfeed&utm _campaign=tiles.

Saeed, N., Yang, Y., & Sinnappan, S. (2009). Emerging web technologies in higher education: A case of incorporating blogs, podcasts and social bookmarks in a web programming course based on students' learning styles and technology preferences. *Educational Technology & Society, 12*(4), 98-109.

Server, M. (2012). A critical look at the theories of sociology of education. *International Journal of Human Sciences* [Online]. 9(1), Retrieved from http://www.insanbilimleri.com/en.

Siemens, G. (2005). Connectivism: A learning theory for the digital age. *International Journal of Instructional Technology & Distance Learning, 2*(1).

Siemens, G. (2006). *Knowing knowledge.* Retrieved from http://www. elearnspace.org/KnowingKnowledge_LowRes.pdf.

Skjuve, M., Haugstveit, I. M., Følstad, A., & Brandtzaeg, P. B. (2019). Help! Is my chatbot falling into the uncanny valley? An empirical study of user experience in human-chatbot interaction. *Human Technology, 15*(1), 30–54.

Statista (2018). *Most popular mobile messaging apps worldwide as of October 2018, based on number of monthly active users.* Retrieved from https:// www.statista.com/ statistics/ 258749/ most-popular-global-mobile-messenger-apps/.

Subrahmanyam, K., Reich, S. M., Waechter, N., & Espinoza, G. (2008). Online and offline social networks: Use of social networking sites by emerging adults. *Journal of Applied Developmental Psychology, 29*, 420-433.

Swanson, J. A., Renes, S. L., & Strange, A. T. (2017). I might not be as tech as you think: Digital versus print preferences. Paper presented at the 14th International Conference on Cognition and Exploratory Learning in the Digital Age (CELDA), Vilamoura, Algarve, Portugal.

Swanson, J. A. & Walker, E. (2015). Academic versus non-academic emerging adult college student technology use. *Technology, Knowledge, and Learning, 20*(2), 147-158.

Tapscott, D. (2009). *Grown up digital: How the Net generation is changing your world.* New York, NY: McGraw-Hill.

Vincent, J. (2006). Emotional attachment and mobile phones. *Knowledge, Technology & Policy, 19*(1), 39-44. doi: 10.1007/s12130-006-1013-7.

Vatel, B. (2014). Social media use: A closer Look at the real meaning of friends. *Psychiatric Times, 31*(9), 1-14.

Wang, W. (2017). Smartphones as Social Actors? Social dispositional factors in assessing anthropomorphism. *Computers in Human Behavior, 68*, 334–344. doi: 10.1016/j.chb.2016.11.022.

WebMD (2009). *Skin problems and treatment health center.* Retrieved from: http:// www.webmd.com/skin-problems-and-treatments/picture-of-the-skin.

ABOUT THE EDITOR

Michelle F. Wright, PhD
Research Associate, Penn State University and Maryk University
Centre County, PA, US

Michelle F. Wright, Ph.D. is a Research Associate at The Pennsylvania State University and a research fellow at Masaryk University in Brno, the Czech Republic. Her research focus is on the contextual factors which influence children's, adolescents', and young adults' involvement in aggressive behaviors, with a special interest in social goals, peer status, and cultural values. She has published on these topics, with her most recent work focused on culture and anonymity, and their role in cyberbullying among adolescents.

INDEX

D

E

T

Related Nova Publications

CYBER-SECURITY AND INFORMATION WARFARE

EDITOR: Nicholas J. Daras

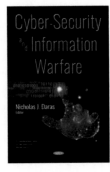

SERIES: Cybercrime and Cybersecurity Research

BOOK DESCRIPTION: A variety of modern research methods in a number of innovating cyber-security techniques and information management technologies are provided in this book along with new related mathematical developments and support applications from engineering. This allows for the exploration of new approaches, useful practices and related problems for further investigation.

HARDCOVER ISBN: 978-1-53614-385-0
RETAIL PRICE: $230

WHY CYBER SECURITY IS A SOCIO-TECHNICAL CHALLENGE: NEW CONCEPTS AND PRACTICAL MEASURES TO ENHANCE DETECTION

EDITOR: Mils Hills

SERIES: Computer Science, Technology and Applications

BOOK DESCRIPTION: This book is a provocative manifesto of disruptive thinking about cyber security. It presents cutting-edge thinking and professional reflection and is designed to be a source of ideas and approaches that can be adopted for application in the real world by those who recognize that conventional ways of defining and considering cyber-attack are insufficient.

HARDCOVER ISBN: 978-1-53610-090-7
RETAIL PRICE: $160

To see complete list of Nova publications, please visit our website at www.novapublishers.com

Related Nova Publications

IoT: Platforms, Connectivity, Applications and Services

Abdulrahman Yarali, Ph.D.

Author: Abdulrahman Yarali

Series: Computer Science, Technology and Applications

Platforms,
Connectivity,
Applications
and Services

Book Description: In this book, there are 16 chapters which cover a broad range of topics such as platforms, technologies, generating business value, delivering smart, sustainable energy solutions, smart communities and citizens, manufacturing, healthcare, security and privacy, commercial drones and many other related IoT topics.

Hardcover ISBN: 978-1-53613-400-1
Retail Price: $230

The Internet of Things (IoT): Applications, Technology, and Privacy Issues

Author: Silvia Watts

Series: Internet Theory, Technology and Applications

SILVIA WATTS

THE INTERNET OF
THINGS
(IoT)

Book Description: This book examines architectures, technologies and applications in the Internet of Things. It presents the development and implementation of an industrial communication system for remote monitoring and management of industrial processes as well as the current IoT governance scenario, its main challenges, the role of the governments and the need to develop public-private partnerships for technical cooperation in the governance of IoT resources.

Hardcover ISBN: 978-1-63484-626-4
Retail Price: $110

To see complete list of Nova publications, please visit our website at www.novapublishers.com